REFLECTING GOD

Wes Tracy, Gary Cockerill,
Donald Demaray, Steve Harper

ISBN 978-0-8341-1866-9

Printed in the
United States of America

Cover Design: Sharon Page

Library of Congress Cataloging-in-Publication Data

Reflecting God / Wesley Tracy . . . [et al.].
p. cm.
Includes bibliographical references.
ISBN 0-8341-1866-1
1. Spiritual life—Christianity. 2. Christian life. I. Tracy, Wesley.

BV4501.1 .R4239 2000
248.4—dc21

00-049394

10 9 8 7 6 5 4 3

Foreword

The "me generation" is how we often refer to the current generation. When faced with major choices, people overwhelmingly make their decisions based on the question "What's in it for me?" Unfortunately, this self-centeredness is too prevalent among believers and affects their walk with God.

As Christians we often focus on experiencing God. We state our desire to "have more of Him." But if we are to become all that God desires, we must elevate our focus. Corrie ten Boom nailed the core principle when she declared, "Don't tell me how much of God you have. Tell me how much of you God has." That is the issue.

God's desire is not simply that we experience Him, but that we become a reflection of him. We can never cast a clear reflection, however, until we have given ourselves completely to Him. This complete surrender opens the door to a wonderful journey of holiness.

Our excellent *Reflecting God* writers have provided us a clear map to guide us on this journey toward Christlikeness. Whether used in small-group Bible study or for personal spiritual enrichment, it is our belief and prayer that God will use this book to raise up a new generation committed to being entirely His.

Set out on this venture. Allow God to work through the pages of this book to change you, to help you discover the joy and peace that can be yours when you are *reflecting God*. Let the journey begin.

—Marlin R. Hotle, Ph.D.
Christian Holiness Partnership
Executive Director

Contents

Introduction

“I *must* break through this deadness. . . . At times this . . . crushes the very soul.”

Fridtjof Nansen, Norwegian explorer, penned these words in his ship’s log. Many expeditions to reach the North Pole by sea had ended with icebound ships and frozen sailors, but Nansen had studied the ocean currents. He believed that the best thing to do was trust the current of the Arctic Ocean. Therefore, in the summer of 1893, he set his ship, the *Fram*, adrift in the ocean current. His goal was to drift to the pole and beyond it, coming out on the other side into the sun-sparkled Pacific.

But soon the *Fram* was locked into frozen solidarity with millions of acres of ice in the polar ice cap. He sat there all winter. Then came a short spring and summer that thawed almost nothing. Winter found him with deck, riggings, and rudder frozen in uselessness. In the middle of that second dark arctic winter he wrote: “Life seems as dark as the winter night outside; there is sunlight upon no other part of it except the past and the far, far distant future. . . . I *must* break through this deadness.”[1]

Nansen could remember the sunlight, and he hoped to see it again in a future too far distant to be of much help in a six-month polar night.

Think of Fridtjof’s voyage as a parable. Do you see your own spiritual voyage pictured there? Is sunlight just a memory, maybe a dim hope fading on the far horizon? Oh, you have encountered the sunlight of God’s love. You have clutched at fleeting glimpses of the glory of God. In surprised moments of sacred solitude you have seen visions of a land aglow with Light.

But as life’s winters have built one upon the other, the dark “deadness” of the night has crushed your soul. The clouds of family problems blackened your sky. The chill of second jobs, overtime, and too many bills squeezed out the light. Perhaps the howling blizzard of failure buried your hopes beyond spring rejuvenation. Has the ache of dreams surrendered brought deadness that only the crushed soul knows?

Perhaps you are one of those who doesn’t even realize that the ship is locked in fatal frozenness. Maybe the sheer busyness of soccer practice, seminars, classes, kids’ performances, and church committees has dulled your heart to the bleak winter that reigns within. Or maybe you are having so much fun making angels in the snow and building snowmen with carrot noses—chasing pleasures and making money—that you are not aware that icy talons are closing around your heart.

Wake up!

You may be a veritable bustle of religious activity, dashing from one workshop, ministry, or good cause to another. In fact, you may be using this whirl of “service” to mute the call to bask in the true Light. Yet in moments of unbuttoned leisure—as scarce as they are—or in times of forced solitude, you experience something such as what happens when a honeysuckle vine cannot keep from sending its tendrils toward the sunlight. In those unrushed moments a voice that says, "Listen to me—there is something missing in all this. You long to be in a love affair, an adventure. You were made for something more. You know it."[2]

Have you sought to fill the longing for the sun by fribbling with false lights? The true Light is fearsome as well as fascinating, so some settle for artificial lights such as drugs, pornography, an affair, an obsession with sports, or gambling. These offer a cheap substitute for transcendence, but soon they are as weak as a flashlight left on all night. You can squelch the light, you know. It's possible to feed a puppy and starve a lion until the puppy can whip the lion.

Do you, like Nansen, have hopes that in some far, far distant future the sun will shine again in your soul?

After two years, the soul-crushed Nansen tried to "break through this deadness" by leaving his ship. With one companion he set out to *walk* to the North Pole. Fat chance. The jagged, icy terrain pounded them into submission. The two trudgers took refuge in a shell of a cave and shivered through the third winter, eating polar bear meat and remembering the sunshine and hoping to feel it again in some distant future.

Back to the parable: At what points, if any, does this polar hike describe your spiritual journey? It's not as if you haven't tried to break through the deadness. You, too, have hiked and vowed and trudged—and failed to reach your destination.

Fridtjof's story has a happy ending. After three years of frozen oneness with the polar ice cap, he was rescued and went home.

Imagine his feelings on a spring morning when he roused from a nightmare of the frigid Arctic and realized that a shaft of May sunlight had slipped through a half-opened curtain and nudged him awake. Think what he experienced when he opened his window to be greeted by a May morning ablaze with sunlit beauty, dancing daffodils, nodding tulips, and dew-freshened rosebuds bathing in the golden ambience of the sun.

You can find yourself in a land ablaze with the sunlit beauty of a May morning.

Fridtjof had broken through the deadness. The sun was no longer hidden in some far, far distant future, but was a present blessing that provoked a dance of gratitude and joy.

Your voyage can have a happy ending too. You can find yourself in a land ablaze with the sunlit beauty of a May morning. This book is your chart out of the spiritual Arctic to the sun-sparkled waters of divine grace, love, and joy.

Since childhood, May has been my favorite month. Toward the end of the month I could not concentrate on long division or pronouns! During the last week of May I couldn't wait for the school bell to end the agony and set me free to head for the creek.

You see, in my part of the world between the last week of May and about the fifth of June, the crawdads shed their shells. And God has not yet created a smallmouth bass that can keep from gobbling a soft-shelled crawdad! Even if it has just dined as sumptuously as the rich man in Lazarus's story, a smallmouth simply can't turn down one more soft-shelled crawdad.

That's great news for boys with Zebco reels and a Styrofoam box of soft-shelled "dads." But that is bad news for the crawdads. They make themselves scarce. They sense their vulnerability and hide from schoolboys and schools of smallmouth bass under rocks and driftwood. In their hiding places, the crawdads grow a new, tougher shell as fast as they can. By the second week in June they will be strutting upstream braver than ever.

Every season the crawdad sheds its old shell and grows a bigger one. It is a protection like a coat of armor. Season after season the crawdad gets better and better at growing tougher and tougher shells.

Then one season it produces the hardest shell of all. Now it is king, the biggest crawdad with the toughest shell. The young ones get out of its way. It gets first choice at feeding time. After all, it is the one with the shell as hard as limestone.

All too soon that superb shell becomes its coffin.

The season comes to change. The warm May sunshine calls, and the crawfish begin to shed their shells, preparing to grow stronger ones. They all change —except the crawdad who in its maturity has grown a shell too tough, too hard to shed. The time comes to change, and it can't. Trapped in its own shell, unable to change, it dies.

That's a parable of people too.

One characteristic of most of us adults is that we are set in our ways. We find out a way to handle problems, explain life, and work things out. We don't like it when someone pipes up and says he or she has a better way. Change is uncomfortable for us. We have grown a shell that has more or less protected us through layoffs, raising teenagers, burying and marrying loved ones, and jousts with the IRS. We don't want someone to tell us they have a better way. Been there, done that.

Something like that happened to the people to whom Jesus preached. The threshold verse of this whole book is about that very thing.

> And we, who with unveiled faces all reflect the Lord's glory, are being transformed into his likeness with ever-increasing glory, which comes from the Lord, who is the Spirit *(2 Cor. 3:18)*.

A tough to translate phrase is lodged in this verse, so please consider this rendition also:

> All of us, with unveiled faces, seeing the glory of the Lord as though reflected in a mirror, are being transformed into the same image from one degree of glory to another; for this comes from the Lord, the Spirit *(NRSV)*.

Paul is speaking about people who should have seen the glory of God in Christ as they read the ancient Scriptures. They were devout, sincere, and thought they were doing right. Many of them were full-time religious professionals, Levites, priests, Pharisees. They read the Scriptures, memorized the Scriptures, hugged the Scriptures, and on occasion danced with the Torah, the Law of Moses. They expounded the Torah, wrote commentaries on it, venerated it, worshiped it. They added subsidiary laws, nearly a thousand of them, and tried their best to keep every one.

But there was one problem. Like us, they were set in their ways. They looked at the Law of Moses as the one ultimate and final revelation of God. They could not conceive of anything new coming along that would supersede the Torah. That belief became their spiritual coffin.

When God fulfilled the Law and the Prophets by sending Jesus Christ His Son into the world, these people were so busy reciting commandments and judging others by them that they did not even see the Christ. The letter of the Law blotted out the spirit and promise of the Law. They memorized prophecies that Jesus would come, but their theology blinded them to the Savior. When God sent His very own Son to reveal the new covenant, they were so busy cramming on the minutiae of the old covenant that they didn't even look up. When God sent the Holy Spirit at Pentecost, they were still poring over the Levitical code of outward ceremonial purity and missed the purification of their hearts by faith.

As Christians gaze into that Light, it transforms them more and more into the very image of Christ.

In 2 Cor. 3 Paul explains that their minds were hardened by their preoccupation with outward appearance—legalism, we call it. The belief that the Law of Moses was the peak of spirituality became a veil over their eyes that prevented them from seeing the Light of Jesus. Those who believe in Jesus know that the glory of God in Christ beams forth from the Word.

As Christians gaze into that Light, it transforms them more and more into the very image of Christ. They are renewed, for "if anyone is in Christ, he is a new creation; the old has gone, the new has come!" (2 Cor. 5:17). Theirs is a new center of life, a new value system, a new *agapē* lifestyle. They are free from legalism, for "the letter [of the Law] kills, but the Spirit gives life," and "where the Spirit of the Lord is, there is freedom" (3:6, 17). The more they bask in the sun of the Son, as in a mirror, the more they reflect that sacred image to all the world.

You aren't set in your ways?

Legalism comes in many forms—religious, cultural, and personal. Perhaps you are not a slave to the Levitical code, but do the traditions of men, denominational culture, or unexamined assumptions blind you to what God wants today? Some have made a legalism about being saved. They went forward along with the rest of the kids at Vacation Bible School when they were seven or eight and assume that they are Christians. That "conversion" experience has become their Torah, the ultimate thing God can do. And among other things they miss God's call to the adventure and romance of sanctification, even though God promises blessings, satisfactions, and fulfillments that they have never seen or even imagined (see 1 Cor. 2:9).

The new Israeli film *Kadosh* testifies that being held hostage to our old ways of looking at things is still alive and well in the homeland of Jesus of Nazareth. The film is set in the Orthodox quarter of contemporary Jerusalem. The main characters, Meir and Rivka, have a good marriage, but no children after 10 years. The rabbi tells Meir that if he is to fulfill the commandment to insure the future by being fruitful and replenishing the earth, he must divorce Rivka and marry a fertile woman. Meir, at first, declines. The rabbi insists. In the meantime, Rivka goes to the doctor and discovers that she is not the sterile partner. Given the culture, she can say nothing. She doesn't even speak up when the divorce is carried out despite their love. A hard line wins again.

Our tendency to legalism is not just a religious problem; it is a human problem. Many of us live daily in shells that protect but eventually are nothing more than living tombs. Thousands pay homage to the creed of cynicism. "You can't trust anyone these days," we say, "not politicians, not bankers, not doctors, not preachers, not even your wife." Soon the shell will be too hard to open to faith or love.

Some of us have been labeled "worthless" or "no good" so long that we believe it, imprisoned within a shell of self-loathing. Trapped in self-deprecation, we do not know that God this very moment is calling us to attain "to the whole measure of . . . fullness of Christ" (Eph. 4:13).

We are surrounded by expectations that threaten to blind us. I recently read an intriguing book titled *Can Asians Think?* The author, an Asian himself, has no doubts about the intelligence of Asians. His point: Asians are not required to think because powerful cultural traditions make the decisions for them. Whom they will marry, what their status in the family will be, their personal conduct, their vocation, and what they will do with their money—all this and more will be dictated by the culture.

Some fixation will try to ambush you too. It may be your personal limitations, the notion of victimization, or the vow never to love again once betrayed. Your challenge may be disillusionment with God, who seemed to sit on His hands when you needed Him the most. It may be that your failures have conditioned you never to try again. Perhaps you think that your substance or sex addiction is hopeless. Maybe you think you'll be a lousy parent because your parents made a lot of mistakes. All of these are traps that, if left unchecked, can build a protective shell so strong that you die long before you breathe your last.

All legalisms, whether religious, cultural, or personal, have certain drawbacks. For one, no code of conduct, not even the Ten Commandments, ever transformed anyone. Second, keeping a code of rules can give you scruples. That is, you have your daily list of dos and don'ts. If you miss one on either side of the ledger, you feel guilty. Further, busily keeping your scruples against doing or not doing some things may cause you to miss what Christian love would ask.

Third, code keeping focuses your eyes on outward performance rather than inward formation. Fourth, legalism provides presumptuous pats on the back. You set out your daily rules and regulations and scrupulously keep them all. Therefore, you presume that you are "good." C. S. Lewis wrote, "Nothing gives one a more spuriously good conscience than keeping rules, even if there has been a total absence of all real charity and faith."[3] Like a spell checker on your computer, it gives you false confidence.

All these brittle shells will give way to freedom if you linger long enough in the presence of the God who is in the business of gently peeling away the layers of our pain, and who reaches out to you in the touch of the Holy Spirit. A friend of mine describes himself as a "recovering legalist." You can be one, too, whatever your religious, secular, or cultural fixations have been. "It is for freedom that Christ has set us free" (Gal. 5:1).

Welcome, embrace, the transforming Light.

We are to stand with unveiled faces gazing upon the Light of God. Think about your face. It is the most public part of your body. You don't cover it very often when you go to the store or to see the kids. School yearbooks are not filled with photos of feet, but faces. Our faces are almost always the most distinctive and recognizable feature about us. Max Lucado says, "God invites us to see his face so he can change ours. He uses our uncovered faces to display his glory."[4] Lucado points out that the sculptor of Mount Rushmore had a lesser challenge. But God is up to the task. "The one who calls you is faithful and he will do it" (1 Thess. 5:24).

In Part One of this book, "Searching for the Light," you are invited to explore your yearning for the Light and come to understand your own journey better. These chapters will set your face toward the Light, the way home.

Part Two, "Transformed by the Light," brings encounters with the fearful, holy, loving, and transforming Light of God. Prepare to be challenged and changed.

The personal and community practices that nourish the spiritual light within comprise the chapters in Part Three, "Nurtured by the Light."

Part Four, "Sharing the Light," will teach you ways to share the spiritual life, joy, and peace that you have received.

This book is a part of a family of products that aim at helping us find and live our spiritual potential. This student textbook is to be used in conjunction with the *Reflecting God Bible*, the *Reflecting God Workbook* with daily lessons derived from this text, and the *Reflecting God Leader's Guide*, which provides weekly group sessions based on the daily lessons from this textbook and the student workbook.

—Wesley D. Tracy, on behalf of the *Reflecting God* team

Part 1

SEARCHING FOR THE LIGHT

We all shrivel up like a leaf, and like the wind our sins sweep us away (Isa. 64:6).

"A seed upon the wind."

According to Howard Thurman, the beloved former chaplain at Boston University, humankind without God is "a seed upon the wind."

What a picture!

A tiny, living thing awaiting its moment of fulfillment . . .
caught up in the tremendous energy of the wind . . .
at the mercy of forces not responsive to its own ends . . .

In the grip of something like this, what is a seed—
no more than a particle of dust,
a nameless nothing.

Here is the abandonment of all purpose,
stark helplessness . . .

The fact that there is locked within the seed
a private world of pattern and design
makes no difference to the fierce velocities
that sweep it on the reckless, relentless way.

Humanity without God is a seed upon the wind.
A victim of the currents of life
that carry him or her where they will
with a bland unmindfulness of purposes and ends
which belong to living, thinking, feeling creatures.

Such a person has no sense of center.

All clues to meaning and value must come from the passing moment,
the transitory event,
the immediate issue of the day.

Such a person is at home "nowhere" because he or she is not at home "somewhere."

What would such a person give in exchange for his or her soul?[1]

A seed upon the wind. Perhaps a more apt metaphor for us who cling to the postmodern cusp of the new millennium would be "a wail in cyber-space."

Like the seed we sense a private pattern and design within, but like an undeliverable E-mail we drift through cyberspace sifting, searching for the cyber port that will connect us to purpose, destiny, and identity before our dimming hope is unplugged and the screen goes dark.

Will you join us in a search for the Light?

Can you still hope? Dare? Believe?

Would you listen, really listen, to those who have found their way home?

The journey is long, but there's good news ahead.

> God, who said, "Let light shine out of darkness," made his light shine in our hearts to give us the light of the knowledge of the glory of God in the face of Christ *(2 Cor. 4:6).*

— 1 —

Somehow I Expected More . . .

First Window on the Word

We were under great pressure, far beyond our ability to endure, so that we despaired even of life (2 Cor. 1:8).

The most frequently reproduced work of art in history?

That's easy. Mona Lisa, right?

Right—if you count all of history. But what if we are talking about the last 10 years?

Not Mona Lisa, but *The Scream*.

Edvard Munch of Germany painted *The Scream* in 1893. At its first exhibit in Berlin the critics found it uncivilized, barbaric, insane, even subhuman! The critics and the public drove *The Scream* into abandoned obscurity. It was out of joint with the times.

Apparently it is not out of joint with our times. During the 1990s that painting decorated more T-shirts, posters, note pads, calendars, night-lights, beer bottles, inflatable dolls, mouse pads, and coffee mugs than any other piece of art!

Michael Parke-Taylor, the curator of a Toronto gallery that houses a major Munch exhibit, claims that *The Scream* stands as *the* "image of modern man—totally stressed out and angst-ridden."[1]

Beware of Falling Idols

Window on the Word

When you cry out for help, let your collection of idols save you! The wind will carry all of them off, a mere breath will blow them away (Isa. 57:13).

The December 6, 1999, edition of the *New York Times Magazine* gave most of its pages to a discussion of suggestions of items to pack into a time capsule for the 20th century. What should we pack into the capsule to help students 200 years from now understand our soul and spirit? Should *The Scream* go in it? How about the John Updike novel that shows a character sitting on a crate of self-help books plotting his own suicide? Perhaps we should include rock star Kurt Cobain's declaration before he shot himself: "Jesus wouldn't want me for a sunbeam."

Maybe the unknown poet had it right when he described those of us who survived the 20th century as "poor unprayed for wanderers hiding in the shadows of their fright." Isaac Asimov said that the motto of the 21st century would be: "No more 20th centuries." Maybe Jean-François Lyotard was right when he declared that modernity has given us "as much terror as we can take."[2] Surely we would include in our time capsule Joan Didion's pathos-filled and reality-packed "How Do I Tell Them There's Nothing Left?" Maybe Saul Bellow's comment in *Herzog* fits: "This generation thinks—and this is the thought of thoughts—that nothing faithful, vulnerable, fragile can be durable. . . . Death awaits these things like a cement floor waits for a dropping light bulb."[3]

Perhaps nothing sums up the despair of Munch, Updike, Cobain, Asimov, Didion, and Bellow more accurately than "Somehow we expected more . . . more than the stressed out, angst-ridden existence that makes us want to scream." Or maybe we should just laugh at the absurdity of our situation and, like the *New York Times*, put a David Letterman Top 10 list in our time capsule.

It's not that we haven't hoped—we used to do a lot of that. We expected more. It's not as if we haven't searched. We wore ourselves out chasing dreams, phantasms, and phony messiahs. By the time the Statler Brothers made the dreams of the "Class of '57" famous, we had already dismissed our old set of idols. Modernity had declared human beings free from the supernatural, free to fashion their own self, free to conquer nature through science, free to produce an always growing economy. All this sprang from faith in the religion of human progress.[4] But these were exposed as impotent saviors, every one of them. A pile of money, nonstop pleasure, self-centered living, and science and technology still left a big hole in your heart, empty and aching.

In the main, society has moved beyond the modern mind-set. There are, of course, still tribes of greedy grabbers, pleasure hounds, egomaniacs, and science and technology worshipers. But they are old-fashioned, out of tune with the times and as dumb as Dr. Faustus, who in Marlowe's tale, traded his soul to the devil for the privilege of criticizing the pope without reprisal, being able to gorge on grapes out of season, and a chance to go to bed with the voluptuous Helen of Troy.

The idols of modernity—materialism, hedonism, narcissism, scientism, and reason—became the establishment against which postmodern searchers have rebelled. These forces became as hopeless as Frank Sinatra's confession. Asked if he believed in prayer, he declared, "I'm for anything that will get you through the night, be it prayer, pills, or a bottle of Jack Daniels."[5]

The Postmodern Search for Meaning

Window on the Word

My soul yearns, even faints, . . . my heart and my flesh cry out for the living God (Ps. 84:2).

The inhabitants of the 21st century are done with mere rationality and empty tradition. They seek something beyond the natural, above the rational, something mysterious and beyond their control. "Our age . . . makes the materialism of the past look picayune. People crave something larger in concepts than the data of this world, something mysterious, ambiguous, nonmaterial."[6]

Rita McClain's pilgrimage speaks for the culture. Her spiritual search started in a Pentecostal church in Iowa, but the guilt was too heavy there. She packed her spiritual bags and moved to a mainline Protestant congregation, but it was too "shallow." She rejected all organized religion and spent years seeking peace in nature, mainly hiking in the mountains and meditating in the desert. A painful divorce moved her to scout her "inner landscape" again. This expedition led her into Unity (a blend of Christian Science, Hinduism, and pop psychology). From there she journeyed into Native American spirituality, and then she came to bow before the Buddha.

If you visited her home (as *Newsweek* did), you would find a truly postmodern altar. Currently it sports "an angel statue, a small bottle of 'sacred water' blessed at a women's vigil, a crystal ball, a pyramid, a small brass image of Buddha sitting on a brass leaf, a votive candle, a Hebrew prayer, a tiny Native American basket from the 1850s, and a picture of her 'most sacred place,' a madrone tree near her home."[7]

Consider Cara Seeger of Victoria, British Columbia. She doesn't go very many days without a magical ceremony of Wicca. She reads tarot cards, immerses herself in Taoism, and practices Buddhism. Like an echo of our pluralistic culture she says, "I believe all attempts of mankind and woman kind to reach the divine are valid."[8]

I read about New York psychotherapist Nancy SantoPietro. She has, it seems, all but abandoned her practice of traditional psychotherapy in favor of *feng shui* ("wind" and "water" in Chinese). *Feng shui* helps her patients find jobs, lovers, and other good things. To cure relationship problems, Santopietro counsels: "Hang a pink shui crystal on a nine-inch red string in your relationship corner."[9]

Our postmodern time is a "consumer culture choosing from a smorgasbord of worldviews."

—Richard Middleton and Brian Walsh

These seekers, like many postmodern gurus, seem to teach four doctrines. First, salvation will come from within you—not from some God or Savior "up there." Books like the *Celestine Prophecy*, films like *The Color Purple*, and songs like Mariah Carey's "Hero" reinforce this. Second, God is in everything, and everything in the universe is connected—and thus good. As one missionary, Agnes Sanford, preached, "God is actually *in* the flowers and the growing grass and all the little, chirping, singing things. He made everything out of himself and then put a part of himself into everything."[10] Third, we are virtual gods, evolving toward divinity as taught by a host of teachers and authors. Fourth, our destiny is to escape conscious personhood. We will rise above the strife and suffering of this life only when we lose personal consciousness and become absorbed into nirvana, the great impersonal oversoul of the universe. Then our personal identity will get lost like a drop of water flicked into the ocean.

So, for postmoderns, the god-rush is on. Spirituality, any spirituality will do, it seems. "Never before has a society allowed its people to become consumers of belief, and allowed belief—all belief—to become merchandise."[11] Our postmodern time is a "consumer culture choosing from a smorgasbord of worldviews."[12]

But increasingly seekers experience disappointment as one after another of the new idols fail to deliver the promised goods. More and more the weary searchers echo Stephen Crane's experience:

A learned man came to me once.
He said, "I know the way—come."
And I was overjoyed at this.
Together we hastened,
Soon, too soon, we were
Where my eyes were useless,
And I knew not the ways of my feet.
I clung to the hand of my friend;
But at last he cried, "I am lost."[13]

In these days of confused and frantic longing for God, gods, some god, any god, despair rises like a dark tide. The efforts of the human race to exist in autonomy have failed.

How do we pack the frantic search for spiritual truth into the *New York Times* time capsule? Whatever we choose to represent these times of empty hearts and failed gods, we must include something that represents another group of people: those who have anchored their hopes in the God of the Bible. Those who have turned to Jesus Christ for new life, hope, and salvation.

There are those among us who do not dwell in the land C. S. Lewis described as "always December but never Christmas." They have found the deeper spiritual life "in Christ."

Not enticed by get-rich gimmicks, these souls are content with bread and bed and roof and family circle.

Not tempted by impromptu messiahs, they walk with the confident pace of those who know a wise and gentle Shepherd who leads them to still waters and green pastures.

Not tortured by fears of tomorrow, they face the future like the sea at rest.

Not despairing because of past shame, they rejoice in the grace of sins freely forgiven.

Not devoured by lust, they keep the sensual subordinate to sanctity.

Not disillusioned by pain, they embrace the assurance that God will surely use their suffering redemptively.

Not devastated by rootlessness, they build on a sure foundation.

Not destroyed by selfishness, they pour out their lives for Christ and others.

These optimistic pilgrims have discovered that holiness and happiness are twins. With Thomas Kelly they have found the joys of the holy life ravishing and its peace profound.[14] Their secret is described in the Bible. They are the ones who, "with unveiled faces, see . . . the glory of the Lord as though reflected in a mirror, [and] are being transformed into the same image from one degree of glory to another" (2 Cor. 3:18, NRSV).

No matter who you are, no matter what sins weigh down your soul, no matter how many times you have failed, no matter how many false idols you have bowed to, you, too, can find the holy and happy life.

"But I'm a sinner," you say.

That's good news; you're in the very group that Jesus came to save.

— 2 —

Who Am I?

First Window on the Word

What is man that you are mindful of him . . . ? You made him a little lower than the angels; you crowned him with glory and honor and put everything under his feet (Heb. 2:6-8).

Rebecca Thompson, 37, sits on the edge of the Fremont Canyon Bridge near Casper, Wyoming. She looks at the North Platte River flowing 112 feet below in the rocky canyon. She gazes at the rocks and the water and begins to cry.

She tells her friend, who is holding Rebecca's 2-year-old daughter, that she has been here before, 19 years before, when she was just 18.

Rebecca chokes out the story between sobs.

On that awful night she and her 11-year-old sister, Amy, went to a convenience store in Casper to buy potato chips and Cokes. They were going to go home and watch a movie on television. When they came out, they found someone had slashed a tire on their car with a knife. Jerry Lee Jenkins and Ronald Leroy Kennedy offered to help.

Rebecca, 18, went back into the store, phoned her mom, and told her that two nice men were going to help them get the tire fixed.

But instead of helping, Jenkins and Kennedy grabbed the girls and hauled them off in their car. Beating them up to keep them quiet as they drove, they headed for the Fremont Canyon Bridge 40 miles away. When they found that lonely bridge on that dark night, the two men took turns beating and raping Rebecca. Her face was pulp. Somehow Rebecca was able to beg them not to do the same to her horrified little sister. They didn't. Instead they threw her off the bridge. She hit a boulder at the river's edge 112 feet below and died instantly. The rapists threw Rebecca off the bridge too. She hit a ledge, then bounced into the water with her hip broken in five places. She dragged herself ashore, hovered between two big rocks, and waited through the shivering night. A man and his wife on a fishing trip found Rebecca about 10 A.M. the next day.

The doctors at the Casper hospital set her broken bones by surgery, using pins and a body cast. But they could not heal her mind and spirit. They could not bring her little sister back. They could not stop the nightmares. Rebecca couldn't either.

The police caught Kennedy and Jenkins. Rebecca testified against them, pointing them out in open court, describing the details. What shame. Everyone now knew of her violation, her humiliation. One of the killers taunted her right there in the courtroom by smirking and sliding his finger across his throat in a slashing motion.

The jury sentenced Kennedy and Jenkins to death. But the U.S. Supreme Court overturned the ruling and reduced the sentence to "life in prison with the possibility of parole."

As soon as they were eligible, Jenkins and Kennedy began to apply for parole. Twice every year they applied. So every six months Rebecca had to return to court and relive that shameful experience. Year after year she recited her shame.

You see, Rebecca had not been assaulted just once but repeatedly. Every time a nightmare woke her up, every time she thought of her dead sister, every time she had to testify again at a parole hearing, the shame came flooding back. Every time she walked down the street, she lived it again as people on the street whispered. Some pointed and avoided her. What do you say to a rape victim? Maybe you cross the street so you don't have to look her in the eye. But everybody knew who she was.

Rebecca could not find the light after that dark night. She lived in the shadows of her guilt and her rage. But the humiliation and shame were the worst. The shame, the eternal shame. It came to dominate her. Every holiday was mutely celebrated in the shadow of that reality. Every morning, afternoon, and evening came and went under that cloud of shame.

"So why after all these years did you want to come back here to the Fremont Canyon Bridge, Rebecca?"

"I know the parole board meets again tomorrow. But surely they won't let those thugs out, Rebecca."

Rebecca is still weeping, out of control now.

The friend does not want the two-year-old to see her mom like this, so she turns to take the baby back to the car.

That's when she hears Rebecca's body hit the water 112 feet below in the bottom of the canyon. The Fremont Canyon Bridge claims Rebecca Thompson one final time.

If Rebecca had only known that she was so much more than her shame.[1]

There are Fremont Canyon Bridges all over the landscape. And there are Rebeccas in every town—men and women acquainted with humiliation, violation, shame. Each thinks his or her name is spelled Worthless, Stained, Hopeless, Humiliated, Violated, Shamed. But God has quite a different spelling.

WHO DO YOU THINK YOU ARE?

Window on the Word

The L*ORD . . . formed the man from the dust of the ground*
and breathed into his nostrils the breath of life,
and the man became a living being (Gen. 2:7).

From Sophocles' *Oedipus Rex* to Alex Haley's *Roots*, classic literature has recorded our longing to solve the riddle of personal identity. From the wanderings of Odysseus to the birth-mother search of the adoptee next door, we have sought with all our hearts to answer the haunting question, "Who am I?"

This is not a trivial pursuit. Psychologist Rollo May asserts that the lonely search for internal identity "is a widespread need which gives rise . . . to . . . the many forms and promises of psychotherapy and the multitude of cure-alls and cult, constructive or destructive as they may be."[2]

Are you a beast?

Some learned folks say that describes you best—the best of the beasts, but still a beast. Hamsters, horses, humans all chained to the same drives and behavior patterns—or so say the sociobiologists.

I heard Joe Bayly, a giant among Christian publishers a generation ago, tell of an encounter at the doctor's office. Joe's faith survived the tragic loss of two sons. He was taking his dying boy for one more treatment. While in the waiting room he met a mother whose son was also dying. Joe spoke words of comfort and inspiration about meeting her son in heaven. But this woman had bought the "animal" definition of human beings. She would have nothing to do with God and heavenly reunions.

"Listen, Mister," she said, "sometime in the next month my son will die. Then we will put his body in a box, dig a hole in the ground, and cover him up with dirt. That will be the end of that."

Are you a human computer?

Some thinkers believe that you are more than a beast; you are a complex and intelligent machine. Theologian Stanley J. Grenz points out that the *Star Trek* series "moves a giant step beyond the wedding of brain and computer chip to the humanization of the computer itself."[3] The 1999 film *Matrix* goes even farther. Personified Artificial Intelligence (A I) enslaves the human race, drawing its existence from the very life of humans.

Are you an immortal soul?

Careful—think before you answer. Part of you may be described as "immortal soul," but you are much more than that. The people who use this phrase to define you and me sometimes talk as if the immaterial part of our being is all that counts, that the body is just the prison house of the soul. Shirley MacLaine, in one of her out-of-body experiences, said, "I now understood how irrelevant my physical body was."[4] One day your immortal soul will shed this body and fly free, and you can then become your true self. You hear this kind of talk at funerals a lot. Remember the 1989 film *Steel Magnolias*? Shelby has died, and Annel makes a wonderful speech about the bliss the deceased will enjoy in her new disembodied existence. But it is sub-Christian.

The notion that death is a doorway to eternal bliss conjures scary implications. Is suicide the route to trouble-free happiness? This idea also aligns with the teaching of reincarnation that our true humanness resides in some mysterious spiritual element called the soul.[5] This notion is at least as old as Plato and several ancient Eastern religions that have emerged into our culture. But the popularity of this presumption does not change the Bible teaching that you and I are embodied creatures, and that we will remain so throughout eternity —just as, many believe, Jesus will be.

Defining yourself as an immortal soul is also unbiblical when immortality is understated as something that we have or are, something we possess. "There is nothing within us that is intrinsically immortal. . . . We simply don't have within ourselves the power to live forever."[6] Eternal life, all life, is something we receive, not something we are. It is a gift of God.

Are you a god?

In multiplied examples the Bible shows that God is distinct from and above all created things and beings.

Some of the most popular gurus today tell us that we are virtual gods. I remember hearing John Denver say in a radio interview, "I'm making progress. I'm getting better and better. Someday I'll be a god." Sadly he became an air crash victim at age 47 before he could claim godhood. Carol Riddell challenges us all to transcend our status as homo sapiens and join her in becoming Homo Divinus.[7]

Millions more, including some within the Christian community, urge us to discover God within. They echo the notions of *The Aquarian Gospel* and its heresy that "all things are God; all things are one."[8] Such self-aggrandizing teachings sound so warm and cozy that it is hard for some to examine them critically. But those who do find them unbiblical and at odds with the Christian faith.

In multiplied examples the Bible shows that God is distinct from and above all created things and beings. In fact, while bearing the image of God, we are "fundamentally one with all that is not God, whether trees, galaxies, animals or the earth. Indeed, our solidarity with the non-human realm is indicated by our creation along with other land animals on the sixth day [Gen. 1:24-31] and our sharing the same food with them."[9]

THE CHRISTIAN VIEW OF WHAT IT MEANS TO BE HUMAN

Window on the Word

Children of God . . . that is what we are! . . .
When he appears, we shall be like him (1 John 3:1-2).

So if you are not an animal, a sophisticated computer, an immortal soul, or a god, what is your real identity?

1. You are an embodied person created by God and in the very image of God (see Gen. 1:27). The Lord arranged that when Adam and Eve produced offspring, the image of God was passed to all generations. Echoes of God's own

image include our ability to love, to transcend self, to reason, to make moral decisions.[10]

2. You are the object of God's love. Max Lucado put it this way: "If God had a refrigerator, your picture would be on it. If He had a wallet your photo would be in it. He sends you flowers every spring and a sunrise every morning. Whenever you want to talk He'll listen. . . . And the Christmas gift He sent you in Bethlehem? Face it, friend. He's crazy about you."[11] The Bible reveals how far God will go to express His love for you. The suffering of Christ is the supreme example. God's love does not fluctuate; it is steady. It is not permissive, gushy, and sentimental; it is redemptive. "Perhaps a good Christian response to Descartes's dictum *cogito ergo sum* (I think, therefore I am) is *sum amatus ergo sum* (I am loved, therefore I am)."[12]

3. You are a unity of body, soul, spirit, mind, and heart.[13]

4. You are male or female. Theologians such as Karl Barth, Paul Jewett, and Kenneth Grider see our maleness or femaleness as part of the image of God.[14]

5. You are a person who is free and responsible. Though you are marked by sin and by the Fall, God has graciously given you the ability to choose God and good. This is called prevenient grace.

You are not free to choose your parents, birthday, physical characteristics, or mental capacity. But you are able, in spite of sin, to choose God and good. Even this ability is the gift of God. John Wesley wrote, "He [God] made you free agents; having an inward power of self-determination, which is essential to your nature. And he deals with you as free agents from first to last."[15]

Environment influences you, but because of grace given to each one of us, it does not have the final word. Some teach that whether you are a missionary or a murderer, you should not be praised or blamed because you are merely what society (environment) made of you. But this is not the picture of humankind that the Bible or experience reveals. You are given the capacity to choose good, and you are held responsible for your choice. You cast the deciding vote in choosing good or evil.

— 3 —

What Am I Searching For and Why Am I Here?

First Window on the Word

LORD . . . we wait for you. . . . My soul yearns for you in the night; in the morning my spirit longs for you (Isa. 26:8-9).

Graduation, Stanford University—a student speaker addressed the celebrating crowd, describing his class as not having any idea how "it relates to the past or the future, having little sense of the present, no life-sustaining beliefs, secular or religious" and consequently having "no goal and no path."[1]

Everywhere you see people lost, lonely, hungry, and searching for something. As confusing as this life is, they often do something as dumb as the three car thieves in Larkspur, California, who tried to break into a pickup truck. The owner saw them and chased them yelling. He hailed a policeman, and he, too, gave chase. The thieves made a valiant effort to escape. They scrambled over a tall fence with barbed wire ripping their pants and scratching blood out of their shins. But it was worth it. The rotund truck owner and the middle-aged cop could never scale a fence like that.

They didn't have to.

The cop looked through the wires and said, "Congratulations, men. You just broke into San Quentin!"[2]

Our attempts to save ourselves are usually about as smart as breaking into prison. Ever feel like that yourself? Have you ever broken into a homemade jail?

The Longing Heart's Cry

Window on the Word

Among those nations you will find no repose, no resting place. . . .
There the LORD will give you an anxious mind,
eyes weary with longing, and a despairing heart (Deut. 28:65).

Many of us feel alone in a world of broken relationships. Our friendships are casual, our commitment to others superficial. Our interchanges come only from the surface of our lives. Remember the scene in George Orwell's *1984*, where the conversation flowed from the speakers' throats, not from their hearts or minds? We ask, "How are you?" but we don't expect a serious answer. It seems we can't find anyone to really care about the deepest needs within us. So we pay a psychiatrist or counselor to listen to us. All around us, we see people in similar pain, with longings like ours. They live in our neighborhoods, away from family and friends. They are our coworkers, reeling from the pain of broken marriages. They are our children's schoolmates, enduring secret abuse at home. We wonder what life is all about anyway and why we should face tomorrow. Our hearts cry out for meaningful intimacy with another.

Let's fill this emptiness with something. That's what the world around us is saying: Let's fill it with material things! Some of us seem to have so many of them. In his book *Lead Us into Temptation*, James Twitchell proposes that acquiring material goods is the modern religion. The acquisition of things gives us status, security, and a sense of belonging. Millions play the lottery and enter sweepstakes.

Doing our own thing has become synonymous with finding meaning. Some even compromise their values and endanger their lives for fleeting experiences of superficial acceptance. Can indulgence in sex, stimulants, or gambling really make us feel better? Can we fill the aching void with entertainment? Recently a teenager who had gone through a period of depression told me how she felt about TV sitcoms: "I see why people watch them," she said. "They may be pointless and empty, but when you're depressed and life has no meaning, you can watch them and try to forget your pain. You can laugh and pretend you're happy." From deep within, our hearts yearn for intimacy and meaning.

Programs can't muffle the cry of innumerable hearts longing for a meaningful relationship with the Almighty and an experience of community with the people of God.

Enough of us feel like that to make Alanis Morrissette's song "All I Really Want" a top hit. Of course, you're not sure the singer knows what she wants. Is it peace, patience, or something to "calm the angry voice"? By the last stanza it sounds as if she longs for a kindred spirit, a soul mate, anyone who "understands."

Why do so many watch the television series *Friends*? Notice the theme song: "I'll Be There for You." Like the "Class of '57" these generation Xers found that "life gets complicated when you get past 18." As "pathless" as the Stanford graduating class were, they pledge to be there for each other. Why? "Because our deepest desire isn't to possess things but to belong. This leads us to seek out friendships that (we hope) can provide us with the sense of 'belonging' we crave."[3]

Many voices tell us that this inner need is a spiritual need. Ours is an age of intense spiritual hunger. People long for closeness with a higher power, with "god" as they understand Him. Bookstores provide entire sections for seekers. Tapes and compact discs offer messages and music to soothe the soul. Spirituality is a hot topic for talk shows. Gurus can be reached via 800 numbers. Retreat centers report record attendance, many with waiting lists. Stadiums and auditoriums are packed with all sorts of people seeking all sorts of things.

Many of us in mainstream Christianity have tried to fill our inner longing with the programs and activities of the church. Christian entertainment competes with its secular counterpart. We become religious consumers who hop from church to church, seeking the programs that meet our needs. Churches compete in this market-driven economy, striving to be "full-service congregations." They provide seven-day-a-week programs that respond to a wide spectrum of felt needs. But programs can't muffle the cry of innumerable hearts longing for a meaningful relationship with the Almighty and an experience of community with the people of God. We hunger for something deeper and more radical than mere religious activity.

Few works of fiction have depicted the superficiality of our relationships and the meaninglessness of modern life more forcefully than Samuel Beckett's *Waiting for Godot*. The entire play, a pointless conversation between Vladimir, Estragon, and several other characters, implies that every relationship and every human endeavor appears to be without meaning. The unifying element in the play is that the two main characters are always "waiting for Godot." Several times the following dialogue is repeated:

"Let's go."

"We can't."

"Why not?"

"We're waiting for Godot."

"Godot" is the one who will give meaning to life. But "Godot" never comes! Whatever Beckett's intention, the play is a vivid depiction of the meaninglessness of our lives without God.

Douglas Coupland is on to something. This man who coined the phrase *generation X* wrote in *Life After God*, "My secret is that I need God—that I am sick and can no longer make it alone. I need God to help me give, because I can no longer . . . be . . . giving; to help me be kind, as I no longer seem capable of kindness; to help me love, as I seem beyond being able to love."[4]

Our deepest hunger is for fellowship and intimacy with God, the triune God, who is the perfect demonstration of community, relationship, and outreaching love.

Why Am I Here?

Window on the Word

What does the L*ORD require of you? . . . Act justly . . . love mercy and . . . walk humbly with your God* (Mic. 6:8).

When the new millennium arrived, people were still asking, "Why am I here?" The 1999 film *Dogma* (a combination of sacrilege and comedy, banned in some cities) ends with the main character asking God, "Why are we here?" God, played by pop singer Alanis Morrissette, just grins, tweaks the questioner's nose, and disappears. Is existence a joke? Our purpose a mystery? Does God even know why we are here?

But in your heart of hearts you know there is a purpose to life. We find that intuition confirmed in the Bible.

1. *The Bible says that the Lord put us in authority over the earth.*

"Then God said, 'Let us make man in our image . . . and let them rule over . . . all the creatures'" (Gen. 1:26). We are part of creation, and we are to be caretakers of the earth. Christians sometimes develop an antinature bias that views nature as something to be exploited, strip-mined, and used up. We must realize that "creation is more than our larder, our playground, our sports arena, our theatre of war. It is God's handiwork; we depend on creation more than creation depends on us; it should command our respect."[5] Psalm 8:6 says, "You made him [humankind] ruler over the works of your hands."

2. *Another part of our purpose is to develop a godly community of faith.*

Maria Harris had a point when she wrote, "A solitary Christian is no Christian. We come to God together, or we do not come at all."[6] The church, the family of faith, is to reflect the Trinity. The Three-in-One God models the perfect community, and Christians on earth are to echo that ideal community.

The genius of the early Wesleyan movement was the *community* achieved in the face-to-face groups (classes, bands, select societies, etc.). They discovered the wisdom of the New Testament that urges the "bearing of one another's burdens, of confronting, correcting, encouraging, exhorting, comforting and edifying one another; of provoking one another to love and good works, of confessing our faults to one another; of weeping with those who weep and rejoicing with those who rejoice; of sharing . . . the same love and unity that Jesus shares with his Father."[7]

God has authorized His children to be His signet ring, His representatives on earth.

3. *We are also here to reflect the image of God.*

The kings of the ancient Near East often left images of themselves in the parts of their kingdom where they could not often be present in person. In a similar manner, God placed you and me on earth to represent our King and Creator. "Our purpose is to show all creation what God is like, especially as we mirror the divine character."[8]

Indeed, God has authorized His children to be His signet ring, His representatives on earth. "'I will take you, my servant . . . and I will make you like my signet ring, for I have chosen you,' declares the LORD Almighty" (Hag. 2:23). We are to reflect the image of God on earth. That is why we must stand with unveiled faces beholding the glory of the Lord as in a mirror. Thus we will be transformed more and more into His image, as 2 Cor. 3:18 teaches.

4. *God's poem.*

Ephesians 2:10 tells us, "We are God's workmanship, created in Christ Jesus to do good works, which God prepared in advance for us to do." The basic Greek word translated "workmanship" is *poiēma*. Our word *poem* comes from that ancient term. Think about it; you are God's poem! His work of art. His masterpiece. God is writing a poem in and through your life!

Three important questions were raised in chapters 2 and 3: Who am I? What am I searching for? Why am I here? You are an embodied person created in the image of God. You are hungering for a vital, intimate relationship with Him. And you are here on earth to reflect the image of God as a work of art reflects the heart of its creator. Your destiny is not absorption into some impersonal nirvana, but full community with the God who invites you to the heaven He has prepared for those who bear the signet ring of faith in His Son Jesus Christ.

Now there's a calling for you. Much more lofty than the "divine" tweaking of the nose in *Dogma*. Much more meaningful than the bleak Fremont Canyon Bridge that shut out the light for Rebecca Thompson. Do you need to ponder Paul's plea to the Ephesian believers? "I urge you to live a life worthy of the calling you have received" (4:1).

— 4 —

What Went Wrong, Anyway?

First Window on the Word

The god of this age has blinded the minds of unbelievers, so that they cannot see the light of the gospel (2 Cor. 4:4).

"I ran out of *at leasts*," Scott said without emotion.

"I used to say, when I would see other people doing wrong, 'At least I don't do that.' Now I have run out of *at leasts*. Nothing matters anymore," he mumbled from his hospital bed.

Scott's suicide attempt had failed. He would live—at least physically. A year earlier he had lost his wife and two children because of an adulterous affair with his secretary. A few weeks later, both he and his secretary were fired from their jobs. Then the lovers discovered they did not want each other anymore—at least, she didn't want him. Scott sought refuge from the gnawing anguish in the stupor of drugs and liquor.

"I had such a great start," he said, "voted 'most likely to succeed.' But now—and this is the hardest part—I turned out to be what I always said, and really believed, I would never be."

We, the very ones intended to reflect God's image in this world, so often end up like Scott—unholy and unhappy.

"Me? God's work of art! God's poem? Surely you jest. Mirror God to the world? Are you kidding? I am so lost I wonder if I will ever find my way. The more I try, the worse I get. I am ashamed of what I do and even more ashamed of what I want to do."

Look at the artwork on the cover of this book. Notice the light. Focus on the light so delicately reflected and refracted. Notice the leaf, its tip sending out gentle ripples in the deep pool. The ripples reflecting the glow murmur the redemptive peace and light of God that move out to a thousand generations. Evil, on the other hand, goes on only to the third and fourth generation (Exod. 34:6-7). The light, the leaf, the pool, the ripples—what a peaceful scene. You can almost hear the twilight tones of a flute with an ethereal cascade of strings in the background that set the tired heart "aglow with the Spirit" (Rom. 12:11, RSV).

"Aglow with the Spirit? Peaceful? Calm? My heart is more like a traffic jam on a hot day. If I am supposed to reflect the image of God, if I was meant for a holy, intimate walk with God, something has gone terribly wrong."

You are right. Something has gone wrong with the human enterprise.

ALIENATION IS EVERYWHERE

Window on the Word

Their mouths are full of cursing and bitterness. . . . Ruin and misery mark their ways, and the way of peace they do not know (Rom. 3:14, 16-17).

Sin has frustrated our destiny of walking in harmony, holiness, and happiness with God. Instead of relationship we find loneliness. Instead of intimacy with our Creator we find *alienation.* Millions feel separated from anything that really matters.

We find ourselves alienated from our families and friends. Why does the family reunion seem so unpleasant? Even if divorce has not ground its teeth on your soul, you and your spouse may live in a parched "isolation for two." One indicator of our alienation from family is the number of television programs featuring one-parent families, divorcés, blended families, and searching singles.

In the world at large we see multitudes living by the creeds of "Nice guys finish last" or "If you don't look out for old number one, no one else will." We live and lunch every day with persons addicted to acquisitiveness—compulsives possessed with possessing more than the Joneses. So what if one must lie, cheat, steal, manipulate, and exploit to build a stack of goodies? The wars that rage on our planet are further testimony to the sinful greed and hatred that can capture the human heart.

Worse than the alienation from others is our estrangement from God. Like Adam and Eve we have distrusted and disobeyed God. Therefore "presuming that God is hostile toward us we project our enmity toward God on God."[1] When we hear His voice in the silences of our hearts, we run away and hide in our busy schedules. When He calls us back into healing, into spiritual relationship, we flee to our soul-numbing pleasures or drown out His still small voice with conscience-soothing games.

We find ourselves alienated from others, from God, and even from our own best selves. We do not find ourselves alone with God, and, therefore, we do not find ourselves at all.

Out of ancient India comes a fable about a motherless tiger cub. The orphaned beast was adopted by goats who taught him to bleat and eat grass. The cub thought he was a goat.

One day a king tiger came along. The goats scattered in fear. But the cub, fascinated by the tiger, stayed behind, afraid, yet not afraid. The tiger asked the cub why in the world he was acting like a goat. The confused cub could only bleat nervously—he couldn't even talk tiger—and continue to nibble grass.

The king tiger picked up the cub and carried him to the edge of a clear lake. He made the cub look at their two images reflected in the water. The tiger thought that the little fellow would make his own correct conclusions, but the cub just kept on bleating like a goat.

Next, the king tiger made the cub eat raw meat. At first he couldn't stand it, but as he ate more and felt it warming his blood, the truth about what he really was became clear to him. Lashing his tail and digging his claws into the earth, the young beast raised his head high, and the jungle trembled at his exultant roar.

In India the tiger represents all that is strong, graceful, and noble in life. We were created for the noble, lofty, and holy life—but because of sin we live like goats. Alienated from our best selves, we struggle along failing and falling, even when we aim high. God has planted His image within us. It guides us, goads us, woos us toward God and good. But we also discover a traitorous "foeman's heart" within.

We were created for the noble, lofty, and holy life —but because of sin we live like goats.

Picture a medieval castle—tall stone walls, strategically placed parapets, strong swordsmen guarding the gate. The castle is surrounded by a deep moat. Safe and secure, right? But what if there is an enemy within the castle who in the still of the night keeps letting down the drawbridge so the enemy can attack? The sinful human heart is like that. Sin keeps betraying our lofty aspirations, our firmest resolutions, our most energetic effort to walk in righteousness with God.

Sin is an inside job. The problem is the enemy within our own hearts. Sin does not exist all by itself. It has no life apart from human motives and actions. Sin is not some external defect or flaw. It is not some chunk of toxic material that pollutes our body and soul. It is not something that can be removed by surgery. No, sin is what fills the spiritual vacuum created by the loss of right relationship to God.

Where Did Sin Come From?

Window on the Word

The fruit of the tree was good for food and pleasing to the eye, and also desirable for gaining wisdom (Gen. 3:6).

The first 11 chapters of your Bible apply ancient wisdom to the great human questions: Where did we come from? Who are we? Why are we here? Genesis chapter 3 answers the question: "Why is there so much sin and misery in the world?"

Adam and Eve, our first parents, were deceived in the Garden of Eden, where they lived in holy and happy relationship with God, each other, and creation. But the serpent convinced them that God was maliciously reserving certain beneficial things for himself; that He was handing out commands: "Don't touch that tree!" The "deprived" pair took steps (or bites) to grab their fair share. "They aspired to be like God, and they succeeded in becoming their own god."[2] That first sin plunged humanity into sin. Adam and Eve bequeathed to all their descendants a tainted world, a fragmented nature, and a propensity to follow selfishness rather than God and good. Since that day "no longer do we experience creation, our co-pilgrims, our creator, or ourselves as friends. Instead . . . the fellowship without flaws, wholesomeness without a history of hurt . . . is gone for all time."[3]

The very nature of sin, its living portrait, emerges from that ancient and yet ever so modern story. The problem began with *unbelief*, that is, with distrust or "unfaith" in God's goodness. This spirit says, "How could God really have my best interest at heart and deprive me of that fine fruit that is so good for food, so pleasing to the eye, and so desirable for gaining wisdom?" (see Gen. 3:6).

Pride or *egocentricity* also struts like a drum major through the story of the first sin. Eager to claim everything that God had, they exalted themselves to the control tower of their own beings. Egocentricity expressed as self-idolatry is the very nature of sin—theirs and ours. Sinful selfishness is crowned king of the heart. Self-gratification prowls the slums of the soul, dragging what was meant to be holy into the dens of sin and sensuality. Though there is no evidence that sexual immorality was the offense of this Edenic couple, many sinners since have cried out with Augustine, "I polluted the spring of friendship with the lust of concupiscence."[4]

The third intrinsic element in sin is *disobedience*. Eve and Adam put their distrust and egocentric longings into action and deliberately disobeyed God. They destroyed their relationship with God, creation, and each other. From that day until the most recent tick of the clock, sin has hounded human life on earth. How up to date is this description written by John Wesley more than 200 years ago.

> Open your eyes! Look around you! See darkness that may be felt; see ignorance and error; see vice in ten thousand forms; see . . . guilt, fear, sorrow, shame, remorse, covering the face of the earth! See misery, the daughter of sin. See, on every side, sickness and pain . . . driving on the poor, helpless sons of men, in every age, to the gates of death!"[5]

IS THAT FAIR?

Window on the Word

We all, like sheep, have gone astray, each of us has turned to his own way (Isa. 53:6).

It doesn't seem fair that I should suffer because of the wrong choices of Adam and Eve at the dawn of human history. I wasn't even there. How can I be held responsible for their antics?

Ever since (and even before) the church fathers Pelagius and Augustine squared off about this subject, theologians have debated the whys and wherefores of sin that universally imprisons every generation. Not all the issues have been settled, but candid consideration makes one thing clear: the story of Adam and Eve is our story—mine and yours. They not only preceded us but also represented us.

You and I have repeated the exact sins of Adam and Eve. We have destroyed our intended destiny of holiness and happiness in close relationship with God. Unbelief, distrust, pride, selfishness, disobedience—every one of them has lounged at your table and laughed at your jokes. You have often ordered them to stay out of sight in the basement of your heart. But the gang downstairs is a disorderly bunch. They threaten to make a scene at any moment. Don't you wish you could control them? Some days you wonder if they actually may be in charge of your whole house. Dietrich Bonhoeffer warned, "We think we are pushing and we are being pushed. We do not rule, we are ruled."[6]

Sin Is an Abusive Master

Window on the Word

At one time we too were foolish, disobedient, deceived and enslaved by all kinds of passions and pleasures (Titus 3:3).

Sinners can quickly become like the demoniac of Gadara (Mark 5), who was controlled by forces stronger than himself. Ask anyone who has fought addiction to alcohol, drugs, tobacco, or sexual perversion. Sexual appetites, John Wesley observed, "lead [a person] captive: they drag him to and fro; in spite of his boasted reason . . . good breeding, and other accomplishments [the man] has no preeminence over the goat."[7]

The sinful self is not only *unwilling* to submit to the rule of God but also *incapable* of submitting to the will of God.[8] The harder we try, the more we fail. "But though he strive with all his might he cannot conquer, sin is mightier than he. . . . He resolves against it, but yet sins on: *He sees the snare and abhors [it] and runs into it!*"[9]

I'll call her Marcia. She has a husband and a one-year-old son at home. But that did not stop her from going on a three-day binge. She ran out of money after a day or so of drinking and shooting up, so she sold her engagement and wedding rings in order to buy one more packet of cocaine. Before the weekend was over, she landed in police custody. On Monday she sat between her husband and her mother as they drove her to the county detox unit. Marcia cried and cried. Over and over she kept saying the same thing: "I don't want to be this way, Mama. I don't want to be this way."

Sin touches every part of our being. That prompts theologians to talk about "total depravity." An ancient Yoruba (Nigerian) proverbial greeting goes, "May your secret never be discovered." But our secret is out, mine and yours. We have destroyed our relationship with others, with creation, with God, and with our own best self through sin—not Adam's sin, ours. The Bible tells our secret: our foolish hearts are darkened (Rom. 1:21), our minds corrupted, and we have made God our enemy (1 Tim. 6:5; Rom. 8:7-8). Jesus tells our secret too. He said that we love darkness better than light. We are drawn to the Light—not to embrace it, but to smash it, to kill it, for the Light exposes our wickedness (John 3:19-21).

What dominant commonality do we all share? Sin!

Paul describes the pervasiveness of sin:

> They have become filled with every kind of wickedness, evil, greed and depravity. They are full of envy, murder, strife, deceit and malice. They are gossips, slanderers, God-haters, insolent, arrogant and boastful; they invent ways of doing evil; they disobey their parents; they are senseless, faithless, heartless, ruthless. Although they know God's . . . decree . . . they . . . continue to do these very things *(Rom. 1:29-32).*

Some say that universal sin is the most practically verifiable of all the Christian doctrines. What dominant commonality do we all share? Sin!

WHY DOESN'T SOMEBODY DO SOMETHING?

Window on the Word

I know my transgressions . . . my sin is always before me. . . . Cleanse me . . . wash me, and I will be whiter than snow. . . . Blot out all my iniquity. Create in me a pure heart, O God (Ps. 51:3, 7, 9-10).

Can't we do something about the mess we are in?

It's not as though we haven't tried. During the "modern" period we put our messianic eggs in the arrogant basket of reason and its chicks: education, science, and technology. In the "postmodern" period the basket has been dropped and abandoned by many.

In the new millennium people are chasing self-help gurus, New Age practitioners, and Eastern religious rites. All the new messiahs tell us with great assurance that the power to save ourselves lies within us. Some even quote the old translations of Luke 17:21, where Jesus says, "The kingdom of God is *within* you." However, the term and the context demand that it be read, "The kingdom of God is *among* you."[10] Singers like Mariah Carey, in her recent hit, "Hero," assure us that we can find a "hero" within, a savior within ourselves, if we just look hard enough.[11]

But biblical history and our own personal journeys into darkness tell us that to believe that we can save ourselves is, once again, to have "no preeminence over the goat." We may deny our sin, we may hide it, we may deceive ourselves about our own alienated condition, but sooner or later we must admit our sin.

In *Scandalous Risks*, Susan Howatch tells the compelling story of Venetia Flaxton. She falls in love with a man, and a secret love affair develops. The two lovers rationalize their sin. "Love" is justification enough for them. After all, they reason, the ancient biblical language no longer describes the contemporary God. But doubts about the affair begin to bother Venetia. She seeks the counsel of an elderly priest.

The old priest tells her the story of the victims of the Hiroshima atom bomb. Some of the survivors thought they had escaped. But they were contaminated by an invisible pollutant that entered their flesh and settled in their bones. It was slowly but surely killing them. He spelled out for her the insidious way sin contaminates all of life. She made elaborate arguments to justify her desires.

Finally the priest made Venetia look in the mirror. She saw in her own face the destruction of sin. She finally admits that the damage is so serious that she can no longer find God.[12] Like Scott at the start of this chapter, she had to admit that she had become what she always said and really believed she would never be. She, too, had run out of "at leasts."

What can I hope for? Can anyone help? Yes, salvation, holiness, and happiness are offered. But when the Bible speaks of salvation, the first thing we learn is that it is not of ourselves (Eph. 2:8).

Part 2

o

And we, who with unveiled faces all reflect the Lord's glory, are being transformed into his likeness with ever-increasing glory, which comes from the Lord (2 Cor. 3:18).

Once there was a king who wanted his two sons to grow up to be courteous, well-mannered gentlemen. But in their youth their behavior made him wonder if they would ever reach such a goal. In order to help them think about the matter, he challenged them with this proposition: Suppose a man had a son and wanted him to become a gentleman. Could he make a gentleman of him by proper training and education?

The first son answered, "Indeed, with good educational training he could make whatever he liked out of the boy."

The second son declared, "No, you are wrong. No amount of mere training would produce a gentleman."

The king, seeing that they disagreed, gave the boys a month to think and study. Then they would be summoned to appear before the king again, and each would have to prove his case. The one who proved his case would be given his father's throne when the king passed to the other world.

The first son decided to think it over by meditating in a tavern. He ordered a soft drink. To his surprise he saw that his drink was served to him by a cat, a cat dressed in a waiter's uniform and walking on its back legs. If you can train a cat to be a waiter—well, the first son knew he had a winning argument. He purchased the trained cat from the tavern owner. Soon he would be the king of all the realm.

The second son saw what had happened. He, too, thought that his brother had won the argument and would be the one to wear the king's crown. How the second son wanted to be king. But how could he compete with a cat trained as a waiter—and a good one at that? Then one day as he walked sadly down the street thinking of the lost throne, he saw something in the store window that made him smile.

The day came for the hearing before the king. The first son presented his trained cat. The cat was dressed in royal attire, walked on its back legs, and daintily served the king a plate of three chocolates.

Next the elegant, trained cat was to serve the king hot tea. But just as he approached the king with the steaming potion, the second son opened the bag he was carrying and emptied it on the floor. Five frightened mice went running for cover. The elegant, trained cat dropped the tea, scalding the king. On all fours, the cat pounced on the nearest mouse, snarling, and growling and gobbling its favorite food!

As valuable as education, discipline, and training are, when it comes to our hearts, it's transformation we need!

Do not conform any longer to the pattern of this world,
but be transformed by the renewing of your mind *(Rom. 12:2).*

— 5 —

Is It True What They Say About God?

First Window on the Word

Praise be to the . . . Father of compassion . . . the God of all comfort (2 Cor. 1:3).

"Is it true what they say about God?" my 10-year-old patient asked through tears. Sheila Burns was sick, very sick. She had heard one of the doctors at Children's Mercy Hospital half whisper to me, "Life threatening. We will know by this time tomorrow." That confirmed what her own intuition had told her. She might be meeting her Maker soon, very soon.

"Is it true what they say about God?"

Curbing my own panic and calling on my professional nurse's training, I said, "Well, dear, that depends on what they say about God."

"That He never forgets any sin you ever did—not even one. Is it true?"

"Well, I—"

"That He sends you to hell to make you pay . . . Like the preacher said, 'Be sure your sin will find you out'?"

"Honey, I think—"

"I'm afraid, Mrs. Mayfield. I'm afraid of God!"

I held Sheila for a long time. Then I explained. "It's true, honey, that God knows everything. He knows about your sins and mine. True, He never forgets them until—until He forgives them. But when He forgives our sins, they are cast in the sea of God's forgetfulness and remembered against us no more."

From the Gideon Bible in the room we read Isa. 43:25: "I . . . am he who blots out your transgressions . . . and remembers your sins no more." Then I told Sheila something I remembered from Corrie ten Boom: When God throws our confessed sins into the sea of His forgetfulness, He puts up a sign on the shore: No Fishing Allowed.

Sheila and I prayed and read John 3:16-17. Sheila wasn't afraid of God anymore. God brought her through the illness. She is a college student now and "aglow with the Spirit" (Rom. 12:11, RSV). She knows God as Friend—not fiend.[1]

What is your God like?

GOD IS HOLY

Window on the Word

Be holy, because I am holy (1 Pet. 1:16).

Sheila Burns is not the only one worried about facing a God of blazing holiness. What sinner would dare lift his or her head in the presence of God?

Not Isaiah for sure. He wrote, "I saw the Lord seated on a throne, high and exalted, and the train of his robe filled the temple. Above him were seraphs, each with six wings: With two wings they covered their faces, with two they covered their feet, and with two they were flying. And they were calling . . . 'Holy, holy, holy is the LORD Almighty; the whole earth is full of his glory.' At the sound of their voices the doorposts and thresholds shook and the temple was filled with smoke" (Isa. 6:1-4).

It was as if Isaiah could see the Lord on His throne in an eight-story IMAX theater, even bigger. Step into the scene with him.

See the throne of the King, the Sovereign of the universe filling the IMAX screen, towering over us. All else shrinks to a tiny proportion at the foot of the throne. We look up, and our eyes burn from the blazing brightness of the One engulfed in glory. His robe unfurls, and the mere hem of His royal garment fills the theater where we sit in awe.

Now we can see the throne no longer. It is high above us. We see God's royal attendants, the great seraphim. These powerful, supernatural creatures are so bright that humans can hardly stand to look at them. Dwelling in God's presence, they reflect His dazzling glory like a sun. No science fiction film has ever matched this majestic, regal, awe-inspiring encounter with the *numinous*, the Holy One.

Yet even the mighty seraphim are overwhelmed by the blazing holiness and majesty of God. They cover their faces because they cannot bear to behold His holiness. They cover their feet in abject humility and deference. They shield us from, while directing our attention to, the Holy One, whose radiance we cannot endure.

Hear their powerful voices resonating in celestial surround sound, "Holy, holy, holy is the LORD Almighty." Their entire activity is proclaiming the holiness of God to any who can hear. God is holy. God is almighty.

As the words "the whole earth is full of his glory" reverberate around us, the camera moves. Far beneath the throne lies a panoramic view of the earth spinning out before us. Breathtaking—the whole earth is ablaze with God's glory. Creation is His beautiful handiwork. This, too, speaks of His power and majesty. God's glory fills the earth, and the universe brims with His presence. There is no place for any other god. Our own sin is so out of place in the radiance of God. With awe-inspiring impact the realization hits us that there is no place to hide from His presence. He knows exactly who and where and what we are.

We look again toward the throne of the holy God. The images on the screen begin to shake. An earthquake rumbles. Doorposts tremble, thresholds vibrate. The very foundations of our building, our lives, are beginning to collapse. Incense, like perfumed smoke, wells up and fills the theater. Our knees turn to rubber, our tongues dry up like a desert wind that parches the skin and raises the hair on the neck. We are filled with awesome dread. We tremble in fear but linger in fascination with the holy mystery of God.

Our assumptions about God, the world, and ourselves have been shattered. Like Isaiah we cry out, "Woe to me! . . . I am ruined! For I am a man of unclean lips" (v. 5). We would put it in our own words, of course: "What a sinner I am. I am in big trouble. Lord, have mercy on me, a sinner."

Isaiah was a prophet, a man of God; but when he saw himself in comparison with God, his own righteousness looked puny and insignificant. He realized that he, and the people with whom he lived, were pursuing their own way instead of reflecting God's character. In the face of God's all-consuming holiness he grasped the dreadfulness of his sinful condition. All he could think of was, "Woe to me! . . . I am ruined!" "In our culture, a chatty familiarity with 'the Man upstairs' has displaced the speechless awe that dares not move in the presence of the Almighty."[2]

When we draw near to God's majestic, mysterious, and tremendous holiness, our goodness doesn't even show up.

My neighbors enjoyed a California vacation. They showed me pictures of the redwoods in Sequoia National Park. The first photo was nothing special, just a close-up of a tree in the forest. "Giant redwood," Fred said, noting that I was unimpressed. Then he handed me a picture of the same tree with his wife standing beside it. Wow! The tree totally dwarfed her—rotund lady that she is, she looked absolutely tiny next to that huge tree.

When we look at our own goodness compared to that of the next-door neighbor, we look pretty good. But when we draw near to God's majestic, mysterious, and tremendous holiness, our goodness doesn't even show up. It is totally dwarfed by the blazing holiness of God. That's why Sheila Burns, Isaiah, you, and I tend to shiver and tremble in God's presence. How can we ever walk in friendship and intimacy with such a God?

A word used hundreds of times in the Bible to describe God's holiness is *Qodesh*. It means "separate," or "separated," or "wholly other." This simply indicates that God is above and beyond, different and distinct from any other being, from all creation. God inhabits a category all by himself. God alone is holy. Any holiness that we receive will be a gift derived from His holiness. Nothing about us is inherently or naturally holy.

Holiness is not something God "has" or something that we "attribute" to Him. That is, holiness is more than an attribute of God. Holiness is what God *is*. As theologian J. Kenneth Grider says, "Holiness is what God is in His *isness*."

When theologians say that God is *transcendent,* they mean that God is above and beyond what we can ever think, know, or say about Him. Transcendence has to do with the power, majesty, energy (a flaming fire)—the supernatural, dreaded, and compelling presence of God the Creator of the universe.[3] Since God dwells in a completely exclusive category, He is sharply distinguished from all the natural world. The rocks and hills, the plants and animals, men and women are all created and can never be called *God.*[4]

God Is Love

Window on the Word

God is love. Whoever lives in love lives in God (1 John 4:16).

In His very essence God is not only blazing holiness but also *agapē* love. Holiness alone would annihilate us. Love alone would trivialize our sin. "It is a holy God *against* whom we have sinned, but it is a loving God who *forgives* our sin and remakes us from within."[5]

Fortunately for us God has spoken His holiness in a *human idiom,* or expression. Jesus Christ is the grand miracle of God's story of redemptive love. "For God so loved the world that he gave his one and only Son, that whoever believes in him shall not perish but have eternal life" (John 3:16). God's glory, majesty, and awe are not diminished, but heightened in Jesus. The holy, transcendent God is above and beyond us; the loving, immanent God reaches out to us.[6]

"As holiness is the starting point, so love is the high point in the Biblical unfolding of the nature of God."[7] Charles Wesley wrote,

Pure, universal Love Thou art. . . .
Thy nature and Thy name is Love.[8]

But what does all that mean to you and me? Everything—because, as Augustine put it, God "loves each one of us as if there were only one of us to love."[9]

God Is Good

Window on the Word

He is good; his love endures forever (2 Chron. 7:3).

Unlike the Force in *Star Wars,* the deities of traditional African religion, the Hindu gods, and the New Age "godlings," the Christian God is good—all good. The Force in George Lucas's classic space story can produce a moral model like Luke Skywalker and at the same time make an arch villain like Darth Vader. Lucas's Force is "beyond good and evil, encompassing both."[10] New Age and Eastern gurus teach that negative experiences such as hunger, abuse, and rape are just as much a part of God as those experiences that seem good. Hindu teacher Swami Vivekananda tells us that God may "manifest Himself as Evil as well as Good."[11] Eshu, the nearest thing in traditional

African religion to the Satan of the Bible, is, strangely enough, also capable of great good.

The "godlings" of many metanarratives are both good and evil. But the Christian God is good through and through. His constant righteousness is the measure for all moral conduct for human beings. The adherents of the gods who are good on Mondays and Wednesdays and evil on Tuesdays and Thursdays will have to stand in bewildered silence when Christians sing "God Is So Good." The same applies when Christians testify:

Yet in the maddening maze of things
And tossed by storm and flood,
To one fixed hope my spirit clings,
I know that God is good.[12]

God Is Three in One

Window on the Word

May the grace of the Lord Jesus Christ, *and the love of* God, *and the fellowship of the* Holy Spirit *be with you all* (2 Cor. 13:14, emphases added).

If we could master God, He would be less than God. Therefore, our attempts to define Him will always fall short. But Christians believe that the one God of the Bible has revealed himself to us as Father, Son, and Spirit.

Though pluralists today naively claim that Christians and devotees of pagan gods from Han spirits to Ogun to Vishnu are all worshiping the same God and will end up in the same heaven, Christians have another idea. At the heart of our faith is the proclamation that the only true God is the one revealed in the Bible through Jesus Christ. Stanley J. Grenz summarizes belief in the one and triune God in these words:

> Christians can conclude that according to the revelation in Jesus, the only God is Father, Son, and Holy Spirit. This God is one, for the three share the same will, nature, and essence. Christians are not polytheists, for we do not worship three distinct Gods, . . . we do not serve some generic "God" but the God who is Father, Son, and Holy Spirit.[13]

The declaration of belief in the Trinity is more than saying that there are three ways of experiencing God. The three Persons of the Trinity are eternally united in the ideal Divine Community. "God is the eternal community of love, and God is love even apart from the universe."[14]

A proper doctrine of the Trinity keeps us from pitting one Person against another within the Divine Community. Some people speak as if the Father, Son, and Spirit act independently. We cannot separate the one God. "All the Persons of the Trinity are involved in all divine operations."[15] The Athanasian Creed declares, "Such as the Father is, such is the Son, and such is the Holy Spirit. . . . The Father is God, the Son is God, and the Holy Ghost is God."

That's why it is ludicrous for a Sunday School paper that I once read to say, "God killed Jesus for your sins!" The second graders for whom this was intended would doubtless feel sorry for Jesus and resent God the Father. No, every Person within the Trinity acted in unison as God absorbed within himself the suffering required for our redemption.

God calls us to fellowship within the family of faith that echoes the Divine Community above.

Further, the doctrine of the Trinity protects us from an icy deism or a sentimental pantheism. The deists' God is "watching us from a distance," as Bette Midler's song says, but never gets involved. Pantheism teaches that "all is God and God is all." Thus, the crucial doctrine of the Trinity keeps a wholesome balance between the transcendent holiness and the loving immanence of God.[16]

In addition, the teaching of the Trinity shows us that isolated, individual discipleship is not what God intended for us. While honoring our personhood, God calls us to fellowship within the family of faith that echoes the Divine Community above. Whatever else the church is, it is a community of faith.

The Celtic Christians of old spoke of the Trinity in such natural and devotional terms that faith is not strained:

Three folds in the cloth, yet only one napkin is there,
Three joints in the finger, but still only one finger fair,
Three leaves of the shamrock, yet no more than one shamrock to wear,
Frost, snow-flakes, and ice, all in water their origin share,
Three Persons in God; to one God alone we make prayer.[17]

God Is Sovereign Creator

Window on the Word

By him all things were created (Col. 1:16).

"In the beginning God created the heavens and the earth" (Gen. 1:1). No white-frocked scientist laboring in the lab, no fevered vision of a New Age sycophant meditating in the noonday sun can ever change that. British scientist James Lovelock has, he says, discovered that the earth sort of gave birth to itself in a kind of "Virgin Mary" action and is part of God. "The living things, the rocks, the air, the oceans merged to form a new entity, Gaia. Just as the sperm merges with the egg, new life was conceived."[18]

Visionaries who declare that they, their rosebush, and the snake under it are all a part of God promote sub-Christian teachings that the doctrine of the Trinity corrects.

Since God is love, all His acts are loving. Thus, creation was a gracious act of divine love. But neither the earth nor humankind was created to meet some lack, some need in God. "God does not need the world to be who God is.

. . . God does not need the world to be a God of love."[19] God was already a Triune Community of love before He spoke our world into existence.

Since God is Creator, He is also Sovereign. The Creator-Owner of the world alone sets the standards for our world. Our Sovereign is unchangeable. That is, His loving intention for creation never changes. Ever and always, He seeks what is best for us.

God Is Personal

Window on the Word

The LORD *appeared . . . and said, "I am God Almighty"* (Gen. 17:1).

Since we were created as *persons*, we can only relate to God through the prism of *personhood*. Since God, who created us in His own image, is also personal, we can relate to Him. If God is not personal, no vital experience of Him is possible for us. This truth is assumed, if not clearly stated, again and again in Scripture. "God is love. Whoever lives in love lives in God, and God in him. . . . We love because he first loved us" (1 John 4:16, 19). This clearly describes a relationship among persons.

The fact that God relates to us Person to persons eternally affirms our distinct personhood. And that makes all the difference. Buddhists, Hindus, New Age practitioners, and many postmodern spiritualities speak of a god who is impersonal. If God is all and all is God, if our ultimate destiny is to merge mindlessly into some impersonal nirvana, human personhood is merely heavy baggage to be lugged on an endless journey to extinction.

God Is Truth, Righteousness, and Mercy

Window on the Word

The LORD *is righteous, he loves justice* (Ps. 11:7).

Holiness and love form the essence of who God is. They are expressed in truth, righteousness (justice), and mercy. "The arc of the universe is long," said Martin Luther King, "but bends toward justice."[20]

These are often called the moral attributes of God. The Lord reveals His truth, righteousness, and mercy to us so that we, who are to reflect His character, will know how to behave. Consider just one example of His mercy.

Max Grimes struck you as a "man's man." He talked tough, loved sports, cursed, spieled dirty jokes, and could hold his liquor. He owned a barbershop in a small Missouri town. Most days his shop was an arena of macho talk by braggadocios.

Max didn't like the new preacher. When "the Rev" came in for his regular haircut, Max would turn the cursing and filthy talk to triple volume. The other barbers and some customers were embarrassed. Not Max.

Then Max got really sick. After his surgery his wife brought him to the shop in a wheelchair. He couldn't work. He just sat on the sidewalk outside the shop and watched the people go by. Weak but cheerful, he greeted old friends.

The preacher came by and spoke to Max. Barber Max was ready to talk to the pastor now. "Reverend," he said, "I was layin' up there on the operating table. I couldn't move or talk. I could hear, but they didn't know that. I heard the doctor tell my wife, 'I don't see how he can last another hour.'"

Max paused to get his breath. "Reverend, I prayed for the first time in my life. I prayed, *O God, if there is a God, please help me now.* The instant I prayed that prayer in my heart—I couldn't put it in real words—the instant that I prayed, I was flooded with peace, I mean floating in peace, and assurance. I felt the presence of God all through me. Regardless of what the doctor had said, I knew I was going to live."

Max stopped again, dabbed a tear with a big thumb. "Do you know what that means, Preacher? Do you *know* what that means? I kicked God in the face every day of my life for 50 years! But the first time I called His name in prayer —the first time I called His name—He came!"

So, is it true what they say about God? If they say He is holy love, if they say He is full of grace and truth, if they say that He is good and that He loves mercy, then it is true what they say about God.

— 6 —

Invitations from God: RSVP

First Window on the Word

God . . . has called you into fellowship with his Son Jesus Christ our Lord (1 Cor. 1:9).

If you are like most postmoderns, you don't care much for rules and regulations. You're not a child. After all, you are a responsible adult. You can be depended on to do your Christian duty, to do the prudent and loving thing each situation demands.

Jeff Litchfield used to feel the same way. Hear his story, "Old Friends."

> Flight canceled! Four hours to kill. Why not call Kevin and Shelby Naughton? I had not seen them in ages. We had been college friends 20 years ago. Kevin and I spent 2 years on the golf team. Shelby and I had dated for two very exciting months. Then came summer vacation and my transfer to another school.
>
> Shelby answered the phone. "Stay right there. I'll pick you up in 20 minutes. Can you stay for dinner?"
>
> As she served the stroganoff she explained that Kevin was out of town. During the chocolate mousse she added, "Kevin is not coming back . . . not my idea, but the divorce is final a month from today."
>
> "I'm so sorry . . ." I tried to comfort her with words, then with hugs. One thing led to another. Old college flames rekindled, blazed—almost out of control now.
>
> "Thou shalt not commit adultery" rose in the recesses of my mind like a banner out of the fog. "Thou shalt not . . ." right there in the old King James as I had memorized it as a kid too young to appreciate its meaning. But we were all but past the point of no return. I managed a one-second prayer, "Jesus, help me." Instantly, the spell was broken. I walked away.
>
> Two years later, I saw Shelby at a conference. Wedding ring on her finger—she and Kevin had called off the divorce and mended their marriage. She told me, "Thanks, thanks for . . . for not taking advantage when I was vulnerable."
>
> I didn't feel like a hero, but I did feel grateful for the seventh commandment.[1]

In His wisdom God knew that people like you and me need both law and grace. He has always provided both. You could say that the Old Testament is about law and the New Testament about grace—but you would be wrong. From Eden to eternity God's grace shines through as He leads His wayward people back to wholeness and holiness. Even His laws, such as the Ten Commandments, are bestowals of grace.

God Invites You to a Tour of His House

Window on the Word

Fix these words of mine in your hearts and minds (Deut. 11:18).

If I invite you to my house, you will learn a lot about me, even if I don't say a word. The pictures on my walls, the books on my shelf, the magazines in the rack, the food on my table, and the video games stacked on top of the VCR will tell you plenty.

Some people call the Ten Commandments of Exod. 20 God's house. That analogy is not perfect, but it can be helpful. God invites us to tour His house. We won't learn all there is to know about God by memorizing the Ten Commandments. No moral code can exhaust the meaning of God. But if we pay attention, we can learn something of how He wants us to live and what His holy love looks like in daily life. Ready for the tour?

Four Cornerstones

The foundation of this house of God rests securely on these cornerstones.

1. *Worship Only the True God*. "You shall have no other gods before me" (Exod. 20:3). The phrase "before me" actually means "against my face." You shall raise no other gods "against my face."

2. *Avoid Idols*. "You shall not make for yourself an idol" (Exod. 20:4). We must not give god status to any man-made thing. We know that material possessions, success, pleasure seeking, and money chasing are worthless as "gods." But even good things such as a church, a spouse, an education, or even the Bible can become an idol.

3. *Honor God's Name*. "You shall not misuse the name of . . . your God" (Exod. 20:7). Beyond cursing and swearing by God's name, we are here warned not to take God lightly!

4. *Keep Sacred the Time for Rest and Worship*. "Remember the Sabbath day by keeping it holy" (Exod. 20:8). Both rest and worship are as essential to the welfare of God's people as food and drink.

A Solid Floor

"Honor your father and your mother" (Exod. 20:12). Learning to respect parents can be the threshold for learning reverence for God. The word for "honor" is sometimes translated "glory." Thus we are to esteem our parents by living in a way that brings credit or glory to them.

The term translated "honor" has the connotation "to be heavy." In ancient times only the rich could afford to be "heavy." The Bible is, therefore, telling us to treat our parents with all the respect and deference that is usually given to the rich. How would that make your folks feel?

Tension between parent and child is too often a problem today as it was then.

Paco, all is forgiven. If you forgive me, too, please meet me at La Estrella Café at noon on Thursday. I love you. Your Father.

This newspaper ad was placed in Madrid, Spain, by a father pleading for his son to come home. According to *Pursuit* magazine, 800 Pacos showed up at La Estrella Café at noon on Thursday! All were seeking reconciliation with their fathers.

If you were to place an ad like that, to what name would you address the message: all is forgiven?

Four Protective Walls

1. *Forgiveness—Not Revenge.* "You shall not murder" (Exod. 20:13). This wall has a window that lets in the soothing breeze of forgiveness. As we shall see later when we are invited to God's "class," this word forbids harboring or enjoying the hatred from which spring acts of murderous revenge.

2. *Purity and Fidelity—Not Adultery.* "You shall not commit adultery" (Exod. 20:14). Sexual purity and faithfulness to marriage vows ring true with something in God's own character.

3. *Generosity—Not Stealing.* "You shall not steal" (Exod. 20:15). The window in this wall lets in the "kindly light" of generosity toward others as opposed to robbing others. "He who has been stealing must steal no longer, but must work . . . [so] that he may have something to share with those in need" (Eph. 4:28).

4. *Integrity—Not Dishonesty.* "You shall not bear false witness" (Exod. 20:16, NKJV). This wall reminds us that we serve a God of truth. "God is not a man, that he should lie" (Num. 23:19). Further, "it is impossible for God to lie" (Heb. 6:18).

The Roof: A Heart like God's

"You shall not covet" (Exod. 20:17). Coveting may be the most forgotten command and the most broken. Even with the house on a firm foundation, the walls decorated nicely, the windows washed—we may have a leaky roof that can ruin everything. "No coveting" is the roof that holds the whole house together. It summarizes all the other commands. Further, it rebukes the attitude that produces the violation of all the other commandments. Murder, stealing, adultery, and most other sins begin with the sinful longing for some position, possession, honor, or privilege that belongs to someone else.

The Hebrews, to whom this command not to covet was first given, provide a dramatic example of how covetousness leads to other sins. First, they coveted the land, the livestock, and the wives of their neighbors. They even coveted the "king" form of government that other nations had. And in astonishing violation of the first commandment, they lusted after the pagan gods of their neighbors!

Laurence Shames, in *The Hunger for More*, says, "More. If there's a single word that summarizes American hopes and obsessions, that's it. More money. More success. More luxuries and gizmos. We live for more . . . the things we already have . . . pale in comparison with the things we still might get."[2] Robert South observed, "Covetousness is both the beginning and end of the devil's alphabet—the first vice in corrupt nature that moves, and the last which dies."[3]

Well, how comfortable do you feel in God's house? Are those your feet on the coffee table? Tense? Guilty? How well does your life reflect the values so much in evidence in God's house? Perhaps you should accept God's invitation to come to His class for instruction.

JESUS INVITES YOU TO HIS CLASS

Window on the Word

The letter kills, but the Spirit gives life (2 Cor. 3:6).

From the very first, God intended the Ten Commandments to be internalized. God said, "I will put my law in their minds and write it on their hearts" (Jer. 31:33).

God's plan was that out of loving, holy hearts persons would honor God, respect parents, ruthlessly resist adultery, and not grab for possessions. But you know the human tendency to reduce principles to mere rules. The ancient code keepers developed schemes to avoid—at least technically—lying, cheating, stealing, or actually committing physical adultery, whatever lustful fantasies might be allowed to romp free. They even found loopholes to avoid supporting their parents.

Jesus gathered a class of interested parties together to consider authentic Kingdom living. His teaching that day is often called the Sermon on the Mount. The educational objective of the Teacher was to help students understand that while the Law was not to be abolished, it was to be internalized and lived from the heart, not observed as an external code by which to judge others.

Jesus' introduction shocked the class and provoked the scribes and Pharisees to disgust. He said something like this: "Look around you. Notice the full-time saints, the religious pros among you. Look at their uniform robes, their leather phylacteries neatly mounted on their foreheads. Haven't you noticed them reciting their prayers in public? You know they can quote Scripture for an hour without stumbling over one shibboleth. I'm telling you, those Pharisees are something else."

A scattering of applause starts, but Jesus raises His hand to squelch it. He is speaking louder now. "But I am here to say that unless you are a whole lot more righteous than the Pharisees, a lot more holy than they are, you will be eternally lost. You will certainly not enter the kingdom of heaven."[4]

The people are confused, the Pharisees seething. The applause starts again, this time at the expense of the professional rule keepers.

If they had used overhead projectors then, Jesus' first transparency would have had two columns. Over the left column, written in red, would have been this header: "What You Have Been Taught." Over the right column, written in blue: "What God Really Wants."

Watch Jesus write on the "What You Have Been Taught" side in red: "No murder!"

"But I say unto you"—as He writes in blue on the "What God Really Wants"—"No anger, hatred, or name calling." Then Jesus goes on to explain that if anything stirs anger between you and your brother or sister, reconciliation in God's presence is the way to go. To nurse hatred against your brother, Jesus declares, is as sinful as killing him! (See Matt. 5:21-26.)

A new transparency goes up. Left column in red: "No adultery!" Right side in blue: "No lustful looks." The one who savors lustful desires has, in God's sight, committed the sin of adultery already, Jesus informs them.

"This does not mean that it is a sin to notice a woman of beauty. But there is no room in the 'holy heart' for leering looks, undressing her with your eyes, or harboring lustful fantasies."[5]

The Bible word that Jesus uses contains the idea of "possessing" the woman who is the object of lust. Jesus explains that the sinful desire to have another man's wife corrupts one's very heart.[6] He is a condemned breaker of the law, though he has never touched the one for whom he burns.

Red side again: "Easy divorce."

Blue side, "What God Really Wants": "No divorce!" Jesus spells it out. "You men have been writing out a 'bill of divorcement' whenever you want a younger wife. Moses let you get by with that because your perverse hearts were as hard as rock. But God never intended, never approved your sinning against your wives in this way." (See Matt. 5:31-32; 19:3.)

The crowd is getting restless. The Pharisees sneer. Their teaching of the Torah as an external code of conduct is being seriously undermined by this popular, revolutionary Rabbi from Nazareth. What Jesus is saying makes so much sense the Pharisees' doctrine is exposed as rules without relationship, legal code without life. Yet they will not let Him forget this. They cannot wait until they can corner Him in private, under cover of darkness.

But at least for now the people are believing what the Pharisees surely labeled "liberal theology." They just might believe this notion that code keeping does not make you holy. And what about this curious theory that religion should be a matter of the heart lived out of the spirit of the Law? That was what God intended, not the pinched-souled rule keeping and the "proud humility" that the Pharisees paraded!

A new transparency goes up in big red letters: "Corban is sacred." On the blue side: "Honor your father and mother!" Jesus denounces *corban*—the practice of putting money in a sort of trust fund for the Temple to avoid supporting aging parents. "Surely, Mom and Dad, you don't want me to take the money I pledged to God to pay for your prescriptions, do you?" With stunts like this, and a dozen others, Jesus tells them they are fracturing the fifth commandment and stand condemned for breaking both the letter and the spirit of the Law. "Thus you nullify the word of God by your tradition" (Mark 7:13).[7]

Jesus goes on conducting His class about what really matters. He condemns the practice of transgressing two commandments by an elaborate system of oaths. They had devised an intricate scheme of double-witness oaths sworn in the name of God (or a substitute for His name) that played out in bald-faced dishonesty. If the promise or agreement was not validated with a God-bound oath, one didn't have to keep it or even intend to. This, Jesus declared, abuses the name of God (third commandment) and transgresses the law of false witnesses (ninth commandment).

Jesus proceeds to inform them that to be holy, they must love even their enemies.

Jesus proceeds to inform them that to be holy, they must love even their enemies. They had been taught by the Pharisees and others to love their neighbors. But they were to hate the "Gentile dogs"—the Greeks and Romans —who had invaded their land and extracted taxes. But Jesus tells them that the spirit of the Law requires them to love even Roman soldiers. Fists begin to clench and teeth start to grit as He tells them not to retaliate or resist when the invaders abuse them! "If someone strikes you on the right cheek, turn to him the other also. . . . If someone forces you to go one mile [carrying his luggage], go with him two miles" (Matt. 5:39, 41).

Just a minute! This is really too much. Love your enemies . . . Maybe the old legalistic system of the Pharisees isn't so bad after all. Who says the letter of the Law is so bad? Just how far does God expect us to go with this "spirit" theme? With this religion of the heart?

Class is over. Will there be a test on this? What do you think?

An Invitation to Intimacy with God

Window on the Word

Whoever is thirsty, let him come; and whoever wishes, let him take the free gift of the water of life (Rev. 22:17).

The whole Bible looks like an engraved invitation to friendship with God. From the moment Adam and Eve sinned themselves into hiding, our Lord has been a seeking God. "Where are you?" God called to Adam (and Eve) in Eden (Gen. 3:9).

Abraham became the "friend" of God. Noah and Enoch were invited to "walk" with God. David became "a man after God's own heart." Moses, talking with God on Sinai, knew that relationship with God was what really mattered for his people. He prayed, "If your Presence does not go with us, do not send us up from here. How will anyone know that you are pleased . . . with your people unless you go with us? What else will distinguish . . . your people from all the other people . . . ?" (Exod. 33:15-16).

But God does not invite just spiritual heroes such as Moses, Abraham, and Noah. He does not just invite members of the Righteous Top 10. He calls hopeless sinners too. Look at Jacob. He was such a crook that they named him "Deceiver." His credentials included liar, cheat, schemer, manipulator, and bigamist! He stole his brother's blessing and birthright—which was considerably more than getting to sit on Daddy's lap in the family portrait. What he snagged from Esau meant, among other things, a double portion of the inheritance. Yet God invited "Deceiver" to intimacy with himself. In two dramatic encounters Jacob's name and nature were graciously transformed. Deceiver became "Prince having power with God" (Israel).

Throughout the Bible God intercepted wayward men, women, tribes, and nations with His invitation to come home. To sin-sick Israel He promised that He would subdue their wickedness and "hurl all [their] iniquities into the . . . sea" (Mic. 7:19). "'Come now, let us reason together,' says the LORD. 'Though your sins are like scarlet, they shall be as white as snow'" (Isa. 1:18).

Hear God, the wounded Parent, say to a rebellious tribe, "How can I give you up, Ephraim?" and to a whole nation gone wrong, "How can I hand you over, Israel?" (Hos. 11:8). Over one sinful nation God said, "My soul moans like a lyre for Moab" (Isa. 16:11, RSV).

Welcome *is a big word to God!*

God extends invitations to all us Jacobs, Ephraims, and Moabs. Hear the language of the Word: "Come, *all* . . . who are thirsty" (Isa. 55:1). "Come to me, *all* you who are weary and burdened" (Matt. 11:28). "*Whoever* is thirsty . . . *whoever* wishes . . . take the free gift" (Rev. 22:17). "Here I am! I stand at the door and knock. If *anyone* hears my voice and opens the door, I will come in" (3:20, emphases added).

God's invitation is acted out for us, demonstrated in images we cannot misunderstand.

—The Good Shepherd searching for lost sheep.

—The woman trying desperately to find the lost coin.

—The grieving father welcoming a wayward son back home.

—Jesus on the Cross, through whom God is saying, "I love you this much!"

The Bible is a 66-book-long invitation. *Welcome* is a big word to God! Will you RSVP today?

— 7 —

What's So Special About Jesus?

First Window on the Word

You are in Christ Jesus, who . . . is, our righteousness, holiness and redemption (1 Cor. 1:30).

Jesus, Jesus, Jesus everywhere—on T-shirts, coffee mugs, posters, book covers, and bumper stickers.

On television: *Jesus of Nazareth*, *Jesus*, and *The Greatest Story Ever Told*. And, like it or not, televangelists hyping their brand of "Jesus saves, Jesus heals, and Jesus prospers," as if He were a brand of cola or shampoo. In the theater: *The Last Temptation of Christ*. On stage: *Jesus Christ, Superstar* and *Godspell*.

At the eve of the millennium *Time* magazine gave its cover (December 6, 1999) to Jesus. He had been there at least three times before. Jesus made the cover of the April 24, 2000, *U.S. News and World Report*. In one year's time He had appeared on the cover of *Time*, *U.S. News and World Report*, *Newsweek*, *Life*, and *Atlantic Monthly*.

Remember back in the '60s when the Beatles declared they were more popular than Jesus? How things change. Jesus is everywhere; the Beatles golden oldies. The Bible is still the best-seller, and the *JESUS* film, distributed by Campus Crusade for Christ, has now been viewed by 3.5 billion inhabitants of the earth.

So what's so special about Jesus? Who is Jesus anyway? Two thousand years ago Jesus asked His disciples, "Who do people say I am?" The answers came back—John the Baptist, Elijah, maybe one of the prophets. Then, as now, there were a lot of notions floating around about just who this remarkable Man was. Jesus then framed the question more personally. He confronted the disciples with the question you and I must answer: "Who do you say I am?" (Mark 8:27-29).

A lot of people have stepped up lately to answer that question. Most of them have remade Jesus into what they would like Him to be with little regard for historical evidence or the message of the Bible.

Norman Mailer, the secular novelist, stepped up with a first-person historical novel in which the lead character, Jesus himself, corrects some of the supposed exaggerations produced by the Bible writers Matthew, Mark, Luke, and

John.[1] Helen Schucman, creator of *A Course in Miracles*, calls Jesus and other spiritually advanced avatars "our evolutionary elder brothers." Shirley MacLaine labeled Jesus an adept yogi who can teach us how to do everything He did. Some of the deconstructionists of the Jesus Seminar imagine that Jesus, like one of the Cynic philosophers, preached getting back to nature and meditation as the cure for a sick society.[2] Others say He was a refugee from the Essene conclave.

Some folks, trying to build an ecumenical bridge between Buddhism and Christianity, have come up with the notion that during His youthful years Jesus left His father's carpenter business and strolled off to India, where He encountered the wisdom and compassion of the Buddha. He then returned to Galilee, they conjecture, intent on interpreting the Buddha for His own kind![3]

And then there is the big crowd who claim that Jesus was a great teacher —but certainly no divine Savior. All those who jump on the great teacher but not God bandwagon need to ponder seriously these words from C. S. Lewis:

> I am trying to prevent . . . the really foolish thing that people often say about Him: "I am ready to accept Jesus as a great moral teacher, but I don't accept His claim to be God." That is the one thing we must not say. A man who was merely a man and said the sort of things Jesus said would not be a moral teacher. He would be a lunatic—on a level with the man who says he is a poached egg—or else he would be the Devil from Hell. You must make your choice. Either this man was, and is, the Son of God: or else a madman or something worse. You can shut Him up for a fool, you can spit at Him and kill Him as a demon; or you can fall at His feet and call Him Lord and God. But let us not come up with any patronizing nonsense about His being a great human teacher. He has not left that open to us. He did not intend to.[4]

In this chapter we shall not chase the fantasies about Jesus. We will, instead, probe what the Bible says about this remarkable Being.

JESUS: BOTH GOD AND MAN

Window on the Word

In the beginning was the Word . . . and the Word was God (John 1:1).

The Bible clearly teaches that Jesus is God become flesh. Like no other person who ever lived, Jesus is coeternal and coequal with the Father and the Holy Spirit. Many scriptures testify to Christ's divine nature. "You are the Christ, the Son of the living God," Peter said (Matt. 16:16, NASB). In John we read, "You [Christ] are the Holy One of God" (6:69). In Matt. 3:16-17 and 17:5 God himself supernaturally proclaims, "This is my Son." In perhaps the most profound passage in all of Scripture, John 1, Christ is identified as God before time even began. "In the beginning was the Word . . . and the Word was

God" (v. 1). The judgment of the Church in the 1st century and the 21st century is that Christ is God.

But Jesus Christ is also fully human, as the Bible records and history confirms. "The Word became flesh and made his dwelling among us" (John 1:14). As a man, Jesus faced the same physical, psychological, and spiritual needs that you and I struggle with every day. Yet He did so without sin (see Heb. 4:15).

How could the human Christ and the "fully God" Christ live in the same person? We cannot fathom the mystery of how God became a human being. The earliest Christians believed this truth, not because they understood it; rather, they believed it because they saw it demonstrated. Jesus was obviously a man—eating, drinking, breathing, sleeping, laughing, and crying just as they did. And yet, Jesus did things that only God could do. An authority that belonged only to God characterized the whole of Jesus' life and ministry. Others taught, but He taught with insight unlike the teachers of the Law (Mark 1:27). He could heal by just speaking a word, just as God had created the world (vv. 40-42; cf. Gen. 1:3, 6, 9, 14, 20, 24). He could drive out evil spirits with a mere command (Luke 4:31-37). Demon-possessed people fell before Him and called him the Son of God (Mark 5:6-7). He had authority to forgive sins (2:1-12).

Ultimately, this God-man Jesus rose from the dead. After throngs of people watched Him be crucified and buried, they assumed it was the end of the story—a good man victimized by the system. Not so. Three days later, witness after witness testified to seeing the same Jesus they buried—now alive. He was not a vision, a spiritual illusion, or an angel. His disciples felt the scars in His hand and side (John 20:19-29; cf. Luke 24:36-43). They saw, heard, talked with, and touched the risen Christ (1 John 1:1-4).

Early Christians and recent ones have experienced Christ as fully human, and yet they know that in Him they encountered God. In the risen Christ we see what God's vision for humanity is, and in Christ we see what God himself is like. We cannot explain the wonder of the Incarnation, yet we believe. And by faith we join Ignatius of Antioch in glorying in the mysteries, antitheses, and paradoxes of Christ's being.[5]

So what's so special about Jesus? "God himself, God the Son, became human in order that and on our behalf He might complete the at-one-ment [atonement] from the human side too."[6] God became flesh in order that He might remove our sin and bring us back to himself through the Cross. That makes Jesus very special.

Jesus Identifies with Us

Window on the Word

We do not have a high priest who is unable to sympathize with our weaknesses, but we have one who has been tempted in every way, just as we are—yet was without sin (Heb. 4:15).

As our High Priest, Jesus builds a bridge across the great gulf of sin that separates us from God. The Latin word for "priest" (pontifex) means "bridge builder." At once we think of the Cross as the bridge to God, and it surely is, but the full extent to which Christ identified with us is worth considering.

1. *The Incarnation* is an astounding act of identification with the human race. *In-carn-ation* means coming "in the flesh," with all of its limitations. God becoming human is a dramatic identification with sinners such as you and me. "For God so loved the world that he gave his one and only Son, that whoever believes in him shall not perish but have eternal life. For God did not send his Son . . . to condemn . . . but to save" (John 3:16-17).

Yea, Lord, we greet Thee, born this happy morning.
O Jesus, to Thee be all glory giv'n:
Word of the Father, now in flesh appearing!
O come, let us adore Him!

—John F. Wade

2. *The Baptism of Jesus* is another take-your-breath-away act of identification with us. Consider the biblical scene: In the murky waters of the Jordan, John the Baptizer is baptizing those who respond to his call for a "baptism of repentance for the forgiveness of sins" (Luke 3:3). "You brood of vipers," John thunders, "who warned you to flee from the coming wrath? Produce fruit in keeping with repentance" (vv. 7-8).

Those wearied with the weight of their wickedness step into the Jordan as an act of repentance. (The word for repentance is *metanoia,* which means to change your mind and turn in a new direction, that is, turn *from* your sins and *to* God.)

Person after person, man and woman, young and old, rich and poor, in godly sorrow for their sins, wade out to meet John. He prays for them and then baptizes them. Their hearts are changed. *Metanoia* has happened, and forgiveness is received.

Standing quietly somewhere in John's baptismal line is Jesus the Nazarene. In line with the repenting sinners? Why would the Son of God, "who knew no sin" (2 Cor. 5:21, KJV), be baptized in a service like this? There is no doubt about the invitation given by the preacher. This "baptism of repentance" is for guilty sinners! So why would Jesus Christ, who has never sinned, not ever, not even once—why would He wade into the river as if He were just another sinful man?

Only one answer makes sense. Jesus so identifies with the transgressors whom He has come to save that He walks into the baptismal waters with them. Christ so identifies with human need that He, who will one day bear our sins to Calvary, now experiences in behalf of all humankind the washing of baptism!

3. *Jesus Battling Temptation* also shows His identity with humanity. Many times we are tempted to do things our way instead of God's way. Doing what we want and looking out for number one seems less painful than pouring out our life in sacrifice for others. The Bible tells us that Jesus faced temptation too. Immediately after His baptism the Holy Spirit led Christ into a desert, where He fasted for 40 days in preparation for His ministry (Matt. 4:1-2). Then the devil came to Jesus, who was weakened by hunger, and tempted Him.

"How can the Son of God be hungry? If you really are the Son of God, use Your power to help yourself; turn these stones into bread," the tempter says. But Jesus refused to let physical needs elbow out spiritual priorities (vv. 2-4). He who came to "give his life as a ransom for many" (Mark 10:45) would not invoke divine power to alleviate His own human suffering.

Jesus next declines the temptation to secure His following through the sensational. "Jump off the Temple turret, and come floating down unhurt," the devil suggests—that will get their attention better than a sermon. Satan then quotes a psalm to Jesus to make his point (Matt. 4:6). But Jesus has the devil's number. He knows his name: *diabolos*, the one who "tears apart," the one who causes "division." Sensationalism for its own sake was not part of God's plan for Jesus. Instead, He was to reveal God by serving others, by healing, by casting out evil spirits, and by going to the Cross.

Satan's third temptation was the most direct. "You have come to be King of Kings and Lord of Lords. Why go to the Cross to win Your crown? Fall down and worship me. I have the kingdoms of the world and will give them to You right now" (see vv. 8-11). Satan always promises to give us what we want if we follow him—pleasure, money, fame, and happiness. His promises are always hollow. Jesus withstood the temptation to strive for worldly success. He rejected the power whereby Satan ("the prince of the power of the air" [Eph. 2:2, KJV]) rules the kingdoms of the world.

Jesus identified with us in battling temptation. He refused to use His power as the Son of God to give Him an advantage in overcoming Satan that we do not have.

What a comfort to know that the Lord who is our Guide and Judge has also walked in our moccasins. He knows the temptations that will bait us tomorrow, the burdens that weigh us down today. He sympathizes with our human weaknesses by enabling us to overcome (see Heb. 4:15)!

4. *The Sacrificial Death of Jesus* is the ultimate act of identification. He who knew no sin *became* sin for us so that we could be reconciled to God (see 2 Cor. 5:19-21). Christ experienced the agony of the ultimate loneliness that surges into the soul when sin separates us from God. That sense of separation from God pierced Him to the core of His being. He cried out, quoting Ps. 22, "My God, my God, why have you forsaken me?" (Matt. 27:46).

Surely God had not truly forsaken Christ, for where one Member of the Holy Trinity is, all are present. And on the Cross "God was in Christ, reconciling the world unto himself" (2 Cor. 5:19, KJV). Yet in the human depths of His soul, Christ experienced death and separation on our behalf.

Jesus Represents Us

Window on the Word

Christ Jesus . . . who was raised to life—is at the right hand of God . . . interceding for us (Rom. 8:34).

Our Lord not only identifies with us but also represents us. Some called Jesus Messiah, Christ, Anointed One, King, Lord, and Son of God. But what Jesus called himself most often was Son of Man. This surely stood for Christ as the Representative Man, the Second Adam. Apparently Jesus identified himself as the "son of man" of Dan. 7:13-14 to whom all authority, glory, and power were given by the Ancient of Days.

In His resurrection and triumph over death, Jesus Christ represents us. His resurrection means that we, too, will be raised from the dead. "Christ has indeed been raised from the dead, the firstfruits of those who have fallen asleep. For since death came through a man, the resurrection of the dead comes also through a man. For as in Adam all die, so in Christ all will be made alive" (1 Cor. 15:20-22). "The trumpet will sound, the dead will be raised imperishable, and we will be changed. For the perishable must clothe itself with the imperishable, and the mortal with immortality. . . . 'Death has been swallowed up in victory.' . . . Thanks be to God! He gives us the victory through our Lord Jesus Christ" (vv. 52-54, 57). Many Christians focus their faith on the Crucifixion and suffering of Good Friday; perhaps we should focus our hope more on the hope of Easter.

Jesus also represents us in heaven. In glory "Christ Jesus . . . is at the right hand of God . . . interceding for us" (Rom. 8:34). If we yield to a sinful temptation, we turn to our Advocate, our Representative, in heaven where "we have one who speaks to the Father in our defense—Jesus Christ, the Righteous One" (1 John 2:1).

JESUS' SACRIFICE DISPLAYS HOLY LOVE

Window on the Word

For all have sinned and fall short of the glory of God, and are justified freely by his grace through the redemption that came by Christ Jesus (Rom. 3:23-24).

The cross of Jesus is the final solution to the world's sin problem. The God of holy love offered up His Son, says Paul, "as a sacrifice of atonement" for the sins of the world. "He did this to demonstrate his justice, because in his forbearance he had left the sins committed beforehand unpunished—he did it to demonstrate his justice at the present time, so as to be just and the one who justifies those who have faith in Jesus" (Rom. 3:25-26). The death of His Son demonstrates that God is indeed "just," despite the fact that in His forbearance He had overlooked sins committed before the Cross. God could afford to endure human ignorance and "sins committed beforehand" (see Acts 17:30-31) because *beforehand* He had purposed to offer up His Son "as a sacrifice of atonement" for fallen humanity. God's offering up of Jesus to die is conclusive proof that He is "just, and yet the justifier" (Rom. 3:26, Wesley's NT) of everyone who has faith in Jesus. By offering up His Son as the world's atoning sacrifice, God found a way to maintain the integrity of His holiness while at the same time pardoning all who put their saving trust in Christ. At the Cross He demonstrates His judgment against sin and His love for sinners.

The Cross is itself a graphic symbol of God's character as holy love. Its upright beam symbolizes God's *justice* (grounded in His holiness), which will veer neither to the right nor to the left. "The soul who sins shall die" (Ezek. 18:4, NKJV). The outstretched beam depicts His *mercy* (expressive of His love), which would embrace every penitent believer. "He . . . did not spare his own Son, but gave him up for us all" (Rom. 8:32). "Mercy and truth have met together; righteousness and peace have kissed each other" (Ps. 85:10, NKJV) in the death of Jesus!

Jesus Reconciles Us to God

Window on the Word

But now he [God] has reconciled you by Christ's . . . death to present you holy in his sight, without blemish (Col. 1:22).

The Bible word for "reconciliation" *(katallagē)* is translated "atonement" in Rom. 5:11 (KJV). Bible translator William Tyndale invented the English word that means "at-one-ment."[7] The death and resurrection of our bridge-builder High Priest, Jesus, makes it possible for us to again be in a relationship of at-one-ment with God. That is the meaning of Rom. 3:25, where Jesus is described as a "sacrifice of *atonement*."

The benefits of Christ's reconciling us to God are so many and so splendored that theologians have developed a whole vocabulary to describe them. Let us note these blessings in simple language.

1. A *Healed Relationship with God.* The term "reconciliation" implies that a broken relationship has been healed. God in Christ, reaching out to us from the Cross, takes the first step to mend the broken relationship.

It is always that way, isn't it? If a wounded relationship is to be healed, the offended party, the innocent party, must forgive and in vulnerability bear the painful cost of reconciliation. In Jesus Christ, God takes the redeeming step toward us. God is the one sinned against—yet He willingly bears the cost of creating a new at-one-ment. "Jesus bore the cost of transforming us from God's enemies to God's friends."[8]

The New Testament never speaks of God being reconciled to human beings—far from it—but always of people like you and me being reconciled to Him. God's love moves Him to reach out to save and heal us.

2. *Pardoned and Set Free.* James S. Stewart tells of a famous chess painting. Faust gambled his soul away to the devil for worldly pleasures. After tasting the pleasures, the time came for Faust to fork over his soul.

An artist painted a picture based on Faust's dilemma. Satan and Faust sit at a chessboard. The game is almost over, and Faust has only a few pieces left—a king, a knight, two pawns. On his face is a look of abject despair. On the other side of the board is a leering devil.

Many a chess player has looked at the picture and agreed that the position is hopeless; it is checkmate! But one day in the gallery a great chess master stood gazing at the painting. He was fascinated by the black despair on Faust's face. Then his gaze went to the pieces on the board. He looked at them a long time, absorbed. Other visitors to the gallery came and went; still he studied the board. Then suddenly the gallery viewers were startled with a ringing shout, "It's a lie! The king has another move—the king has another move!"

I stand in the hall of divine justice—guilty, condemned, hopeless, despairing. I confess my miserable sins, I plead guilty. The gavel sounds. The inevitable verdict is on the way. But suddenly a voice rings out, "The King has another move. The King of Kings has another move!" Jesus slips in and quietly stands by my side. In a voice as calm as a silent sea and as deep as all eternity He says, "I became sin for him. I suffered in his behalf."

Miracle of miracles, the court proceedings change from the prosecution of a transgressor to a joyous adoption proceeding.[9]

Since God is both the injured party and the judge, He can justly pardon our sins through the price paid by His Son. He does not forgive us or justify us because we have made ourselves good. Only God's grace can make us righteous —and it does.

Justification is not simply a matter of God regarding the born-again Christian as righteous; it is a matter of God making us righteous. Justification is the gracious and judicial act of God by which He grants full pardon of our guilt and releases us from the penalty of our sins. He accepts us as righteous. When He justifies us, God transforms our hearts through Christ's atoning work. He declares the new believer righteous because His grace has made us so! "Since we have been justified through faith, we have peace with God through our Lord Jesus Christ, through whom we have gained access by faith into this grace in which we now stand" (Rom. 5:1-2).

God not only pardons our sin and declares us in right relationship with Him but also makes us righteous.

3. *A New Start with a New Heart*. "If anyone is in Christ, he is a new creation; the old has gone, the new has come!" (2 Cor. 5:17). Isn't that what you need?

Theologians call this delightful reality *regeneration*. Most of us just say "born again" because it is something like the new start that a newborn has. In regeneration we are changed from the inside out.

I heard about Romie Paday of Daet, a city in the Philippines. He was a heavy drinker, a brawler, a rage-filled man, and no stranger to jail. But today he is a patient father, attentive husband, and a Bible study leader. He has even started a churchlike fellowship in his house. Why the change? Six months ago he was "born again." "Before, my heart was as hard as a rock," Romie said. "But when I surrendered to Christ, He gave me a new heart and a new life. Only God could change a man as wild as I."

Unfortunately, some in the Christian community have shied away from proclaiming God's transforming grace. Living in a New Age culture and amid human potential movements galore, they are fearful that people might misinterpret regeneration to mean humans becoming gods. They don't want to ascribe more to human nature than they should. But biblical teaching about the new birth is not about the potential of human nature. It's about the power of the life of God in the human heart. God not only pardons our sin and declares us in right relationship with Him but also makes us righteous. What if He forgave our sins and left us to go on in the same old way? A new start does us no good without a new *us!* Paul's words that we are "being transformed into his likeness" speak of a genuine transformation, not just a declared one. We do not become gods, for there is always a categorical distinction between the Creator and the created. But we do become internally what we're called externally. We do experience a transformation of character, not just a change of name. Because this is always the work of God, we don't swell with pride; rather, we become consumed with gratitude and live in humble dependence on God's grace.

4. *Adopted into God's Family.* The Bible speaks of being "born of God." It also uses another great metaphor to describe how we become God's children—it says we've been "adopted" into God's family (Eph. 1:5; see also Rom. 8:14-17). These are two ways of describing the same glorious reality. Paul says that we've been adopted by having received God's Spirit into our lives (Rom. 8:14-15). Our adoption means we have the legal rights of God's children, and we can enjoy the blessings of being in His family. One of the greatest of these blessings is the inward assurance that we're in intimate relationship with Him.

JESUS IS LORD

Window on the Word

Confess with your mouth, "Jesus is Lord" (Rom. 10:9).

One of the first Christian affirmations of faith was, "Jesus is Lord." By this testimony the early Christians meant that Jesus is God. He was Lord not only of their personal lives but of the universe. Jesus Christ came to earth, took on Satan and all his "principalities and powers" (KJV), and defeated them. Satan is forever the defeated foe of the human race. "Christ's victory over sin as our Representative makes possible . . . our victory over sin."[10] Jesus dethroned every alien power that seeks to destroy us—the demonic, the depraved, the addictive! Those forces can no longer bind us as God's born-again people—without our permission. Even the "last enemy," death, simply means a more glorious stage of life begins for Christians. "Having disarmed the powers and authorities, he [Christ] made a public spectacle of them, triumphing over them by the cross" (Col. 2:15).

In our resurrected Lord we see the true humanity to which we are heirs. "God has created us not for estrangement, but for fellowship, not for death, but for life, not for bondage, but for freedom."[11]

JESUS, THE SUFFERING REDEEMER

Window on the Word

The Son of Man did not come to be served, but to serve, and to give his life as a ransom for many (Mark 10:45).

Surely, Jesus saw himself as the Suffering Servant of Isaiah. "He was despised and rejected . . . a man of sorrows, and familiar with suffering. . . . Surely he took up our infirmities and carried our sorrows. . . . He was pierced for our transgressions, he was crushed for our iniquities. . . . By his wounds we are healed. . . . The LORD has laid on him the iniquity of us all" (53:3-6). Surely Mother Eve speaks for each of us, male and female, in this old Celtic poem:

I am Eve; great Adam's wife;
It is I that outraged Jesus of old;
It is I that stole heaven from my children;
By rights it is I that should have gone upon the Tree.[12]

Jesus our Sacrifice comes into view when we notice that all through Bible history the covenants between God and humankind were marked with a sacrificial offering. Jesus saw himself as the Sacrifice of the new covenant. Jesus said, "I lay down my life. . . . No one takes it from me, but I lay it down of my own accord" (John 10:17-18). More to the point, Jesus said at the Last Supper, "This is my blood of the covenant, which is poured out for . . . the forgiveness of sins" (Matt. 26:28).

Let us pause in the presence of the One who suffered to redeem us. He who is infinite Love, holy Love bore our sins in His own bosom. He, the One offended by the incomprehensible weight of the sins of the world, bore the cost at the most profound level.[13] Unfathomable Love incredibly gave!

In the Cross we see "God Himself . . . bearing the brunt and paying the price. . . . That is the atonement for our sins that takes place in the very heart and life of God, because He is infinite love; and it is out of that costly atonement that forgiveness and release come to us."[14]

"If there must be a bearing of sin, and the holiness of God requires that there be, there are only two possibilities: Either we bear our own sins, or God bears them himself. Paul . . . demonstrates indisputably the bankruptcy of the former course. Hence, if there is reconciliation between man and God at all, it must occur through the divine sin bearing."[15]

As our suffering Redeemer, Christ brings to us eternal life, something we could never do for ourselves.

> Alas! no man can ever ransom himself nor pay God the price of that release; his ransom would cost too much, for ever beyond his power to pay, the ransom that would let him live on always and never see the pit of death. . . . But God will ransom my life, he will take me from the power of Sheol [the grave] *(Ps. 49:7-9, 15,* NEB*)*.

How do we know that the Divine One bearing our sins effects reconciliation? "The resurrection of Christ . . . is God's validation of this claim. By raising Jesus from the dead, God sets His seal of approval upon the mission of the Suffering Servant that the Son embodied in His total life and death. This is why Paul can say in 1 Cor. 15:17: 'And if Christ be not raised, your faith is vain; ye are yet in your sins' (KJV)."[16]

An old story tells of a boy who carefully built a toy boat. He sawed and sanded and painted until it looked just right. But the first day he put the boat in the water, the swift current of the stream carried it away. A week later he found it downstream lodged in a bank of driftwood just above the falls. Carefully he retrieved the toy boat. And, as he lifted it from the bank, he said, "Little boat, you are twice mine. Mine because I made you, and mine because I rescued you."

That's the way we have experienced God in Christ. He created us, and after we were lost to sin, He rescued us from the river that was too strong for us.

O Love divine! What hast Thou done?
The incarnate God hath died for me!
The Father's coeternal Son
Bore all my sins upon the tree;
The immortal God for me hath died!
My Lord, my Love is crucified.

Behold Him, all ye that pass by,
The bleeding Prince of life and peace!
Come, sinners, see your Maker die,
And say, "Was ever grief like His?"
Come, feel with me His blood applied!
My Lord, my Love is crucified;

Is crucified for me and you,
To bring us rebels back to God.
Believe, believe the record true:
Ye all are bought with Jesus' blood;
Pardon for all flows from His side.
My Lord, my Love is crucified.

Then let us sit beneath His cross,
And gladly catch the healing stream,
All things for Him account but loss,
And give up all our hearts to Him;
Of nothing think or speak beside:
My Lord, my Love is crucified.

—Charles Wesley[17]

What's so special about Jesus? He is both God and man; He identifies with us; He represents us; His sacrifice displays holy love; He reconciles us to God, forgiving our sins and giving us new life; He is both Lord and Redeemer. That makes Him pretty special. So special that "salvation is found in no one else, for there is no other name under heaven given . . . by which we must be saved" (Acts 4:12).

— 8 —

Come Home to the Light

First Window on the Word:

God . . . made his light shine in our hearts to give us the light of the knowledge of the glory of God in the face of Christ (2 Cor. 4:6).

We got off the London underground train at the Charing Cross Station. When we climbed to street level, we found that the ubiquitous London fog had condensed into a chilling rain. Umbrella dripping, I lingered at the famous Charing Cross intersection, lost in thought. My wife urged me to hurry to the shelter of a nearby restaurant. But I just stood there gazing and remembering.

"What's going on?" my wife asked, without trying to hide the irritation in her voice.

"I'm thinking about a sermon," I replied.

"A sermon—in the rain?"

As soon as we were ensconced in a booth at the restaurant, I told her about a British minister who once came to preach at the church I attended as a boy. I don't remember his text, his sermon, or even his name. But I did remember his story about Charing Cross, or as the locals called it for short, "the Cross."

It seems that a five-year-old boy at play wandered away from home and was lost. He tried one street after another. Nothing looked familiar—nothing. Soon the lad was crying as he peered at buildings and signs, searching for home.

A helpful policeman found the frightened boy. He wiped away tears and asked the standard questions. "Do you remember the name of your street?"

"No."

"How about your house number?"

"I don't know."

"Telephone number?"

"It has a *five* in it, but that's all I . . ."

The policeman looked pensive. Suddenly the boy brightened and through his tears said eagerly, "Sir, take me to the Cross. I can find my way home from there!"

You can too. As the Spirit leads you to the foot of the cross of Christ, you are coming to the lights of home. As you stand at the foot of the Cross, you need to know just two things: (1) you are a sinner, (2) Christ is the Savior.

MAP FOR THE JOURNEY HOME

Window on the Word

My grace is sufficient for you (2 Cor. 12:9).

The map is provided courtesy of the *Atoning Grace* of God.

"Because of his great love for us, God, who is rich in mercy, made us alive with Christ even when we were dead in transgressions—it is by *grace* you have been saved. And God raised us up with Christ . . . in order that . . . he might show the incomparable riches of his *grace*. . . . For it is by *grace* you have been saved, through faith—and this not from yourselves, it is the gift of God—not by works, so that no one can boast" (Eph. 2:4-9, emphases added).

Before the foundation of the world God provided atoning grace. This divine "unmerited favor" is not something we can manufacture, produce, earn, or demand. It is a gift from God.

Preparatory Grace is the grace of God at work in your heart right now. By this grace God gently—sometimes loudly—tugs at your heart, inviting you home. Look back over your life, and you will see that all along God has been bringing you to this day in which you long to join His family. Preparatory grace is the Holy Spirit enabling and empowering you to choose God and good. Thus you become responsible; you can choose, so you must choose good or evil. As evangelist Bud Robinson once said, "God voted for me, the devil voted against me, and I cast the deciding ballot for myself."[1]

Some theologians call preparatory grace *prevenient grace*. "God's prevenient grace goes before us—preventing us from sin, awakening in us a thirst for God, surprising us with His providence, convicting us of unbelief, and leading us to trust in Christ and Christ alone."[2] It is the gracious Spirit of God who raises the Philippian jailer's question in your own heart, "What must I do to be saved?" (Acts 16:30).

STREET SIGNS

Window on the Word

The Lord is . . . not willing that any should perish,
but that all should come to repentance (2 Pet. 3:9, KJV).

You are getting close to home now, in the neighborhood. As the streets become more and more familiar, you quicken your step. You want to get home before dark.

1. *Confession*. "We all, like sheep, have gone astray, each of us has turned to his own way" (Isa. 53:6). None are excluded; each of us must deal straightforwardly with the sin problem. This is no time to call sin by a nice name. No

pleading "low self-esteem." No hiding behind "maladjustment." No whining "victim." Don't tell God your corrupt and immoral behavior happened because Dad didn't take you fishing or because Mom did not read you stories. Don't point fingers at the "system." Remember Adam. When confronted with his sin, he first tried to blame others ("The devil and the woman made me do it"). But he finally confessed, "I ate it" (Gen. 3:12). You and I stand without excuse before God's declaration, "All have sinned and fall short of the glory of God" (Rom. 3:23).

The New Testament word for "confess" is made of two Greek terms. One means "same" or "alike"; the other means "word," "speech," or "idea." The compound word means "to speak alike" or "to say the same thing." To *confess* your sins, then, is to speak out your "agreement with God" on the matter of your spiritual condition.[3]

Forgive unconfessed sin? Not even God can do that! On the other hand, "If we confess our sins, he [God] is faithful and just and will forgive us our sins" (1 John 1:9). Do not fear to confess yourself a sinner. Jesus died for sinners, and no one else.

2. *Repentance*. To repent is to turn away from your sins, to utterly renounce them and forsake them in "godly sorrow."

When you add repentance to confession, you are very close to home. Oswald Chambers called repentance the "threshold" to the Kingdom. John Wesley called repentance the "porch" that leads to a life of intimacy with God.

In turning away from self to God, you find your "true self"—the real self that is created in the very image of God.

Repentance is not just sorrow that you got caught, or that you made a mess of your life. Rather, it involves remorse for sinning against God and against the very persons to whom you owed your best. The sins the repentant sinner once prized now appear so revolting as to produce grief.

Four dimensions of repentance beckon to us. The first is intellectual. The sinner comes to the "knowledge of sin." The second dimension is emotional, producing "godly sorrow . . . that leads to salvation" (2 Cor. 7:10). The third element in repentance involves the will. With firm purpose the sinner turns from self toward God and toward others. Just as our pattern, Jesus, was "the man for others," so those who repent no longer live for themselves.

This sounds frighteningly radical—and it is. But it is delightful and fulfilling too. For as you turn from self to God and others, you come to know what Jesus meant when He said, "Whoever wants [seeks] to save his life will lose it, but whoever loses his life for me will find it" (Matt. 16:25). One of the treasures beyond the "porch" of repentance is the discovery that in turning away from self to God, you find your "true self"—the real self that is created in the very image of God.[4]

Repentance has a fourth dimension. When John the Baptizer preached the gospel of repentance, he challenged hearers to "produce *fruit* in keeping with *repentance*" (Matt. 3:8, emphases added). One such fruit is repairing the damage our sin has done to others. If we have stolen money or property, we make *restitution* by paying it back with interest or damages. If we have abused others, brought suffering because of our addictions, or have injured the good name of others, we must not only ask forgiveness but also try to repair the damage.

Sometimes we do not have the opportunity to make restitution. In other situations, where our public or private confession would do more harm than good, we should carry the remorse of our painful secret, keeping quiet about it to our dying day. We accept God's forgiveness, but we forego the consolation of confession to others if it would clearly hurt more than help. Consider Cynthia's story.

Over a period of several months, Cynthia had let a neighbor man make love to her when her husband was away. Feeling rotten about the affair, she finally broke it off, and the man moved away, making the whole thing easier. That all happened 12 years ago. But it still haunts Cynthia daily.

Her husband, Roger, never knew about the sinful affair. One of their children could possibly—not probably—have been fathered by her lover. Cynthia carries a load of guilt. And she has been trying to get closer to God lately. Does this mean that she should tell Roger about the affair? Is that what God wants her to do?

Actually she longs to tell her husband about her betrayal. She needs to get it out in the open so everyone can move on. She thinks Roger can handle it. The children would never know—would they? Aren't couples supposed to share everything? Doesn't Roger have a right to know? She knows she would feel better if she could get the whole thing off her chest.

So Cynthia spoke to her pastor about it. He advised her, "Cynthia, never tell Roger about it. Absorb the pain of that memory yourself, turn the burden over to Christ, and carry that secret to your grave." If public restitution would hurt more than help, then keep quiet, and carry your burden only to God. Offer a prayer of true repentance as David did:

> Have mercy on me, O God, according to your unfailing love; according to your great compassion blot out my transgressions. Wash away all my iniquity and cleanse me from my sin. For I know my transgressions, and my sin is always before me. Against you, you only, have I sinned and done what is evil. . . . Surely you desire truth in the inner parts. . . . Cleanse me with hyssop, and I will be clean; wash me, and I will be whiter than snow. . . . Hide your face from my sins and blot out all my iniquity. Create in me a pure heart, O God, and renew a steadfast spirit within me. Do not cast me from your presence *(Ps. 51:1-4, 6-7, 9-11).*

To know God, you and I must follow David's example, for "God . . . commands all people everywhere to repent" (Acts 17:30).

3. *Trust in Jesus for Salvation.* Recognizing your spiritual poverty, confess your sins, and repent from the bottom of your heart. Now you are just one step

from home. The last stride is a step of faith. Put all your trust in Jesus Christ. Believe that He loves you as if you were the only one to love. Believe that He died for you, and that God's *saving grace* is extended even to a sinner like you.

"For God so loved the world that he gave his one and only Son, that whoever *believes* in him shall not perish but have eternal life. For God did not send his Son . . . to condemn . . . but to save. . . . Whoever *believes* in him is not condemned" (John 3:16-18, emphases added).

The final step into right relationship with God is solid, firmly grounded in the gracious promises of God:

—"If you confess with your mouth, 'Jesus is Lord,' and *believe* in your heart that God raised him from the dead, you will be saved. For it is with your heart that you *believe* and are justified, and it is with your mouth that you confess and are saved" (Rom. 10:9-10, emphases added).

—"To those who *believed* in his name, he gave the right to become children of God" (John 1:12, emphasis added).

—"Jesus said . . . 'I am the resurrection and the life. He who *believes* in me will live, even though he dies; and whoever lives and *believes* in me will never die'" (John 11:25-26, emphases added).

Will you be accepted? If you have been honest with God, do not fear. Jesus, who loved you enough to die for you, says: "Here I am! I stand at the door and knock. If *anyone* hears my voice and opens the door, I will come in" (Rev. 3:20, emphasis added). Quiet . . . can you hear Him knocking?

4. *Receive the Assurance of the Spirit.* You will not be prepared for it. You may not know what to say or how to act. But in the process of confessing, repenting, and affirming your faith in Christ, the Holy Spirit will give you a deep inner assurance that your sins are forgiven and that you have been born into the family of God.

Becoming a new creation in Christ can be a breathtaking experience. Descriptions of it are often feeble compared to the experience itself. But once you have received the witness of the Spirit, you will give the knowing nod of recognition wherever Rom. 8:16 is read at church: "The Spirit himself testifies with our spirit that we are God's children."

The young John Wesley had struggled for years to find peace with God. He became a priest, a missionary, and an Oxford professor in the process. Yet peace did not come—until May 24, 1738, when he . . . well, let him tell his own story:

> In the evening I went very unwillingly to a society in Aldersgate-Street, where one was reading Luther's preface to the Epistle to the Romans. About a quarter before nine, while he was describing the change which God works in the heart through faith in Christ, I felt my heart strangely warmed. I felt I did trust in Christ, Christ alone for salvation: And an assurance was given me, that He had taken away *my* sins, even *mine*, and saved *me* from the law of sin and death. . . . I then testified openly to all there, what I now first felt in my heart.[5]

Wesley knew the date, time, and place of his born-again experience. Note that the Oxford professor, so admirably schooled in logic and reason, found

Christ in heartfelt religion. Note the place he gives to the inner "assurance" that God had saved him. Later he would write in a sermon on the "Witness of the Spirit," "We know . . . that the Spirit of God does give a believer such a testimony of his adoption, that while it is present in the soul, he can no more doubt the reality of his sonship, than he can doubt of the shining of the sun, while he stands in the full blaze of his beams."[6]

Paul captured the essence of assurance: "I know whom I have believed, and am convinced that he is able to guard what I have entrusted to him for that day [of Christ's return]" (2 Tim. 1:12).

Does the Savior Really Want You to Come Home?

Window on the Word

Come to me, all you who are weary and burdened, and I will give you rest (Matt. 11:28).

Max Lucado tells about Maria and Christina in *No Wonder They Call Him Savior.*

Christina wanted more. Seventeen, beautiful, and trapped in a tiny town in Brazil—she wanted more. She looked around the one-room dwelling she shared with her mother—washbasin, dirt floor, wood-burning stove—she wanted more. Her father had died long ago. Her mother, Maria, a hardworking maid, had raised her.

From underneath the pallet that was her bed she pulled the magazine someone had left on the bus. She looked at the pictures of Rio de Janeiro. Glittering lights and happy faces, and the clothes—Christina had only two dresses. Seventeen, beautiful, and only two dresses. Christina looked at the lines in her mother's face and at the fun-filled faces in the Rio pictures.

Maria awoke one morning to find the bed of Christina, her only child, empty, both dresses gone. Maria knew. Her daughter had often spoken of the city. Maria had warned her. "Life is harsh and cruel in the city. How would you eat? What would you do for a living?"

Maria knew exactly what pretty girls would do, would have to do to make a living in Rio. She also knew what she must do. She threw some clothes in a bag, gathered up all her money, and headed for the bus stop. On the way she stopped at the drugstore for pictures. She sat down in the booth, closed the curtain, and put in all the coins she could afford. With a purse full of photos she caught the bus for Rio.

Maria knew that her daughter had no way of earning money. She also knew that she was too stubborn to give up. Maria knew that when pride meets hunger, one will do what before was unthinkable. She began her search—bars, hotels, nightclubs, any place with the reputation for streetwalkers or prostitutes. At each place she left her picture—taped to a bathroom mirror, tacked to a hotel bulletin board, fastened to a phone booth. On the back of each picture she wrote a note.

Before long Maria's money and her pictures ran out. She wept as she got on the bus to go back home, alone.

A few weeks later Christina descended the hotel stairs. Her young face was tired. Her brown eyes no longer danced. Her laughter was broken. Her dream had become a nightmare. A thousand times she had wished to trade those countless hotel beds for her pallet back home. But home was, in many ways, too far away.

You keep bumping into Jesus, the very picture of God.

As she reached the bottom of the stairs, she noticed a familiar face. There on the lobby mirror was a small picture of her mother. Christina's eyes burned and her throat tightened as she removed the small photo. Written on the back was, "Whatever you have done, whatever you have become, it doesn't matter. Please come home."

She did.[7]

You could say that God has put His picture everywhere. According to John 1:18 and Col. 1:15, Jesus is the very picture of God. You keep bumping into Jesus, the perfect picture of God, don't you? God has put His picture in the Bible, in hymns, in sermons, in the lives of Christlike people, even in books like this. On all those pictures, written in the blood of the Lamb, is an invitation, God's way of saying, "Whatever you have done, whatever you have become, it doesn't matter. Please come home."

You have the road map home.

You know the final vote is up to you.

Will you pray the sinner's prayer?

Will you come home? Today?

Why not pray the sinner's prayer right now and come home to the Light?

"O God, I confess that I am a sinner and need Your forgiveness. I believe that Jesus died on the Cross for my sin. This day I ask You to come into my life as my Savior and my Lord. I long to turn from sin and follow You. Thank You for hearing my prayer and making me Your child today. Amen."

— 9 —

The Will of God—Your Sanctification

First Window on the Word

May God himself, the God of peace, sanctify you through and through. . . . The one who calls you is faithful and he will do it (1 Thess. 5:23-24).

Just when the born-anew disciple thinks his or her spiritual life couldn't get any better, it does—dramatically. The guilt and power of sin are gone. You are living a miracle already; what more could you ask for? What more could you expect? What more could you absorb?

Greening Power

Window on the Word

Do not conform any longer to the pattern of this world, but be transformed by the renewing of your mind (Rom. 12:2).

You soon discover that the transformation begun in your conversion continues. The Spirit who led you into the transforming Light now coaxes you to bask in its life-giving rays. Old memories are being healed, resentments are being melted. The things of the Lord become sweet as honey. The closer you draw to Christ, the more the hunger for God increases, and the more God satisfies that hunger.

"There is no top to the divine heights . . . no bottom to the divine depths; there is no shore to the ocean of God's perfections," one man said describing this experience. "The soul bathes and drinks and drinks and bathes, and says, 'I know Him better and love Him more. . . . I stand awe-inspired in the presence of the infinite glory, which, though I come nigh, is ever unapproachable; though I bathe my soul in it and am filled, yet its measureless heights and depths and lengths and breadths overwhelm me."[1] The Bible's description is "And all of us, with unveiled faces, seeing the glory of the Lord as though reflected in a mirror, are being transformed into the same image from one degree of glory to another" (2 Cor. 3:18, NRSV).

You discover the meaning of 1 Cor. 2:9: "No eye has seen, no ear has heard, no mind has conceived what God has prepared for those who love him."

That scripture is not talking about heaven, or at least not *just* heaven. Rather, the unseen, unheard of, unimaginable blessings barge into our present lives as marvelous encounters with God. As you walk close to Him, you discover deep satisfactions and enriching fulfillments you never dreamed of.

How does this happen? As you walk in the Spirit, He begins to share with you what the apostle Paul called "God's secret wisdom," for the "Spirit searches . . . even the deep things of God" (vv. 7, 10).

As the transforming Light radiates Christ's Spirit into your heart, new spiritual sensitivities are brought to awareness, and the thirst to be more like Christ grows. Submerged longings to be free from every stain of sin burst forth like tulips on an inordinately warm spring day. As the sunflower follows the sun, you are drawn to the transforming Light.

What is going on? Some of God's saints have called this gradual sanctification. Others insist on calling it growth in grace. I like Hildegarde of Bingen's description. She labeled this phenomenon *viriditas* or "greening power." This power meant spiritual fertility and growth to her. Hildegarde believed that Rom. 12:11 calls us to *viriditas* when it tells us to be "aglow with the Spirit" (RSV).

Recently a botanist found some 600-year-old seeds in the Arabian desert. He watered and nourished them; they sprouted and blossomed! Through sanctifying grace and spiritual growth, God is performing a similar miracle in your heart. Seeds of God's image long dried out in the barren desert of your sinful heart are being watered, and they are bursting out in the greening power of the Light. Oh, stay close to the Light so those precious seeds of God's image can blossom in love and selflessness.

The Problem of Inward Sin

Window on the Word

It is God's will that you should be sanctified. . . . For God did not call us to be impure, but to live a holy life (1 Thess. 4:3, 7).

As you follow the Spirit into the sunrise of sanctifying grace, you become more aware of the love and holiness of God. The closer you get to Him, the more your own lack of love and your own unholy affections show up. This hurts. You are tempted to shrink from the Light because it makes you look bad, embarrassingly bad.

When I look into Your holiness
When I gaze into Your loveliness
When all things that surround
*Become shadows in the light of You.**

*"When I Look into Your Holiness," by Wayne and Cathy Perrin. Copyright 1981, Integrity Music. Used by permission.

Though you have been born anew, though you have walked away from the acts of sin that plagued your former life, you are now forced to admit that though sin does not *reign* in your heart, it does *remain*.

Inward sin is not something you *do*, A. W. Tozer taught, it is something you *are*. You grieve, for at the deepest level you want to be like Christ. But there's a part of you that treasures lust, or harbors a lurking self-idolatry, or nourishes the "drum major instinct," or thirsts for praise, or protects a touchy ego, or affirms a cultural prejudice, or shelters unworthy motives, or rebels against continual obedience to God. Tozer called these "the hyphenated sins of the human spirit." He named some: "self-righteousness, self-pity, . . . self-sufficiency, self-admiration, self-love."[2]

The Spirit of the Lord is so gentle, yet so firm. Faithfully He confronts you with these un-Christlike affections. At first you may dismiss His gentle revelations or try to ignore, mislabel, or sidestep them. But He keeps bringing you back to the mirror of the divine Light, where you can admit that you need to have your very inmost heart cleansed of sin. You are ready to join Charles Wesley in:

Show me, as my soul can bear,
The depth of inbred sin;
All the unbelief declare,
The pride that lurks within.
Take me, whom Thyself hast bought,
Bring into captivity
Ev'ry high, aspiring thought
That would not stoop to Thee.[3]

My pastor used to say in public prayer, "O Lord, show us the worst of our condition." That prayer I scarcely had the nerve to repeat. I preferred the Wesley hymn "Show me, *as my soul can bear*, the depth of inbred sin." If you pray such a prayer, tighten your spiritual seat belt. You may be in for a jolting ride through some sin-stained slums of your inner world that are as ugly as—well, as ugly as sin.

When that happens, "do not cast away your confidence" (Heb. 10:35, NKJV). Rather, wrap the robe of faith around you, and hold on to God. Recall the wonderful things God has already done for you, instead of sinking into despair over what He has not yet done for you. Never trivialize the miracle of the new birth. You have been born again; you are a child of God. To that truth the Spirit bears witness, as does your changed life.

One of Satan's devices is to so bully the believer who is on the way to sanctification into despair over *remaining sin* that he or she forgets the transformation that put out *reigning* sin. You are not yet all that you will be, but you certainly aren't what you used to be. John Wesley warned that the seeking soul, now conscious of inward sin, may become more ashamed of its most holy duties than former brazen sins.[4]

Keep in step with the Spirit. He will gently lead you to loving submission to God so that you can be cleansed "from everything that contaminates body and spirit, perfecting holiness" (2 Cor. 7:1). Hymn writer W. J. Kirkpatrick called this cleansing being "saved to the uttermost." John Wesley called it "entire sanctification." The Holy Bible calls it being sanctified "through and through" (1 Thess. 5:23).

THE INSTANTANEOUS DIMENSION OF SANCTIFICATION

Window on the Word

God . . . testified to them by giving them the Holy Spirit . . . cleansing their hearts by faith (Acts 15:8-9, NRSV).

God is God, and He will do as He pleases. Sometimes God's ways are mysterious—we will never be able to get our minds around His ways. But when it comes to sanctification, we have strong clues as to how God usually works. We have the Scriptures. And God has bestowed sanctifying grace upon millions of believers. Watching the lives of God's people, we see the "tracks" of the Lord among us. If we can resist the temptation to reduce God's redeeming work to some singsong formula, we can learn how He will deal with us. "What He's done for others, He'll do for you" (Stuart Hamblen).

So how does He work? John Wesley had the same question. Being a practical sort, he sought clear evidence. So between 1759 and 1762 he personally interviewed 1,000 persons who had found the deeper life, the life of holiness.

The Holy Spirit challenges each un-Christlike attitude, each throne of self-interest—every one.

John learned a couple of things in his research. First, without a single exception among them the 1,000 interviewees declared that they had been sanctified in the "twinkling of an eye." In this crisic, instantaneous encounter with God, sin died, the Spirit came in His fullness, and they entered into a deeper experience of God than they had ever known. The same people, however, convinced Wesley that there had been a gradual work of sanctification in process both before and after that "instant" infilling of the Spirit. God appears to work through both gradual and instantaneous methods to make our hearts and lives holy.

Jesus promised that the Holy Spirit would "guide you into all truth" and "teach you all things" (John 16:13; 14:26). Our Guide and Educator faithfully shines the light of the Lord into the dark corners and shadows of your heart. He challenges each un-Christlike attitude, each throne of self-interest—every one. Eventually you must ask God to "break down every idol; cast out every foe" if you hope to become "whiter than snow" (James Nicholson).

The Spirit's goal is to bring you to the point where you "'love the Lord your God with all your heart and with all your soul and with all your mind.' . . . And . . . 'your neighbor as yourself'" (Matt. 22:37, 39). When that blessed state is reached, the Holy Spirit of Christ will bestow sanctifying grace, the fullness of the Spirit, saying "Be clean" and "the blood of Jesus, his Son, purifies us from all sin" (1 John 1:7).

But between you, the believer on the way to sanctification, and that blessed state of "all loves excelling" looms the Cross, the hurdle of total self-surrender. Along the road of growth in grace the Holy Spirit keeps inviting you to surrender the one thing you can't give up. The one thing—or the things—to which you have given "god value." They challenge the Lordship of Christ. Soon you learn that Jesus will be Lord of all or not Lord at all.

The saints of every age from Augustine to Billy Graham report having faced the dilemma of self-surrender. A biographer wrote, "After 30 years of detours and dead-end seeking, St. Augustine found, *in his moment of surrender,* all that had previously eluded him" (emphasis added).[5] Lloyd Ogilvie often speaks of his moment of surrender that came as he paced and prayed on a lonely beach in Scotland. Hudson Taylor, founder of the China Inland Mission and already an important missionary, came to the end of himself and surrendered the sinfulness of his own heart for cleansing.

Frances Ridley Havergal was a woman of learning, charm, and talent. She was already a well-known hymn writer when a booklet called *All for Jesus* came her way. She read it and came to realize the necessity of full surrender. She said, "There must be full surrender before there can be full blessedness."[6] "Take My Life and Let It Be" became her personal prayer of self-surrender. Verses 5 and 6 of her prayer-song read:

Take my will and make it Thine—
It shall be no longer mine.
Take my heart—it is Thine own;
It shall be Thy royal throne.

Take my love—my Lord, I pour
At Thy feet its treasure store.
Take myself—and I will be
Ever, only, all for Thee.

Such consecration is not easy. The Bible calls it being *crucified* with Christ. Still, the Holy Spirit wants to hear from your lips the very words of Jesus in Gethsemane, "Not as I will, but as you will" (Matt. 26:39). Of course, you don't have to make that ultimate self-surrender. Not even God can make you. But in the end "Thy will be done" will rule. Either you say it to God, or God, seeing that your decision to clutch your self-centeredness is firm, will finally say to you, "Not my will, but thine be done."

If that happens, your spiritual voyage will likely be stranded in the shallows. You will probably join the ranks of those nominal Christians who have lost the joy of their salvation; lost *viriditas*, the greening and growing power; and have been defeated at the point of self-denial. You may even drift back into the old life and settle for the leeks and garlics of Egyptian bondage. You would, of course, be joining the mainstream. Robert Bellah, researching *Habits of the Heart*, found that "radical self-interest" is the primary influence in shaping the emerging American character.[7]

But if you make your consecration complete, self-surrender can become the prelude to sanctification. And like the stream surging through a gracile gorge, you will experience expansive freedom beyond the narrows! This is the crisic, the instantaneous, the twinkling-of-an-eye aspect of sanctification.

Some ask, "If sanctification can be gradual, why can't it continue all through life with no need for the instantaneous?" God is God, and He will work with us as He chooses, but the testimony of God's people in every age indicates a pattern of both gradual and instantaneous sanctification. After conversion, the Spirit, in weeks or months or years, brings us to the point where we must surrender all or say no to God. This is a crucial turning point in the spiritual journey. Things will never be the same again—however we respond. If we say no to God, then negative results will ensue. If we say the ultimate yes to God, we may soon receive, by grace through faith, the fullness of the Spirit or entire sanctification. And this appears to be the experience of people in all ages and in various faith traditions or denominations. God does not care so much about our denominational labels as He does about giving us the gift of a pure heart filled with Christlike love.

To receive the fullness of the blessing of God, we must give up godlike allegiance to all self-centered interests.

Therefore, instantaneous sanctification should not be reduced to a dogma to be debated. Scripture and tradition have plenty to teach us about this matter, but so does the simple way relationships work. To receive the fullness of the blessing of God, we must give up godlike allegiance to all self-centered interests. If we will not do this, the relationship between us and God is seriously damaged. That's not a doctrinal affirmation; it is simply the way relationships work.

For example, Jim and Cheryl are planning to get married in two weeks. They look over the wedding vows for the first time. When Jim sees the "forsaking all others" line, he says, "Wow, I didn't know about this! Forsaking all . . . all others . . ."

Cheryl informs him that if they are going to be married, he has to stop dating other women. Jim thinks it over, then announces that he could give them all up except Sally and Meredith. "Not that I want to go out with them all the time . . . but every now and then I would like to date . . ."

The engagement ring lands in his lap.

"Well, I guess I could give up Sally, but Meredith and I go back a long way . . . I can't just dump her . . ."

Looks as if Cheryl's parents just saved all that money they were going to cough up for the nuptials. Talk about damage to the relationship!

While most analogies, including this one, will break down if pushed too far, this one does illustrate the nature of certain relationships. And one of the best views of the need, if not the necessity, of instantaneous sanctification is gained from noticing how relationships work. The born-again believer, walking in the light, sooner or later will have to "forsake all others" and say the ultimate no to sin and self and the ultimate yes to God if he or she wants to continue to stand with unveiled face absorbing and reflecting the light and glory of the Lord. That's the way relationships work; that's one dimension of the way sanctification works.

That is not to say that on the other side of your no, God will desert you. Even after you refuse to surrender whatever it is that you won't give up, God will likely knock on your heart's door again. God's will for you is sanctification. He has called you to holiness (1 Thess. 4:3, 7). He yearns to bring you full fellowship with himself.

When the Spirit calls, respond as William Cowper did. When he faced the crucial turning point of complete surrender, he wrote his decision in a song:

The dearest idol I have known,
Whate'er that idol be,
Help me to tear it from Thy throne
And worship only Thee.[8]

— 10 —

Songs of the Stairway

First Window on the Word

Put on the new self, created to be like God in true righteousness and holiness (Eph. 4:24).

Psalms 120—134 are Songs of *Ascents.* They are processional songs sung by celebrating pilgrims on festive days of worship. In particular, the Psalms of Ascents commemorated the freedom from Babylonian exile. They are sometimes called "Songs of the Stairway" because on some high, holy days the procession of singing pilgrims started on the stairs at the Fountain Gate (Neh. 12:37) and moved up Mount Zion to the Temple. There, on the 15 steps between the Court of Women and the Court of Israel, the priests and other marchers would sing, "Lift up your hands in the sanctuary and praise the LORD" (Ps. 134:2). The Christian song "We're Marching to Zion" picks up the precise theme of the Psalms of Ascents.

Come, we that love the Lord, And let our joys be known.
Join in a song with sweet accord, Join in a song with sweet accord,
And thus surround the throne, And thus surround the throne.
We're marching to Zion, Beautiful, beautiful Zion.
We're marching upward to Zion, The beautiful city of God.

—Isaac Watts, Robert Lowry

The Psalms of Ascents themselves appear to be a praise-filled elaboration of Aaron's benediction of Num. 6:24-26, "The LORD bless you and keep you; the LORD make his face shine upon you and be gracious to you; the LORD turn his face toward you and give you peace." Every major branch of Christianity has its own songs of ascents celebrating God's gift of sanctification. Often neglected in recent years, the commemoration of this sacred gift has enjoyed renewal among many denominations. May the Holy Spirit be the choreographer of the new songs of sanctifying grace. The songs of ascent have begun low and plaintive but are rising to a crescendo in these days. Each faith family has its own tempo, tune, language, and points of emphasis, but many Christians are now in a jubilee spirit extolling the grace of sanctification. For example, Henry Holloman of Talbot School of Theology has authored a book, *The Forgotten Blessing: Rediscovering the Transforming Power of Sanctification.* In it he explores the Reformed and Fundamentalist views of this doctrine. Maxie Dunnam, president of Asbury Theological Seminary, said to the United Methodist denomination, "I am calling for a new look at, and a new commitment to, sanctification, the possibility of holiness or wholeness, the restoration of God's image within us."[1]

Many volumes, thick and thin, have been written on this biblical doctrine. I cannot even begin to summarize them here. Rather, I want to give a few brief notes, ranging from somber to joyous, that carry the melody of the song of sanctification.

GRACE AND FAITH

Window on the Word

By grace you have been saved, through faith (Eph. 2:8).

Every step of our spiritual journey is enabled by grace. Every stage of salvation, including sanctification, is a gift of God's grace revealed in Christ. You cannot boast of a gift nor demand it. You can only be thankful.

Your story and mine is a saga of grace. It starts with *atoning grace*, with the Lamb slain before the foundation of the world. The story moves to *prevenient grace* operating before you even knew it. God was working in the circumstances of life preventing tragedies you did not even know were threatening. Most importantly, God was giving you and me the capacity to choose Him and good in spite of our sinful state. *Saving grace* that rescued from the guilt, shame, and power of sin is the next stop on the journey of faith. With Christ now living in your heart, you discover how serious God is about *transforming* or *sanctifying grace*. Max Lucado observes, "God loves to decorate. God *has* to decorate. Let Him live long enough in a heart, and that heart will begin to change. Portraits of hurt will be replaced with landscapes of grace. Walls of anger will be demolished and shaky foundations restored. . . . It's not enough for Him to own you; He wants to change you."[2] "God loves you just the way you are, but He refuses to leave you that way. He wants you to be just like Jesus."[3] He will go on changing you and me all our lives through *refining* or *perfecting grace*. Even in eternity, in heaven, the grace of God will likely be at work honing, shaping, transforming us from one degree of glory to another.

Even in eternity, in heaven, the grace of God will likely be at work honing, shaping, transforming us from one degree of glory to another.

These stages of grace come to us not because we are good or deserving, not because we work hard or discipline ourselves, but by *faith* in the redeeming love of God in Christ. Hannah Whitall Smith modeled faith for sanctifying grace. She wrote in her diary, "I do give myself up unreservedly to God to be and to do just what He wills, and I do trust only Jesus to keep me moment by moment, to preserve me blameless, to purge me and cleanse me and sanctify me wholly. I know He is able, I believe He is willing, I believe that He will."[4]

LOVE

Window on the Word

How great is the love the Father has lavished on us (1 John 3:1).

The essence of sanctification is love. Divine love conquering sin; love filling the heart and soul to the brim. John Wesley described this as love expelling sin, as "love excluding sin, love filling the heart, taking up the whole capacity of the soul. . . . How clearly does this express being perfected in love! . . . For as long as love takes up the whole heart, what room is there for sin?"[5] When asked to express sanctification or holiness in its simplest terms, John Wesley quoted Matt. 22:37-39: 'Love the Lord your God with all your heart and with all your soul and with all your mind.' . . . [and] 'Love your neighbor as yourself.'"

Oswald Chambers, author of the devotional classic *My Utmost for His Highest*, described the experience of sanctifying grace in these words: "Glory be to God, the last aching abyss of the human heart is filled to overflowing with the love of God. Love is the beginning, love is the middle and love is the end."[6]

Love in the life of the sanctified includes a radical love for others. After all, the world is principally inhabited by *other people*. Wesley taught his people to embrace their neighbors with "the most tender good-will" and "earnest and cordial affection" while "procuring for him every possible good." This love was to be extended even or especially to those known to be evil, enemy, and persecutor. In regard to such persons the Wesleyans were to "thirst after his happiness" and offer "unwearied care to screen him from whatever might grieve or hurt either his soul or body."[7] In this world burning with battles, ethnic cleansing, tribalism, nationalism, and cultural wars, perhaps only a radical love such as this can help.

Those who are tempted to confine sanctification to a neatly packaged doctrine need to read John Wesley's statement on love—at least twice:

> The "heaven of heavens is love." There is nothing higher in religion; there is, in effect, nothing else; if you look for anything but more love, you are looking wide of the mark. . . . And when you are asking others, "Have you received this or that blessing?" if you mean anything but more love, you mean wrong; you are leading them out of the way, and putting them upon a false scent. Settle it then in your heart, that from the moment God has saved you from all sin, you are to aim at nothing more, but more of that love described in the thirteenth of [First] Corinthians. You can go no higher than this.[8]

SELF-FULFILLMENT THROUGH SELF-SURRENDER

Window on the Word

Whoever tries to keep his life will lose it, and whoever loses his life will preserve it (Luke 17:33).

Emlyn Williams, a Welsh actor who has played in *A Man for All Seasons* many times, tells the story of his cousin Bronwen. This attractive young woman was engaged to a young man with very good prospects. But Bronwen felt the call of God to Africa. She surrendered her life to God, broke the engagement and her fiancé's heart, and at age 23 sailed off to Africa "to help the missionaries." Her mother declared bitterly, "She had no business to go. She should have married that nice young man."

The most throw-your-hat-in-the-air joys you will ever celebrate all lie on the far side of loving submission to Christ.

Years later, in a theatrical tour to Africa, Emlyn Williams got to see Bronwen again. She was married to a missionary doctor and the mother of two children. Williams said, "She was worn with work, but she was shining with fulfillment."[9]

The deepest peace you will ever know, the most satisfying fulfillments you will ever experience, the most throw-your-hat-in-the-air joys you will ever celebrate all lie on the far side of loving submission to Christ. The most pleasant hours of self-acceptance or self-approval are found in that same spot. And "an hour of self-approval is worth a week of ordinary living."[10]

God's way up is down. The path to self-fulfillment is not through assertiveness training or winning through intimidation. Rather, according to Jesus, the only path to self-fulfillment is self-denial. If you try to save your life for yourself, you lose it. If you follow Christ in becoming a person for others, you find a richer life than any self-absorbed celebrity or any me-first millionaire will ever find.

The path of self-denial seems frightening at first. You have your plans, you have announced your goals, you have noted the family expectations, you have places to go and mountains to conquer. To drop all these for whatever God calls you to do is scary. But you can trust God. Open your sanctified heart to Him, and He will make the very thing He calls you to do the very thing you *want* to do. A young pastor told me of his call to a slum pastorate.

> I didn't want to go for the trial sermon. My wife did not want to go, either. But I had promised the district superintendent that I would. The plan was to go, preach, let them vote if they insisted, and then say no. On that Sunday morning my wife and I headed out scared to death that the members of that slum congregation would want me to be their pastor. After the morning and evening services we drove home scared to death that they would not want me to be their pastor. The very thing we dreaded, the very thing God wanted, in one day came to be the one thing we wanted to do.

The Holy Spirit makes His will sweet. Do not dread full commitment to Him.

"Become a little child . . . by laying aside all your greatness, self-assertion, self-dependence, wisdom, and strength, and consent to die to your own self-life and be born again into the kingdom of God."[11] Do not think that loving submission to God in consecration does away with your personhood. Far from it; loving submission is the way to find your true personhood, your true self. Self-denial is not the opposite of self-actualization. Self-denial is not the same thing as self-contempt or self-loathing. "Self contempt says that we have no worth; self denial declares that we are of infinite worth, as are others."[12] Further, self-affirmation comes when we accept the fact that God knows us thoroughly and loves us thoroughly. "Knowing that we are . . . affirmed by God . . . makes possible the acceptance of ourselves."[13]

The Self Crucified, Disciplined, and Actualized

Window on the Word

I have been crucified with Christ and I no longer live, but Christ lives in me. The life I live in the body, I live by faith in the Son of God, who loved me and gave himself for me (Gal. 2:20).

The world of the inner self is complex. These categories explored by William M. Greathouse in *Love Made Perfect* may help you understand yourself better. Greathouse bases his remarks on Gal. 2:20. This verse shows that

1. *There is a sinful self to be crucified with Christ*. This sinful self is to be put to death. The believer is dead to sin (Rom. 6:1-2). Though Jesus has been declared Lord, self wants to be prime minister. The call is for total self-abdication. "You have been set free from sin and have become slaves to God, the benefit you reap leads to holiness" (Rom. 6:22).

2. *There is a human [or natural] self to be disciplined in Christ*. God is not at war with your humanity. He does not wish to destroy your "self," but He does want to help you discipline it. God cannot do this alone. You must participate vigorously in controlling both bodily and psychological drives that "bubble" out of the subconscious in an amoral state. Paul wrote, "I beat my body and make it my slave so that after I have preached to others, I myself will not be disqualified" (1 Cor. 9:27). When an instinctual urge or drive seeks illegitimate satisfaction, we must, as W. E. Sangster said, "blast it with a prayer."

3. *There is a true self to be actualized in Christ*. The way of the Cross is indeed the way of fulfillment. Yet true fulfillment is only the by-product of crucifixion with Christ. The end God has in mind is the *actualization of the divine self*. The goal of the New Age movement and of consumer psychology is *self-actualization*. The goal of the gospel is *Christ-actualization*—"Christ lives in me."[14]

At a recent seminar the coauthor of a best-selling book on spiritual formation said,

> It was my duty and privilege to read, over a period of three years, the best writings on spirituality from every Christian century, from the New Testament to the latest book off the press. I discovered one common de-

nominator among the saints of every generation. Whether I was reading the experience of a Catholic or Protestant, an ancient or modern, a scholar or an uneducated person, a man or a woman, a conservative or a liberal, one common denominator stood out—self-surrender.

One priest had written a spirituality of ecstasy. His book donned a pig in a swing with a rose in its mouth on the cover and declared that in feeling good, in the experience of ecstasy, one is most spiritual. The libertines had a heyday for a few pages, then the author revealed that we never know true ecstasy until we transcend self and live for others. One woman had written a two-volume, 1,112-page Ph.D. dissertation on the secret of the holy life. On the last page her conclusion was something like this: 'The secret to the holy life is self-surrender, always has been, always will be.'"[15]

This common denominator was called by slightly different names by the saints—self-denial, self-surrender, self-transcendence, self-crucifixion. Some saints of the Middle Ages called it self-donation.

The saints in Papua New Guinea know this. John Nielson, president of Asia-Pacific Nazarene Theological Seminary in Manila, introduced me to the pidgin English songbook used by Christians in New Guinea. One song struck my heart. It has no title, just hymn number 119. If I were to title it, I would call it "A Song of Loving Submission." The tune is to "Have Thine Own Way, Lord." The following edition of verse 1 is edited to make reading easier:

You boss me, God, You boss me.
You are the Papa, me pickinini (child).
Suppose me got sin, You straighten me.
Me cry long [to] You, You come boss me.[16]

Couldn't you sing that song of ascents all the way from the Fountain Gate to the steps of the Temple?

STAIRWAY TO THE UPPER ROOM 

Window on the Word

Receive the gift of the Holy Spirit. The promise is for you (Acts 2:38-39).

With care not to reduce to a dead formula or a code the glorious path of ascents that leads to full sanctification, let me at least point you to the illumined stairway that has been the way to the deeper life for many.

1. *Know that it is God's will for you*. "It is God's will that you should be sanctified" (1 Thess. 4:3). "May God himself, the God of peace, sanctify you through and through. . . . The one who calls you is faithful and he will do it" (5:23-24).

2. *Invite God to prepare your heart for full sanctification*. The Holy Spirit will faithfully lead you to see the depths of inbred sin—that inward sinfulness that wars against the soul even after acts of sin have been forgiven. God will use the deep hunger of your own heart to lead you toward the Light. Yield

every sinful attachment that the Spirit points out. When He has led you to the point where you love God with all your heart, mind, soul, and strength, expect sanctifying grace that cleanses the heart and fills you with the loving Spirit. The promise is sure. "If we walk in the light . . . the blood of Jesus . . . purifies us from all sin" (1 John 1:7).

3. *Make your consecration complete.* Make loving submission to Christ a priority. You may wish to make this prayer from John Wesley's handwritten prayer journal your own prayer of loving submission:

O Lord Jesus,
I give thee my body,
my soul,
my substance [wealth],
my fame,
my friends,
my liberty, and my life:
dispose of me and all that is mine
as it seems best to thee.
I am now not mine, but thine:
therefore claim me as thy right,
keep me as thy charge, and love me as thy child.
Fight for me when I am assaulted,
heal me when I am wounded,
and revive me when I am destroyed.
Amen.[17]

4. *Expect sanctifying grace instantaneously by faith.* You have been growing both *in* and *toward holiness*. As the Spirit leads you to say the ultimate yes to God, expectantly hope for that moment when He says the second time, "Be clean." Remember, you cannot earn, demand, or bargain for sanctifying grace. It is a gift, a gift that He has promised to you. He will, in His own time, bestow the purging fire and the fullness of the Spirit.

5. *Patiently follow the hunger of your soul.* If you follow the deepest hunger of your heart, God will lead you into sanctifying grace. Seek with your whole heart, without fretting or tormenting yourself. Resist efforts of zealous persons to get you to claim the blessing too soon.

Meanwhile, do not put your Christian life on hold. John Wesley taught that the way to "wait" for sanctification is to throw yourself into "acts of piety" (prayer, worship, Communion, etc.) and "acts of mercy" (visiting the sick, feeding the hungry, clothing the naked, teaching the gospel, etc.).

You can trust God to give you just what you need from Him. He died to make your sanctification possible. He prayed for your sanctification (John 17). It is His will. He calls you to holiness, and the Faithful One will deliver what He promises. Wait patiently for Him.

6. *In faith believing, accept God's gracious gift of the fullness of the Spirit.* Exercise your faith in your Savior who has already saved you from the guilt and power of sin. Now when He calls you to another level of sonship, trust in Him,

weight upon Him. He alone is able to bring about the transforma-
for.

...yer for sanctifying grace*. If you are already a believer, and if you ...ied by the Spirit to do so, make this prayer your own.

O God, I praise you for all that You have done for me and my brothers and sisters in Christ. Holy is Your name! I now open my heart to its depths before You.

Cleanse by the fire of Your Spirit anything that is unlike Christ. Purge my attitudes, my spirit, my affections. Consume all my sinfulness.

Fill me with Your love until I love even those who persecute or mistreat me. Make me a flame of holy love.

Take all that is mine—I hold nothing back. I claim no right to my wealth, position, or reputation. I give You my body, my soul, my freedom, and my life. Do with me as You wish. I wish only to know You better and to serve You better all the days of my life. If in Your sovereign will I am ready to receive full sanctification, please bestow that gift on my unworthy heart. If the time is not yet, if there is work yet to be done to prepare me for the fullness of the Spirit, then, Lord, help me to wait patiently, and give me eyes to see what You are teaching me in order to prepare my heart.

Thank You, Lord, for hearing my prayer. Amen.

— 11 —

In Step with the Transforming Spirit

First Window on the Word

Since we live by the Spirit, let us keep in step with the Spirit (Gal. 5:25).

A 12-pound hawksbill turtle crawled up to die on a Honolulu beach. Concerned environmentalists arranged an autopsy that showed that one-quarter of its weight was plastic. Its intestines contained

several beads,
a comb
a golf tee,
a toy wheel,
a balloon,
a toothpaste cap,
part of a medical syringe,
baggies, and
a plastic flower.

The living turtle became a dead trash barrel.

The worldly environment in which we live is also full of trash. The devil makes sure that to live for God we must continually swim through a swirl of trash at work, at school, in the neighborhood, and even in our homes because of television, the Internet, and so on. That's his job. He loves his work, and he is good at it.

That's one reason God gives us His Holy Spirit to guide us. With the Spirit leading us, we don't have to swallow trash, even if it looks good enough to eat.

Freedom from Sins of the Flesh

Window on the Word

The acts of the sinful nature are obvious: sexual immorality, impurity and debauchery; idolatry and witchcraft; hatred, discord, jealousy, fits of rage, selfish ambition, dissensions, factions and envy; drunkenness, orgies and the like (Gal. 5:19-21).

In describing life in the Spirit, Paul puts the negative sins of the flesh first and then moves to the positive fruit of the Spirit. As Gal. 5:19-21 shows, the "sins of the flesh" are not merely physical but include sins of the mind, heart, and spirit. For Paul "the flesh" meant "human nature weakened, vitiated, tainted by sin. The flesh is man as he is apart from Jesus Christ and his Spirit."[1]

Though sensual sins are not the whole story, Paul starts his list with three sexual sins. He uses the strongest command available to him in Greek to let us know that the life in step with the Spirit is to be free from sexual sins. "You will not gratify the desires of the sinful nature," he declares (v. 16).

The first on his list is translated "sexual immorality." The Greek word is *porneia* and means every kind of illicit sexual intercourse, including prostitution. *Porneia* includes the kind of love that is bought and sold; the sort of love that makes persons into things (or clients?) to be used.

The second prohibition is sexual impurity *(akatharsia)*, which means dirt and filth or uncleanness. It refers to a filthy mind, a polluted personality that can reduce the finest action to a smutty jest that disgusts all decent people. This word was also used in ancient literature for the person who was ceremonially unclean and thus unfit to come into God's presence.

The third sexual sin is debauchery *(aselgeia)*. This refers to the man or woman so recklessly sinful, so set on pursuing lust, that he or she no longer cares what anybody sees or thinks. Such persons will brazenly shock public decency and do so with no sense of shame whatever.

Wait just a minute! Why is Paul preaching so loudly about this? After all, we are Christians. Of course we will avoid *porneia*, *akatharsia*, and that other one, *aselgeia!* Who does he think we are?

Think about the first readers of this letter. Their culture was even more sex-saturated than ours! The cultural god was the "life force" celebrated in the power of sexuality. Religion and prostitution were inextricably linked. The Greek ruler Solon not only legalized prostitution but also created state-owned brothels and dedicated the profits to build temples to the gods. Sex was part of worship. The temple to Aphrodite in Corinth alone employed 1,000 prostitutes. Desmosthenes, the famous orator, wrote, "We keep mistresses for pleasure, concubines for the day to day needs of the body, but we have wives in order to produce children legitimately."[2]

Almost no thought was given to disciplining the sexual drive. Instead, it was celebrated and exploited at every opportunity. Promiscuous sex was the "baseball, apple pie, and Chevrolet" of that culture. William Barclay says that sexual purity was the one completely new virtue Christianity introduced into the pagan world. Observers thought the ability of Christians to live in sexual purity was an almost miraculous power—and it was![3] And it was only possible for those who walked "in step with the Spirit" (Gal. 5:25).

Can you imagine any area of life in which you need more help from the Spirit?

THE FRUIT OF THE SPIRIT—LOVE

Window on the Word

The fruit of the Spirit is love (Gal. 5:22).

The fruit of the Spirit "is one in essence and nine in expression."[4] Love is the singular fruit of the Spirit. Joy, peace, patience, kindness, goodness, faithfulness, gentleness, and self-control exegete and express its meaning.[5]

Agapē is the Bible word used for love that is the fruit of the Spirit. It means unselfish, self-sacrificing, or self-giving love. The Greeks had other terms for sexual love, brotherly love, and family love. The early Christians took over *agapē* to describe Christ's kind of love. When we are filled with the Spirit, we are filled with *agapē* love.

Perfect love drives out fear, the Bible says. It makes heroes of ordinary Christians. Consider the case of Lili Khabel.

May Day celebration, Marburg, Germany.

The town council decides to invite a traveling circus to enhance the festivities. The park at the heart of the city is soon filled with clowns, magicians, jugglers, tightrope walkers, sword swallowers, cotton candy, and fire-eaters. The animals are present too. In a big circle near the pond in the park, caged tigers and lions and bears pace. Monkeys chatter and elephants parade. Presiding over all this is the happy music of the calliope.

Lili Khabel decides to introduce her little girl, Karen, to the excitement of the circus. What fun! I can see it now, can't you? Music, clowns, candy, and bratwurst with brown mustard. But while Lili pays for the second round of snacks, Karen disappears.

"Karen! Karen!" But the rollicking music of the calliope drowns her voice. For 5, maybe 10 minutes, Lili scurries from one exhibit to another. No Karen.

Then she spots her. The toddler has, quite unnoticed by the attendant, squeezed through the bars of the lion's cage! She canters behind the pacing lion. Little legs pump, chubby hands reach out trying to catch the lion's tail.

The lion turns. A throaty growl. Tail twitching in the spring sunlight.

A paralyzing hush falls like a lid. All eyes turn to the toddler and the lion.

"Komme, Katzchen." (Come, kitten.) "Mulie, mulie, mulie." (Kitty, kitty, kitty.)

No one breathes. One reveler drops his beer. The raucous music of the calliope rollicks on as senseless as the dead Greek goddess of the same name.

Little Karen leans forward and smiles into the lion's face. She has found the biggest, grandest kitty in town: "Schoene Katzchen." (Nice kitty.)

The lion does not return the smile. A toothy snarl. A drawn-back paw. Slashing position. Someone screams. The calliope careens into a crescendo. The attendant stares, stunned into frozen inactivity.

Another toothy snarl. A slight twitch at the bushy end of the tail echoes each movement of the child.

Lili snatches the key ring from the slack-jawed attendant. Five keys. The second one works. Lili rushes into the cage, swoops up her baby. A race to the cage door. The calliope pipes on. Lili slams the cage door in the face of the charging lion.

Cheers! Applause! Lili faints.

Lili Khabel is as scared of lions as you are. What made her so brave?

Love, perfect, complete love. She was so full of love that she forgot her own safety. Love is like that. When it fills your heart, it evicts fear. No room. When your whole being is filled with the love *for* God and the love *of* God, it is quite amazing how many of the "lions of life" you can lock up in their cages.[6]

The fruit of the Spirit is *love*.

The Spirit enables the Christian to act in love that is "unconquerable benevolence." This means that "no matter what a man may do to us by way of insult or injury or humiliation we will never seek anything else but his highest good. . . . It [is] the deliberate effort . . . never to seek anything but the best even for those who seek the worst for us."[7] But *agapē* is not a weak word. Do not mistake it for the simplistic notion that to let a person do whatever he or she likes is to be loving. The Bible is clear that at times love demands discipline and rebuke.

In Paul's writings the epitome of love is seen in 1 Cor. 13. There we see that possession of all the spiritual gifts without love is utterly useless. We also learn that love is eternal—knowledge, tongues, and even time will disappear, but "love never fails." Such love is patient, kind, not envious, boastful, proud, rude, or angry. Love gets no thrill out of evil but rejoices in truth. Love protects, trusts, and hopes.

The level of love described in 1 Cor. 13 is not the automatic possession of everyone. The Spirit's nurture, rebuke, and guidance must be joined to strong desire, discipline, and relentless pursuit on the part of the believer. The second mile and the turned cheek take a bit of practice and determination.

Someone has said that the greatest proof of God's love is a life that needs God's love to explain it. A life in tune with 1 Cor. 13 could certainly be explained only by the work of the gracious Spirit of God.

What the Fruit of the Spirit Looks Like

Window on the Word

The fruit of the Spirit is love, joy, peace, patience, kindness, goodness, faithfulness, gentleness, and self-control (Gal. 5:22-23).

The 5 *sensual sins*—including drunkenness and orgies—must be strictly avoided even by every Christian. But Paul lists 10 other "acts of the sinful nature." These are opposites of the fruit of the Spirit. If you live hand in hand with the Spirit, gazing upon the face of Christ, you will be led *from* the 10 remaining works of the "flesh" and *to* the 9-fold fruit of the Spirit.

You will be led *from* the 5 *sinful attitudes*—hatred, jealousy, rage, selfish ambition, and envy—*to* the *inner graces*, those of love, joy, peace.

The Spirit will guide you away *from* the *sins of the spirit*—idolatry and sorcery or witchcraft—and *to* the *inner disciplines*, those of patience, faithfulness or trustworthiness, and self-control. Idolatry and witchcraft not your problem? Think carefully. Idolatry is giving god-value to something (career, education, marriage, money, etc.) that is less than God. What about witchcraft or sorcery? The Bible word is *pharmakeia*, which refers to the use of drugs for magical and religious purposes. Some primitive religions seek "inebriated ecstasy" in magic, drugs, and worship all at once.

Keeping in step with the Spirit, you will detour around the *interpersonal sins*—discord, dissensions, and factions—to the *interpersonal graces*, those of kindness, goodness, and gentleness.

Remembering that the fruit of the Spirit is one in essence (love) and nine in expression, we now survey the way *love* looks in the fruit basket of your life and mine.

Joy: The New Testament is chock-full of joy. The verb form *(charein)* and the noun form *(chara)* appear 132 times. The verb form is a greeting that means "Joy be with you!" When the Jerusalem Council saw the light and decided to let Gentiles in, they sent a message that began, "Joy be with you" (Acts 15:23). James, writing to the exiles under persecution, said, "Joy be with you" (1:1). When the angel announced the birth of Jesus to Mary, he said, "Joy be with you!" (Luke 1:28, BARCLAY). When Jesus Christ arose, He said to the women in the garden, "Joy be with you" (Matt. 28:9, BARCLAY).[8]

The New Testament celebrates several kinds of joy. Joy is that positive element that gives songs in the night. It is the victory that survives persecution, trial, and suffering. James told his readers, "Consider it pure joy, my brothers, whenever you face trials" (1:2). There's nothing giddy or giggly about Christian joy. It is far deeper than a few laughs. An Egyptian proverb says that when we enter the eternal world, we will be asked two questions: "Did you bring joy in life? Did you find joy in life?"[9]

Joy springs up like a fountain at the blessed assurance of sins forgiven. As we mature in Christ and progress in sanctification, that fountain of joy becomes a deep, cool well from which we can drink on thirsty days.

Joy is the reward of Christian fellowship and the camaraderie of shared Christian service.

Joy is the echo of God's life within us, the reflection of spiritual health.[10]

Joy is the gift of Jesus. If your religion is as grim as a stomach cramp, ponder Jesus' words: "As the Father has loved me, so have I loved you. . . . I have told you this so that my joy may be in you and that your joy may be complete" (John 15:9, 11).

Peace: When we are justified freely (saved or born again), we have peace *with* God. As we walk in step with the Spirit, sanctifying grace brings us "the peace *of* God" (Phil. 4:7).[11] The peace of God *(eirēnē)* Augustine defined as "serenity of mind, tranquility of spirit, and simplicity of heart."[12] The peace of God stands in stark contrast to the chaos of the sins of the flesh. Compare a few: "serenity of mind" vs. "fits of rage," "tranquility of spirit" vs. "jealousy," "simplicity of heart" vs. "debauchery."

We are to *pursue* peace as a hunter goes after his prey (1 Pet. 3:11). With burning enthusiasm we are to seek peace with God (2 Pet. 3:14).

Patience: Ever have to work or live around a short-tempered person? Well, patience *(makrothumia)* is just the opposite. It literally means "long-tempered." It is often translated "long-suffering." Patience the Spirit cultivates in us makes us more like God. He is described in the Bible as "compassionate and gracious, slow to anger, abounding in love" (Ps. 103:8; see also Exod. 34:6; Neh. 9:17; Pss. 86:15; 145:8; and Jon. 4:2). God's patience isn't just idle waiting; He works to bring the stubborn to repentance before it is too late.

Sensing God's purpose, patience never loses hope, is slow to retaliate, and endures. Patience is the opposite of the spirit that turns to idols and witchcraft (sins of the flesh) to find a key to magically manipulate the divine in order to get its way. William Barclay defines it as "the power to see things through."[13]

Kindness and Goodness: Kindness *(chrēstotēs)* and goodness *(agathōsunē)* have overlapping meanings. But some nuances of difference appear. Kindness is a milder word, sometimes translated *sweetness*. It has no stern dimension. Goodness, on the other hand, can discipline in love as well as practice kindness.

William Barclay notes that Jesus is said to be acting in *goodness* when He cleansed the Temple by driving out those who had made it a bazaar. He acted in *kindness* when He blessed the sinning woman who anointed His feet with her tears.[14] Ralph Earle points out that *agathōsunē* (goodness) has an action dimension. You are not good because of something you don't do. Refraining from lying, stealing, or cheating does not make you good. You are good only as you "act in love."[15]

Faithfulness: This Bible word *(pistis)* describes a person you can depend on. Under persecution those in step with the Spirit were faithful unto death. This word describes Jesus himself. In Revelation He is the "*faithful* witness" and the "*Faithful* and True" (1:5; 19:11, emphases added). In Hebrews Jesus is the *faithful* High Priest, and He is *faithful* to the divine mission (2:17; 3:2, 6). Further, this term is used about God. God is *faithful* not to allow us to be tempted beyond what we can bear (see 1 Cor. 10:13). He is "*faithful* and just to forgive us our sins" (1 John 1:9, KJV, emphasis added). God will sanctify us through and through, and the One who calls you is *faithful*. He will do it (see 1 Thess. 5:23-24). If your goal is to be like Christ, let the Spirit transform your unreliability into loving faithfulness.

Gentleness: The word for gentleness *(praus, prautēs)* is often translated "meekness" and sometimes "humility." Far from describing the intimidated weakling, however, *prautēs* describes the person in whom strength and humility are perfectly combined. An ancient example pictures the watchdog who is bravely hostile to intruders and gentle and friendly with the members of the family.[16] In the Bible the gentle, whom God will exalt, are often contrasted with the mighty, the proud, and the sinful, whom God will put down.

Gentleness yields a *teachable spirit*. Not even God can teach the proud. The arrogant man who thinks he knows never submits to instruction, but the gentle man can "humbly *[praus]* accept the word planted in you" (James 1:21).

Gentleness is the tone of *accountability* in the church. "If someone is caught in a sin . . . restore him *gently*" (Gal. 6:1, emphasis added). Thus, "correction is a means of hope and not a cause of despair."[17]

Prautēs, gentleness, is the spirit in which the Christian minister is to instruct those who oppose him or her (2 Tim. 2:25).

Gentleness or meekness provides the proper texture for Christian witness. "Be prepared to give an answer to everyone who asks you to give the reason for the hope that you have. But do this with gentleness *[prautēs]* and respect" (1 Pet. 3:15).

Self-Control: The Bible term for self-control is *egkrateia*, sometimes translated "temperance." The root verb means "to grasp, to hold, to grip." The Christian use of this term relates it directly to mastery of human sensual desire. This fruit of the Spirit calls us to something directly opposite to what William F. Buckley Jr. accuses rock and roll lyrics of urging: "instant capitulation to the libido."[18]

In one of the Early Church writings a vision speaks of a great tower being built representing the Church. The tower is supported by statues of seven women who symbolize the seven virtues. The second woman is wearing a garment typically worn by men. Perhaps this was to show that men need this virtue more than women. This second pillar was *egkrateia*, self-control. Whoever shall "follow her becomes blessed . . . he refrains from every evil lust, he will inherit eternal life."[19] Self-control, as a fruit of the Spirit, is chastity. Few can walk this road without the moment-by-moment strengthening of the Holy Spirit. Paul's attitude is worth adopting: "I'm running hard for the finish line. I'm giving it everything I've got. No sloppy living for me! I'm staying alert and in top condition" (1 Cor. 9:26-27, TM).

How Does the Spirit Work in Us?

Window on the Word

Those who live in accordance with the Spirit have their minds set on what the Spirit desires (Rom. 8:5).

How does the Spirit produce fruit in us? Is it like osmosis, where the sun and the rain and the earth bring forth a heavy bunch of Eschol grapes or a bough-breaking crop of apples? Perhaps it is more like a growing, long-term relationship.

In Paul's biblical writings the *spirit* is the part of you that is most distinctly and uniquely akin to God. The "spirit of a man is that part of him which is implanted . . . by God; it is the presence and the power of God in him; it is the coming of the risen Christ into residence within man."[20] This results in a new focus of life. The closer the walk with the Spirit, the more the beauty of holiness shines through.

Paul's most noble passage on the way the Spirit changes us is Rom. 8:1-17. For Paul, it is a *Spirit to spirit thing*. The Spirit sets us free from sin and death, liberating us from the domination of the lower nature (vv. 2, 4). He speaks of the Holy Spirit testifying or witnessing with our spirit that we are the children of God (v. 16).

Three times in those verses he speaks of the Spirit living "in you" (vv. 9, 11). Elsewhere Paul extends this metaphor, saying, "We are the temple of the living God" (2 Cor. 6:16). How intriguing that he uses the term *naos* for temple. One of the uses for this word is of the little cell, the niche in the Greek temples where the image of the god was placed. The believer, then, is the very niche especially designed for God's residence. The redeemed, so to speak, become His shrine, His sacred cell, His holy place, the very sanctuary of God.[21] The new resident Lord of the heart makes all the difference in what that life produces.

Romans 8 tells us twice that the Holy Spirit controls the mind and heart of the sanctified (vv. 6, 9). Also, as we live in step with the Spirit, we have our minds set on "what the Spirit desires" (v. 5). Further, we are led by the Spirit as sons of God (v. 14).

Howard Thurman describes the process of getting in tune with the Spirit. He speaks of the person who has made "the primary surrender . . . yielding to God at the core of his being." This person has relaxed the will to control his or her life. "This does not come without exacting struggle. . . . One by one the outposts of his spirit are captured, retaken, and lost again through hours, months, even years of warfare, until at last the very citadel of his spirit is under siege and he is subjected to utter yielding."

Thurman goes on to say that a long silence may follow when nothing in the soul stirs. "Then out of the quiet of his vanquished spirit something stirs and a new life emerges that belongs to God more than to self. The movement now rests with Purposes that are beyond the little purposes, with Ends that transcend the private ends, the Purposes and Ends of God."[22]

Perhaps a story, a true story, will make the Spirit's ways even more plain.

Ignace Paderewski was Poland's prime minister and most famous pianist. He set up a tour of rural Poland in hopes of cultivating an appreciation for the arts. At one village the concert was about to begin. Imagine the gasp of the audience when the stage lights came on. There was Paderewski's grand piano, all right. But crawling up onto the bench was a little boy. Oblivious to the crowd he began to pick out with two fingers "Twinkle, Twinkle, Little Star."

The audience groaned, the child's mother nearly passed out, and the stagehands surged forward. But Paderewski appeared and waved them away. The world's premier pianist stepped up behind the boy and whispered, "Don't quit. Keep playing."

Leaning over, Paderewski put his left hand around the boy and began to fill in some bass notes. Then his right arm reached around the other side of the boy and began to add a running obbligato. The crowd was mesmerized. They never heard such a magnificent "Twinkle, Twinkle, Little Star."

That is the way the Holy Spirit guides us. Can you feel His arms encircling you as you try to play your simple song? His grace, His power, His counsel helping you make music, instead of a mess, of your life? Can you hear Him now, as you plunk out your tune, saying, "Don't quit. Keep playing"?

PART 3

NURTURED BY THE LIGHT

"I know the plans I have for you," declares the LORD, "plans to prosper you and not to harm you, plans to give you hope and a future" (Jer. 29:11).

What God has planned for you is not just a future, but a rich and radiant future. That doesn't mean that He is going to dump glitz, gold, and notoriety on you in one bedazzling moment. Rather, as you are nurtured by the transforming Light, you will progress from one degree of glory to another. That's meaningful movement toward "the whole measure of the fullness of Christ" (Eph. 4:13).

C. S. Lewis put it this way:

God is intent on making you and me into
"a dazzling,
radiant,
immortal creature,
pulsating all through with such
energy
and joy
and wisdom
and love
as we cannot imagine, a bright stainless mirror that reflects back to God perfectly (though on a smaller scale) His own boundless
power
and delight
and goodness."

What if Lewis is right!

Make every effort to add to your faith goodness; and to goodness, knowledge; and to knowledge, self-control; and to self-control, perseverance; and to perseverance, godliness; and to godliness, brotherly kindness; and to brotherly kindness, love. For if you possess these qualities in increasing measure, they will keep you from being ineffective . . . and you will receive a rich welcome into the eternal kingdom of our Lord *(2 Pet. 1:5-8, 11).*

— 12 —

Nurtured by the Light of the Word

First Window on the Word

All Scripture is God-breathed and is useful for teaching, rebuking, correcting and training in righteousness (2 Tim. 3:16).

They knew that John C. Fitzpatrick wasn't dead—but he soon would be! The grizzly had all but finished him off.

The soldiers trying to chart a better northwest passage through the Rockies had to move on before the winter snows trapped them. They had no time to nurse a wounded man who was all but dead anyway. The captain, in this Richard Harris film reminiscent of *The Song of Hugh Glass*, bellowed, "Leave him!" They covered him with a thin layer of dirt and leaves and left him there to die.

But he didn't.

Somehow he dug himself out before the wolves found him or the bear came back. Fueled by a seething hatred that not even the Rocky Mountain winter could cool, he set out after the men who abandoned him. The dream of wreaking vengeance on the captain who he heard bark, "Leave him!" gave him energy even when he was hungry and aching from his wounds.

Fitzpatrick came across the remains of a pioneer camp. The people had been killed by Indians, their dwelling burned. Sifting through the wreckage looking for a tool, a weapon, a morsel of food, he found a slightly singed New Testament.

He began to read it on that season-long trek. At the end of each grueling day in the waning sunlight or by the flicker of his campfire, Fitzpatrick read the Testament.

By spring he had found the camp of his former comrades. He spotted the captain and shoved a gun barrel in the face of the man who had ordered, "Leave him!" But something had happened to the revenge seeker. All those evenings with the New Testament had changed him. Somehow the hatred had leaked out of his soul, and to the man who had bellowed, "Leave him!" the New Testament was saying, "Love him!" Fitzpatrick lowered his gun. "Captain, I have a gift for you." Then, with trembling hand, he gave him the New Testament and said, "Let's go home, Captain."

The Holy Scriptures have the power to transform. According to 2 Cor.

3:18, our key verse for this book, the glory of God in Christ shines forth from the Bible. Read all of chapter 3. The source of the transforming Light in verse 18 is the Holy Scriptures. It is the image of Christ found in the Bible that we are to reflect.

What does it take to keep a Christian going? E. Stanley Jones obviously knew. He was a leading missionary of the 20th century, with a ministry encircling the globe and reaching millions. For eight decades he tirelessly proclaimed to all who would listen, "Jesus is Lord."

What fueled the fire of his soul and sustained him? He credited his "listening post" time. A rare photograph shows him at his quiet time sitting with his Bible, a notebook, and a pen. His powerful writings flowed from those early-morning periods of reading, meditating, and listening. He knew that the teachings from God's Word are "more precious than gold . . . sweeter than honey" (Ps. 19:10).

Christianity is rooted in revelation. God speaks to us in many ways, but the most definitive is through the Bible. The Bible is God's written Word, serving as the objective revelation by which other revelations are evaluated. We may be inspired by music, art, poetry, the writings of the saints, worship, great literature, a sunset, or a dream. But none of these will surpass the normative revelation found in Holy Scripture. If we are to grow in intimacy with God, we must be nurtured by His Word.

Like many others, John Wesley was a person who "soaked up life" from many different sources. He enjoyed reading as many books as he could get his hands on. But he came to see that while his night sky had many stars in it, there was only one North Star—the Bible. It was his fixed point of navigation on the sea of life. He referred to himself as *homo unis libri*—a man of one book. In his preface to his *Standard Sermons*, Wesley wrote, "O give me that book! At any price, give me the book of God! . . . Here is knowledge enough for me."[1]

We're called to be "people of the Book" as much as E. Stanley Jones or John Wesley were. We're invited to join with the saints of the ages in a regular and sustained contemplation of God's Word. In a culture filled with multiple and conflicting voices, we need to be grounded in revelation. But more than that, we need a word to sustain us and to give us hope. God's wisdom and nurture come to us through the Bible. Therefore, learning to study the Bible is a must for every Christian—every one.

READING AS AN EXPLORER

Window on the Word

Your word is a lamp to my feet and a light for my path (Ps. 119:105).

How we read the Bible is important. If we approach it in haste, the message will seem little more than a blur. If we approach it out of a cold sense of duty, we'll fulfill an obligation while missing an encounter with the Living Word. If we approach it merely to increase our Bible knowledge, our heads will swell and our hearts will shrink. How much better to approach Bible study as explorers.

Think of the famous explorers you learned about in history class. These courageous persons were adventurers and risk takers. Hardships and setbacks did not blunt their vision or hinder the pursuit of their dreams and goals.

As we approach the Bible with an explorer's spirit, we find it "maps" the terrain of God's will for us. Explorers respect their maps, realizing that what's on paper has come only through the effort and expense of others who traveled before them. Explorers pore over maps, looking for the best routes. They compare points on the map with where they actually are, connecting their current surroundings with the printed coordinates. They become so familiar with the map that they internalize a sense of location and direction. Every step they take is in relation to the map that has now become part of them.

We've been educated to read informationally more than formationally. We can't separate one kind of reading from another. The two can happen simultaneously. Most of us read more as students trying to pass a test than we do as explorers seeking to familiarize ourselves with the map that enables us to make the journey. As we learn to explore God's Word, we appreciate the information it gives us, but we understand that the data is for the purpose of *navigation*.

Explorers don't wander randomly over earth, sky, or sea. They have a profound respect for order and handle their equipment in the best possible way. Months before their journey, they begin a calculated process to insure that their trip will be successful. They purchase suitable provisions. They pack instruments to guide them and first-aid kits in case of injury. They're not people who merely "follow their noses" and hope things go well. The drama of exploration unfolds according to a well-thought-out plan.

We will never "find" time to study the Bible; we must make it.

That's the way successful explorers do it. Some of the other kind don't plan so well and pay with their lives. For example, there was Sir John Franklin. In 1845 he set out from England with two ships and 138 seasoned sailors. Their objective: to find a passage through the Canadian Arctic to the Pacific Ocean.

Franklin was a little short in the planning department. Though the trip was to take two to three years, he took only a 12-day supply of coal for his auxiliary steam engines. Rather than coal or heavy coats Franklin toted on board a 2,400-volume library, enough cut glass wine goblets and ornate sterling silver flatware to serve all the seamen, and a custom-made backgammon board, which was a gift from his wife.

Plying their way into the Arctic, the ships from deck to rigging became coated with ice. Ice locked the rudders, and the ships could not be guided. Years later the bodies of the crew were found amid copies of the *Britannica*, *Robinson Crusoe*, and sterling tableware, cannibalized and frozen.[2]

Christian, plan for the voyage; it is a tough, demanding trip. We will never "find" time to study the Bible; we must make it. Exploring the Bible's message should not be left to chance. Let's examine a plan for Bible study that will nourish our minds and souls and help keep the spirit of the explorer alive in us.[3]

Explorer's Bible Study, Step 1: Observation

Window on the Word

The Bereans . . . received the message with great eagerness and examined the Scriptures every day (Acts 17:11).

The beginning point is *observation*. "You can see a lot by looking," Yogi Berra said. I would add, "You can see only what you're looking for." Haven't we all looked past, or failed to see, things right in front of us? Remember the last time you lost your car keys? You were looking for them so intently that you either skipped over or completely ignored other things in your view: the flowers, the jewelry, the breath mints, and the junk under the car seat. Nothing mattered except those keys. The other items were invisible by comparison, because you weren't looking for them.

Exploring a biblical text observationally involves paying attention to as much of it as you possibly can. You may be accustomed to looking for the big picture or the main message when you read the Bible. Sharpening your observational skills will eventually mean that words like "and," "but," "for," and "because" hold as much promise as the big words like "justify" and "sanctify." Approaching the text observationally means that we don't skip over any word until we've held it in our minds, turned it over, and examined it for meaning.

Take Ps. 23:1: "The LORD is my shepherd." Take each word, observe it, and see how the verse shines more brightly with each subsequent examination. Stop your reading and actually experience what happens to you when you read this verse with an emphasis on a different word each time:

The LORD is my shepherd.
The *LORD* is my shepherd.
The LORD *is* my shepherd.
The LORD is *my* shepherd.
The LORD is my *shepherd*.

What happened in you as you observed each word in the verse? As you meditate, God's Word will open a part of your mind and heart, giving you a richer view than if you had merely read the verse once and moved on.

This kind of reading has quality, not quantity, as its goal. By pausing over each word, we have time to let our minds and hearts catch up with our eyes. We ponder the text prayerfully, trusting that the Holy Spirit will allow certain terms to become "bold print" for us.

Observational reading is closely akin to meditation: "I meditate on your precepts and consider your ways" (Ps. 119:15). Biblical meditation is not random stream of consciousness; rather, it's slow and considered examination of the external Word with the prayer that it might become the living Word. It's not coming to God empty-headed, but rather approaching God openhearted.

Explorer's Bible Study, Step 2: Interpretation

Window on the Word

The unfolding of your words gives light; it gives understanding to the simple (Ps. 119:130).

In *observation*, we seek to answer "What does this say?" During interpretation, we're seeking to answer "What does this mean?" Go back to Ps. 23:1. During your observation, you paused to consider the word "LORD." That's what the text says. But what does "LORD" mean? As soon as you ask that question, you enter the world of biblical interpretation. You begin to explore a concept found throughout the books of the Bible that contains rich and varied meanings.

We're prone to focus on a word or an idea and then move immediately to consult a commentary or a scholar who can give us the "real meaning." Resist doing this. Instead, stay with the text yourself as long as you can. You need a good study Bible with a substantial concordance and cross-references. You'll want to have a good Bible dictionary to help you define words and concepts. The point is to glean as much meaning from the text *on your own* as you can. A consecrated interpretation of the text will yield treasures. Trust God to help you use your own abilities to interpret the text. There will be a time to find out what others have said the verse means. For now, focus on what it means to you.

Interpretation includes making connections. Study your selected passage in the context of what precedes and follows it. Look for comparisons, contrasts, continued ideas, changes of direction, and cause-effect relationships. Include the characters in your interpretation. What kind of people were they? What else do you know about them? Put yourself in their shoes, and see what the passage looks like from their vantage point. Also consider the tone of the passage—that is, the emotion underlying the words. Interpretation extends and expands the observational process.

Explorer's Bible Study, Step 3: Correlation

Window on the Word

We have the word of the prophets made more certain, and you will do well to pay attention to it, as to a light shining in a dark place, until the day dawns and the morning star rises in your hearts (2 Pet. 1:19).

Interpretation flows into *correlation*. Now's the time to take what you've discovered on your own and lay it alongside what others have said. Begin by relating your passage to other biblical passages where similar words or ideas are recorded. Then move outside the Bible to see what informed believers have said about the verse you're exploring. Consider stories, poetry, art, and music that connect in some way to the passage you're studying. Hymnals are excellent companions for this kind of correlation. So are books of religious art. Finally, turn to the commentaries to see how the meanings you're discovering have been reflected in the study others have done. Use commentaries written by reputable scholars who treat Scripture as the Word of God to be honored rather than mere literature to be critiqued.

One of the exciting dimensions of correlation includes sharing your insights with others. Let the Bible become part of your conversation with friends, colleagues, your pastor, or prayer partner. Explorers are not lone rangers when it comes to making progress in the Bible. They learn in community.

EXPLORER'S BIBLE STUDY, STEP 4: EVALUATION

Window on the Word

For the word of God is living and active. Sharper than any double-edged sword, it penetrates even to dividing soul and spirit, joints and marrow; it judges the thoughts and attitudes of the heart (Heb. 4:12).

Correlation moves naturally into *evaluation*. All Scripture is inspired (2 Tim. 3:16), but not every verse is equally valuable to us at the same time. After studying a passage for a while, ask, "What part of this passage is particularly important for me right now?" Evaluation is a deliberate move back into the process of personalizing the text. One way to get at this is to ask yourself, "Why am I glad I read this passage today?" This simple question can take you to the heart of the passage. It's important not to leave the message of God's Word disconnected from life.

Return to Ps. 23:1 and ponder its words again. Let's assume you've observed them, interpreted them, and correlated them. You're as full of the verse as you can be. Now ask, "Which of these words is God using to speak specifically to me today?" For example, it may be the simple word "is." Maybe you need a fresh reminder that your Shepherd is not way back in history or way ahead of you in the future—but is with you in the present. If that kind of message is what you need, Ps. 23:1 will be a great blessing. Or maybe your life is somewhat out of control right now. Then pondering the fact that your Shepherd is also "LORD" will help stabilize your life. Evaluation makes you not merely a "sailor on the sea" but also a "lover of the ocean."

EXPLORER BIBLE STUDY, STEP 5: APPLICATION

Window on the Word

But as for you, continue in what you have learned and have become convinced of . . . how from infancy you have known the holy Scriptures, which are able to make you wise for salvation (2 Tim. 3:14-15).

Evaluation turns easily into *application*. This prayerful dimension asks, "God, what do You want me to do with what I've read and internalized?" Is there a promise to claim? Is there an action to take? Is there some attitude adjustment that's called for? Is this a passage to memorize and store in your heart?

(See Ps. 119:11.) Application is our intention to put the Word of God into practice—immediately. It may be clear that there's something for you to do. Application is your commitment to do it.

We live increasingly in a "virtual" environment. Video games and virtual reality "rides" take us into exciting dimensions but are a step short of the real thing. Application is what prevents our Bible study from being "virtual." If there's anything to be said about exploration, it's that we're *really* engaged in what's going on. There are no theoretical explorers!

Reading with Determination

Window on the Word

Take the helmet of salvation and the sword of the Spirit, which is the word of God (Eph. 6:17).

Even explorers have days when all they're doing is simply "exploring." Sailors refer to it as the doldrums periods, when the wind isn't blowing and the ship seems to go nowhere. Expert seamen, who have planned better than Sir John Franklin, don't panic when such times occur. They have both the will and the skill to stay on course. No matter what kind of method we adopt, there will be spiritual doldrums as we read and ponder God's Word. The "wind of the Spirit" may seem to have stopped blowing.

This is an especially critical time. We must maintain the attitude of the explorer, understanding that as we stay the course, the "winds" will blow again. No method is foolproof. No journey is all adventure. One of the secrets to spiritual formation is learning how to get genuine blessings from seemingly insignificant experiences. Don't approach your time of Bible study expecting always to hear great and glorious things. Often you won't get headlines; instead, you'll receive fine print.

Cultivate the habit of bringing your encounter with the Bible into community with others. History reveals that the saints spent much time alone with God—but they also took their inspirations into the community. We're told to "test the spirits to see whether they are from God" (1 John 4:1). This includes interfacing our insights with the larger faith perspectives of the Church and trusted Christian friends.

Listening to the Lord is one of the great blessings of the spiritual life. We've been made in the image of God; consequently, we're able to receive the messages the God of revelation is sending. As His children who have been made new in Christ, living in the nurturing light of the Word enables us to draw closer to Him. As we hear and obey, we reflect His character more radiantly.

— 13 —

Nurtured by the Light in Prayer

First Window on the Word

Pray in the Spirit on all occasions with all kinds of prayers and requests . . . always keep on praying for all the saints (Eph. 6:18).

John Kenworthy delights and amuses me. To hear him pray—well, one does not detect much difference between living room conversation and his prayers. He talks to God in unvarnished language, telling the Almighty everything. I have to control myself to keep from laughing. John has not learned Christianese.

Don't you wish we could all remove the mask of pretense and just talk to God directly and honestly? That's what Brother Lawrence, 17th-century saint, advised. "We ought to act with God in the greatest simplicity," he said, "speaking to Him frankly and plainly."[1] That is what Jesus called us to do, and that helps explain the first two words of His model prayer, "Our Father." He wanted you and me to make prayer a family affair. Can you imagine visiting with your earthly father, using a stained-glass voice?

Authentic Prayer

Window on the Word

But if . . . you seek the L*ORD your God, you will find him if you look for him with all your heart and with all your soul* (Deut. 4:29).

When you talk to the Father out of genuine need, in desperation and openhearted sincerity, He hears you. But don't you sense a "putting on of airs" in the painted-over prayers that telegraph, *I must use these words because I'm in church, and please note the proper ecclesiastical manner, Lord.*

Have you observed the difference between mere technique and authenticity in prayer? Some have developed flowing English and remarkable phrasing—a skill we all admire. When lovely language bonds with grace, ah! a beautiful devotional experience ensues. I have noticed, however, that some have acquired the skill of prayer but lack the grace of authenticity.

What is authenticity in prayer? Here's a checklist that may help you.

1. *Complete trust in the Father, the One with all knowledge, the One who understands your heart*. Hebrews 11:6 clarifies the point: "And without faith it is impossible to please God, because anyone who comes to him must believe that he exists and that he rewards those who earnestly seek him."

2. *Utter reverence in the presence of God*. Ego tripping in group prayer, a nonchalant attitude, carelessness of any kind must not invade your prayer times or mine. Some even think, "If I do my daily time, boring though it may be, I've done my duty." You and I need to check our attitudes, making quite certain of our genuine respect for the Creator of the universe.

Never forget who God is. Don't get too familiar in your style of praying. God is your Father, your Friend, but not a backslapping buddy. So bring to your prayers, private or public, utter respect for God the Father. After all, God is the ultimate authority, the author of both law and grace, the sovereign over your life and mine. Not to recognize Him as Lord robs us of a natural sense of dignity and may even lead to subtle attempts to manipulate Him.

3. *Getting on God's wavelength*. Sometimes this takes moments of silence in His presence. I do not always sense God immediately, do you? The clutter and hassle of life can distract at prayer time. Once you achieve focus, God stands ready to listen. He stands with you before that, too, helping you come to that centering down experience that opens your heart to Him.

4. *Seek the cleansing of your heart*. Let no hypocrisy lurk in the hidden recesses of your mind. God will point out any hidden two-faced posture. He will also give grace to confront and confess it, and then grace to enjoy the subsequent freedom in prayer.

5. *Guard against woolgathering*. In quiet times, any number of scattered thoughts may invite themselves into our minds. What strange and unexpected thoughts can come during prayer!

Here I do not refer to a train of thought that may come to you when focused on prayer for a friend or relatives; that may lead to the concerns of family, job, and a whole circle of needs. God may send those thoughts; often He wants you to embrace the whole concern while praying for friend or family. That is very different from woolgathering, which dilutes your effectiveness in prayer.

BECOME A STUDENT OF PRAYER

Window on the Word

Do not be anxious about anything, but in everything, by prayer and petition, with thanksgiving, present your requests to God (Phil. 4:6).

We live in an age of rich literature about prayer. A nonstop flow of books and articles come off the presses. Because we engage in life at full tilt, few of us have time to keep up with all the volumes on prayer. But fortunately we have easy access to materials, such as Foster and Smith's *Devotional Classics*. The great writers, past and present, show up in that anthology, including Thomas à Kempis: *Imitation of Christ*; Brother Lawrence: *The Practice of the Presence of*

God; John Wesley: *Christian Perfection*; John Baillie: *A Diary of Private Prayer*; and E. Stanley Jones: *Conversion*.

Take a book like *Devotional Classics*, and read just a little every day, perhaps in the morning before going off to work. You will find the very experience of reading such books a lot like actual praying. The words will put you in touch with God.

Do take time, also, to read the Bible, especially the Psalms. A friend of mine commented one day, "Each evening our family reads a psalm. That's more important at our house than TV or even supper." The tone and context of his words let me know evening prayers with psalm reading created a godly atmosphere in the home.

The Psalms, of course, remind us of our own hymns, for the ancient Israelites sang their Psalms in private and public worship. You may want to find songs from your hymnbook that "paraphrase" Psalms. Try using these in your quiet times this week.

"O God, Our Help in Ages Past" (Ps. 90)

"God Is My Strong Salvation" (Ps. 27:1-3)

"The Lord's My Shepherd" to the tune Crimond (Ps. 23)

Singing the Psalms may lead you to other biblically oriented praise hymns such as:

"I Need Thee Every Hour" (John 15:5)

"Take Time to Be Holy" (1 Pet. 1:16)

"Peace, Perfect Peace" (Isa. 26:3)

But whether sung or read, the Bible should come into your prayer times. The Book of Books is your best study guide to prayer. It does more than talk about prayer—it gives us words to pray. Don't just read the Psalms, pray them. Meditate on them. Allow God to use them to form your own prayer life. If you pray five psalms a day, you can pray through them all in a month!

Jesus Teaches Us about Prayer

Window on the Word

One day Jesus was praying in a certain place. When he finished, one of his disciples said to him, "Lord, teach us to pray, just as John taught his disciples." He said to them, "When you pray, say: 'Father, hallowed be your name, your kingdom come. Give us each day our daily bread. Forgive us our sins, for we also forgive everyone who sins against us. And lead us not into temptation'" (Luke 11:1-4).

When the disciples asked Jesus to teach them how to pray, they were not dealing with something at the bottom of the priority list. Jesus was prepared for this "teachable moment." In Luke 11 we have the teaching form of the model prayer, and in Matt. 6 we see the church or public worship expression of that prayer.

When I teach in the seminary classroom, I often put these key words on the overhead projector.

1. *Praise and adoration words: "Father, hallowed be your name."*

"Father, hallowed be your name" signals not only the family spirit of the Christian's faith, not only the respect we must have for God, but also the adoration and praise we ought to give Him. God favors us with food, clothes, family, and so many blessings we have a hard time keeping track of them. Jesus saw Him as a kind and gracious Father. No wonder He asked us to praise and thank the Father!

Note this law of the spiritual life: Praise to God comes right back to us in spiritual blessing.

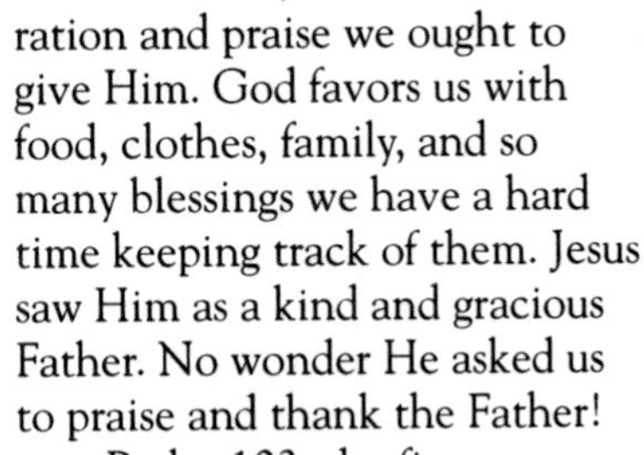

Psalm 103, the first paragraph (vv. 1-5), puts us in the mood of adoration and praise:

> Praise the LORD, O my soul; all my inmost being, praise his holy name. Praise the LORD, O my soul, and forget not all his benefits—who forgives all your sins and heals all your diseases, who redeems your life from the pit and crowns you with love and compassion, who satisfies your desires with good things so that your youth is renewed like the eagle's.

What a mood that creates in your soul! And note this law of the spiritual life: Praise to God comes right back to us in spiritual blessing. We all know that we cannot outgive God. When we express adoration, it comes back to us. Like giving love to a child or spouse, we tend to get what we give.

The opposite happens when we show disrespect for God. Joe swore with the fellows on the construction crew, laughed at religion, and made fun of his devout wife. But Joe did not live a happy life; anger filled his soul. That inner madness showed up in awful ways—fights (broken bones and the loss of an eye), a churning stomach (ulcers), and finally a heartbroken family (he deserted his wife and children).

Jesus instructed us to praise and respect the name of the Father and to hallow His name. What He said is utterly practical, something that makes for joy and peace and the love every human being craves.

Coming at the beginning of the Lord's Prayer, you may think that *adoration* is a mere prelude to praying. But it is far more. Teachers of prayer such as A. W. Tozer, Albert E. Day, Richard Foster, and Frederick Buechner say that adoration is the most lofty level of prayer.

In adoration one worships God, not for what He has done for you, but for His own sake. That is to say, adoration does not spring from the heart because God has forgiven sins, removed guilt, brought peace of mind, purified your heart, or sent the rent money—though He may have bestowed all of these. Rather, adoration rises in love for the God who was before we were born, who He is and will be long after we are gone. Frederick Buechner said, "I loved him [God] not so much in spite of there being nothing in it for me, but almost because there was nothing in it for me."[2]

The followers of Bernard of Clairvaux in the Middle Ages made popular the vision of a woman carrying a pitcher and a torch. With the pitcher she would quench the fires of hell, and with the torch she would burn up the pleasures of heaven. With these out of the way, people would then be free to love God for His own sake.

2. *Intercession words: "Your kingdom come."*

Matthew's version adds, "your will be done on earth as it is in heaven." Jesus taught us that truly interceding makes a difference; serenity takes the place of disruption, order comes out of chaos, problems yield to solution. Jesus seemed to have no doubt that God answers prayer. Nor do people who practice prayer. Henri Nouwen taught that to pray for others was to offer them a hospitable place in my heart, "where I can really listen to their needs and pains." More important, God and the person you are praying for can "meet each other there. Then the center of my heart can become the place where God can hear the prayer for my neighbors and embrace them with his love."[3] How vital is intercession!

Prayer journal books, found in religious bookstores, provide a fine tool for aiding intercession. These books have blank pages except for numbers, with a line up and down the middle. On the left side one can record concerns by number, leaving the right side empty to record the date and the answer to the prayer of intercession. For many years, I have kept such a notebook and have literally hundreds of answers recorded. That inspires my faith! No one can persuade me God does not answer prayer. When I think of "impossible" problems for which God has brought resolution—well, how can I doubt Him when a fresh challenge shows its face?

I have also noticed that God answers by surprise. I can never really guess how He will respond. But inevitably His reply comes in a package more colorful and attractive and exciting than I could have imagined.

Here is a suggestion for interceding. When sitting on an airplane, pray for the people you can see. Take them one by one, in the quiet of your seat, lifting them to God. You may, on occasion, observe a crying baby, a businessman with distress written on his face, even a seat partner who takes up conversation with you.

When I hear a siren, I pray for the persons in need, perhaps in dire need. I also pray for my colleagues at work, sometimes by department to help me remember names and faces. When family members come to mind, I lift intercessions.

The Lord wants to hear our concerns, and He treats us as family. Moreover, God often waits to answer prayers until we lift them into His presence.

3. *Petition words: "Give us each day our daily bread."*

Petition means asking for ourselves, while intercession relates to appealing to God for others. Notice that Jesus puts Kingdom concerns (intercessions) before personal requests (petitions). And before intercessions, He puts praise to God. Notice the order: God first, others second, myself in third place. Our tendency, no doubt because of our inborn selfishness, nudges us to put ourselves first, then others if we get around to them. Often we completely forget to praise God.

Herein we have another law of the spiritual life: God-oriented people pray with perspective, bringing balance to their lives.

Jim serves God with his whole heart. No wonder his prayers are answered. Answers come with a feel for adventure. Jim has a growing family—three young children plus a new baby. He lives with big challenges: school full-time, and work to support the family. Time after time he meets impossible odds. But, according to his own testimony, he gets excited when challenges come: "I'm filled with a sense of adventure, wondering how God will answer prayer." The last crunch time, Jim and his family needed money to go home to New Jersey for Christmas. Jim got an unexpected check in the mail for $300. "Will that cover your expenses?" I queried. "I don't know," he replied, "but God will always meet our real needs." Jim took his family to see his wife's people in New Jersey during the holidays.

No, God does not always respond that way. Peggy wants a baby. She cannot get pregnant. The doctors have failed to help her. Expensive treatments have not worked. The young couple fights depression.

None of us know why some prayers do not come to solution. But sometimes we look back over the years and, with the perspective only time can provide, see why God did not answer. On my own journey, I am discovering that God has many ways to answer prayers that I think He doesn't even hear. Some I have noted in my spiritual life journal include:

Yes; why did you wait so long to ask?
Yes, and here's more.
No, not yet.
No, I love you too much.
No, but My grace is sufficient for you.

The words "Give us each day our daily bread" represent necessities of any kind. Haven't you noticed that God often not only answers our prayers but goes above and beyond requests? We can rest with complete assurance in His all-knowing awareness of our needs and depend utterly on His care. I find this the best kind of news, news that keeps me going day after day.

4. *Confession words: "Forgive us our sins, for we also forgive everyone who sins against us. And lead us not into temptation."*

Today, in the world of counseling, a whole new discipline has emerged: "Forgiveness Counseling." Students study forgiveness in graduate school, and pastors know that in forgiveness lies a major clue to happiness and fulfilled living.

When Jesus added, "And lead us not into temptation," He cautioned us against the deliciously tempting urge to hold grudges. Unforgiving attitudes, harbored even in the hidden recesses of the soul, can create both emotional and physical illness. Recently, I saw an article in a Chicago newspaper that declared that forgiving someone looks on the surface like forfeiting justice, but in point of scientific fact, forgiveness releases one to happiness.

We need to admonish ourselves to take courage, review our relationships, and let the Spirit of God point out any unkind word we may have said to someone. This requires complete honesty, for we can rationalize ever so easily, saying to ourselves, "Well, that person deserved a chewing out," or "I expressed firm love really, not unkindness," or "We did not actually cheat him—he did the same to us in our last business transaction." Tiny misdeeds can lodge in the psyche and, accumulating over time, cause havoc.

I have discovered that God speaks to me in the quiet of the prayer time, revealing anything at all that needs confession, or anything that I must put right with a fellow human being. Jesus warned us that we must forgive others from our heart or forfeit forgiveness from God (Matt. 18:35).

Two temptations lure us when we offer the prayer of confession. Richard Foster presents the poles of tension. "If we are the lone examiners of our heart, a thousand justifications will arise to declare our innocence. . . . At the other end of the spectrum is our tendency toward self-flagellation. . . . It is easy for us to take one good look at who we really are and declare ourselves unredeemable. Our damaged self-image votes against us."[4]

5. *Guidance words: "Deliver us from the evil one."*

This bit of the Lord's Prayer appears in the Gospel of Matthew version (6:13). When we ask God to deliver us, as we pray the liturgical form of the Lord's Prayer in church, we really request His guidance. And He does give it when we ask earnestly.

W. E. Sangster, the famous 20th-century English preacher of an earlier generation, wrote a book titled *God DOES Guide Us*. That title telegraphs, without a single doubt, that God leads His people. How will He lead you? In many ways, but God is known to have guided many people like you and me through:

—His Word, the Bible, illumined by the Holy Spirit
—anointed preaching and teaching
—His saints, often older members of the Church with years of experience
—prayer and quiet times, when we get silent enough to hear His voice
—attendance upon the means of grace like Holy Communion, prayer groups, regular worship with homily and song
—reading of the devotional classics, the time-tested expressions of truth

In such ways God leads, protecting us from evil, even in distressing times.

All Glory to God

Window on the Word

Because your love is better than life, my lips will glorify you.
I will praise you as long as I live, and in your name will I
lift up my hands. . . . With singing lips my mouth will praise you.
. . . I sing in the shadow of your wings (Ps. 63:3-5, 7).

In neither Luke nor Matthew do we find the last line of the Lord's Prayer, the line we always say in public worship: "For thine is the kingdom, and the power, and the glory, for ever." That line may be an echo of 1 Chron. 29:10-11.

Though its historical origin has not been discovered for sure, we nonetheless cherish it because it reminds us that all glory belongs to God, not one tiny bit to ourselves.

Johann Sebastian Bach ended all his handwritten scores with the initials S.D.G., *soli deo gloria* (glory to God alone). He gave full credit to God. Bach believed the Kingdom and the power and the glory belongs to God now and forever.

Every time you receive an answer to prayer, record it in your journal. You could sign answers with S.D.G.

— 14 —

Nurtured by the Light in Worship

First Window on the Word

The true worshipers will worship the Father in spirit and truth, for they are the kind of worshipers the Father seeks. God is spirit, and his worshipers must worship in spirit and in truth (John 4:23-24).

The soul is like an unopened package. Or so said John of the Cross. Only God knows what gifts He has put into that gift parcel. All our private devotion and self-examination only get as far as removing the wrapping and the string. The real contents of God's gift package will never be known even to us, according to John, until the worshiping community helps us discover the contents of the mysterious unopened package of our soul. Among our worshiping brothers and sisters we discover our identity and our gifts.

Whatever else the Church may be, it is a *worshiping community*.

A great vulnerability of the spiritual formation movement with its emphasis on personal spiritual disciplines is that the spiritual life "will be considered an individualized, privatized, and largely hidden experience . . . [that] can be *practiced alone*."[1] As significant as private devotion is, we never outgrow our need for the worshiping community. Evelyn Underhill reminds us that "the true consecrated life, however fully given to God, however deeply it may seem to be transformed is never . . . self-supporting."[2] As individual members of the Body of Christ, we worship as one small cell of that Body, and not as the center of the universe. Thus, corporate worship is not "focused upon consolation, support, or perfecting of the individual soul. . . . All of this may be achieved by it. But [worship] looks beyond every personal satisfaction"[3] to the broader redemptive purposes of God in the world. Maria Harris declares, "One Christian is no Christian; we go to God together or we do not go at all."[4]

WHAT HAPPENS WHEN CHRISTIANS WORSHIP TOGETHER?

Window on the Word

Let us not give up meeting together, as some are in the habit of doing, but let us encourage one another—and all the more as you see the Day approaching (Heb. 10:25).

In cathedrals, chapels, or catacombs the Christian Church has met regularly for worship. The fellowship of the saints and the yearning for God bring them together. "We discover a certain capacity for eternity . . . a deep thirst for the Unchanging, a need for God."[5] Beyond the blessings of private devotion the Church has experienced something unique when the faithful come together and pray, "O God . . . even we cry out . . . Holy art thou in deed, holy art thou in truth, and lofty art thou and exalted above all."[6] As they offer themselves as Church and as individual persons in self-oblivious worship, Christians encounter the Holy One who is "worthy of glory from every mouth, and confession from every tongue, and adoration and exaltation from all creatures . . . glorious Trinity, Father, Son, and Holy Spirit."[7]

Authentic worship is a powerful and dangerous adventure, for the Presence, who fills us with both dread and fascination, might seize us and transform us forever. Annie Dillard, in *Teaching a Stone to Talk*, said, "Ushers should issue life preservers and signal flares. For . . . the waking God may draw us out where we can never return."[8]

This does not mean that every worshiper, every Sunday, will be dazzled with Ezekiel's vision, or knocked out of the saddle like Saul on the Damascus road. Though worship may seem tame, divine purposes are being achieved.

One of the hindrances to true worship in many Evangelical churches is that worship is conducted with little concept of being the people of God, the covenant community. It seems more like a concert, a party, or a boring routine. It makes a difference how we speak and listen to God. "The superficial silliness of many misguided attempts at 'celebration' and the dulled predictability of many traditional Sunday morning services may speak more to our adoration and protection of ourselves . . . than to the living God who calls us together."[9]

In many congregations you see people, isolated from each other, carrying out their private "just You and me, Jesus" type of worship in a public place. About all they share with the others present is that they are doing their private prayer in the same building. Sometimes the liturgists, the worship leaders, or song directors aid and abet the "private worship in public" syndrome. They close their eyes, shutting out the worshipers, and sing and talk and pray as if they were at home alone.

But when we learn to join together in authentic worship, God is glorified, the Church is edified, and the soul of the individual believer is nourished. In spite of our lack of skill at worship God is achieving His purpose. Many wonderful things occur in the life of the family and the individual member. William Temple, the beloved archbishop of Canterbury, wrote this famous description of what goes on in Christian worship: "To worship God is to quicken the conscience by the holiness of God, to feed the mind with the truth of God, to purge the imagination by the beauty of God, to open the heart to the love of God, to devote the will to the purpose of God."[10]

Notice the key concerns of that definition. What does worship mean?

- A conscience quickened by God's holiness—your conscience comes alive before the majestic greatness and superlative purity of God, and you know again that God is the standard, and not public opinion or the guy next door, compared to whom you look OK.

- A mind fed on the truth of God—nourished by the truth recorded in God's Word, the Bible rather than the notions of social science or talk show hosts.
- Imagination cleansed by the beauty of God—from all that is vain, lustful, or self-serving.
- A heart open to the love of God—a love whose very nature demands being passed on to family, friends, neighbors, even enemies.
- A will devoted to God's purposes—yes, God graces us with decisiveness to do His will, including attendance at worship itself.

Talk about being nurtured by the light of worship! What more could you and I ask for—a resurrected conscience, a mind full of truth, a cleansed imagination, a heart brimming with divine love, and a will bent on God's holy purposes. Given this, how do you think attending divine worship stacks up with staying home from church to watch football on TV?

GOD-CENTERED WORSHIP

Window on the Word

For great is the LORD and most worthy of praise; he is to be feared above all gods. For all the gods of nations are idols, but the LORD made the heavens. Splendor and majesty are before him; strength and glory are in his sanctuary (Ps. 96:4-6).

Christian worship is not primarily about us. You don't go to worship to keep your soul in shape. Worship is not about entertainment! The worship leaders are not up front to keep us amused and entertained; they are not performers fishing for call-back encores. They are to guide us in reaching to God. The "audience" in Christian worship is God; we the worshipers offer to God sacrifices that we pray will be acceptable. As Ps. 96:4-6 indicates, we worship because of who God is!

The word *worship* comes from the Anglo-Saxon *weorthscipe*—worth-ship. In other words, God's worth, His worthiness calls us to adoration. Thus, our worship has to do, first, with who God is, and secondarily to who we are and "who we wish to God we were."[11]

Why is God central in worship? This truth is expressed so clearly in Ps. 100: "Worship the LORD with gladness; come before him with joyful songs" (v. 2). Why? Because of who God is: "Know that the LORD is God. It is he who made us, and we are his; we are his people, the sheep of his pasture" (v. 3). Look at verse 4: "Enter his gates with thanksgiving and his courts with praise; give thanks to him and praise his name." Why? "For the LORD is good and his love endures forever; his faithfulness continues through all generations" (v. 5). God's "steadfast love" is God's love that won't quit. Who God is and His care for us motivates Christians to worship Him. It's no wonder we adore Him!

On television I saw a gospel service that turned me off. A man danced about, playing a guitar and singing over and over, "I feel good." I got the clear message that that man did not worship God but himself. This issues in personal confusion and group chaos.

Essentials of Christian Worship

Window on the Word

Let us be thankful, and so worship God acceptably with reverence and awe (Heb. 12:28).

As a boy, I worshiped in a little church of modest size. A crowd of 350 at special rallies always impressed us; normally we had under 200 for worship. We enjoyed choir music only at Christmas or Easter. The people loved to give their testimonies, sometimes with tears of conviction or gratitude. The preacher took the simple stories and truths of the Bible and explained them so even I, as a child, could understand the fundamental truths of the Christian gospel.

As I grew, I learned to love other styles of worship as well—some in other kinds of settings also. I knew little of formal liturgies in childhood; later, I became aware of the Bible background of ritual prayers, choral responses, and litanies. After ordination, I preached in many places: little white churches in rural areas, houses of worship in Africa, and stately Anglican and Presbyterian cathedral-type places. I heard all kinds of music: full orchestras to solo guitarists, sophisticated and perfected Bach chorales to gospel choruses, operatic soloists to untrained teens expressing their love of God. I learned that God loves sincere expressions of adoration; He turns His back on parade and posturing, on all hypocrisy.

This law of worship John Wesley expressed in a single sentence: "All the children of God may unite in love, notwithstanding their differences in opinion or modes of worship."[12]

The current interest in worship styles has sent scholars digging into Early Church times tracing the elements of worship that have survived for some 2,000 years. These classical elements, having stood the test of time, may be called the essentials of Christian worship. They include:

Singing
Prayer
Public Reading of the Scripture
Preaching
Sacraments of Baptism and the Lord's Supper

Some Evangelical, Pentecostal, and contemporary worship diminishes some of these essentials. Many churches neglect the public reading of the Bible. Except for the reading of the pastor's text, the Scripture is not heard. Some denominations have reduced the sacraments to mere "ordinances." In Pentecostal models of worship, preaching is often distinctly separated from worship time. For the first time in history a major worship plan has regarded preaching as less than an act of worship.

The point is this: If Christians for 20 centuries have found that these practices were acceptable to God and that they put them in touch with Him, then they will likely be fruitful for us today. Still, Wesley's law is prudent advice.

The Lord's Supper

Window on the Word

The Lord Jesus, on the night he was betrayed, took bread, . . . and said, "This is my body, which is for you; do this in remembrance of me." In the same way . . . he took the cup, saying, "This cup is the new covenant in my blood; do this, whenever you drink it, in remembrance of me" (1 Cor. 11:23-25).

Two of the most important elements of worship are preaching (sometimes called the sacrament of the Word) and the Lord's Supper. In the Early Church, the Christians took the Lord's Supper frequently. John Wesley took it several times a week. Some denominations require it every Sabbath, others monthly, and still others quarterly.

Some Christian groups never take the bread and wine. Most Quakers do not, nor do Salvation Army worshipers as a rule. Rituals can so easily get in the way of genuine heart experience of God, they believe. Nevertheless, most Christians celebrate the Lord's Supper, often called the Holy Eucharist—the Bible word is *eucharistia*, meaning "thanksgiving as an act of worship."

Millions find the Lord's Supper the apex of their worship experiences. Most followers of Christ believe in what theologians call the "real presence." This means that Jesus comes in a special way at the Lord's Supper. Protestants generally believe in the mystical presence of Jesus. Jesus does not materialize in some difficult-to-explain way, but nonetheless He does come. I do not find this hard to accept because I personally sense Him in the Lord's Supper.

Because the Lord's Supper carries so much significance, we must examine our motivations, our very selves, in preparation. When you take Holy Communion, you make important affirmations.

1. You publicly identify yourself with Christ and His people.
2. You affirm your faith in Jesus Christ as Lord and Savior.
3. You demonstrate your belief in salvation by grace, for no one is worthy to kneel at the Lord's table on his or her own merits.
4. You repent of any known sins, for one cannot bring unconfessed sins to the table of the Lord.
5. You seek purification. In the words of an ancient liturgy you pray, "Consume the thorns of my offenses. Make clean my soul, make holy my mind."[13]
6. Your action says that you are ready to encounter God in soul-shaking dimensions. In the Eucharist it may be that "the soul is led into the very recesses of the Godhead, and by love made visible is snatched up to the Invisible Love."[14]

7. You memorialize the suffering of Jesus Christ in your behalf.

8. You reenact the sacrifice of Christ and commit yourself to share in His sufferings in behalf of the lost for whom He died. Evelyn Underhill declares, "The Church is the Body of Christ, the organ of His eternal self-offering. . . . Each of her members accepts a sacrificial status, is willing to give all for the world's need."[15] In the Lord's Supper, the believers are "stretching out the arms upon the cross . . . that they may embrace the whole world."[16] The question is not, "Am I good enough to take Communion?" Rather it is, "Am I willing to give my whole life in self-oblivious sacrifice in the name of Jesus?"

9. You renew the covenant with Christ. You make the Liturgy of St. Basil your pledge: "Of thy sacramental feast this day, O Son of God, accept me as a partaker. . . . I will not give thee a kiss like Judas."[17]

10. You declare your hope in the return of Jesus Christ.

11. You assert your faith in the resurrection of Jesus and in your own resurrection (Rom. 8:11).

12. You express your commitment to the unity of the church, and your willingness to reach out in love and forbearance to the family of faith.

13. By participating in the Lord's Supper, you are nourished by the Bread of Life and the Blood of the Lamb.

HOLY BAPTISM

Window on the Word

Go and make disciples of all nations, baptizing them in the name of the Father and of the Son and of the Holy Spirit (Matt. 28:19).

Sunday morning brightened as the sun broke through after the early morning tropical rain. The familiar sound of people pounding rice—thud, thud—echoed through the West African village. People walked to the church in twos and threes with anticipation. This Sunday new believers would be baptized. The singing was joyous. The pastor preached from Rom. 6:4: "We were therefore buried with him through baptism into death in order that, just as Christ was raised from the dead through the glory of the Father, we too may live a new life." The pastor called the names of those to be baptized. Thirty people stood with shining faces. Before their friends and neighbors, they were proclaiming their faith in Christ. The pastor and other leaders led the procession through the village to the riverbank.

Loud and clear the pastor asked: "Do you believe that Jesus Christ, who died and rose again, is your Savior, that He has forgiven you of your sins, and you are a child of God?"

"I do."

"I baptize you in the name of the Father and of the Son and of the Holy Spirit. Amen."

Each candidate testified, and the family of God sang praises.

Jesus commanded baptism: "Go and make disciples of all nations, baptizing them in the name of the Father and of the Son and of the Holy Spirit, and teaching them to obey everything I have commanded you" (Matt. 28:19-20).

Some Christians pour water on the one to be baptized, some sprinkle water on the head, while others immerse in water. Some baptize the infants of Christian parents, while others baptize people when they themselves become children of God through faith in Jesus. In any case, it's a solemn act of worship in which the person is identified as part of the Christian family. The water visualizes the old life of sin being washed away so the person enters a new, clean life with Christ. In many churches a baptismal fountain is found near the door. The water of baptism signifies our entrance into the family of God.

When children are baptized, the parents promise to bring them up in the Christian faith and guide them to the time when they'll make what was done for them in baptism their own by giving themselves to Jesus. The whole church welcomes the child into the Christian community. The congregation promises to help the parents "nurture" their children "in the chastening and admonition of the Lord" (Eph. 6:4, ASV).

Baptism is a public testimony of their commitment to Christ.

The baptism of adults or older children is also a great time of Christian worship. These people have given their hearts and lives to Christ. In obedience to Christ, they're taking the step of baptism. Their baptism is a public testimony of their commitment to Christ.

If you've become a Christian believer but have not yet been baptized, talk to your pastor about taking this step in obedience to Christ. You'll be confirmed in your faith, and the family of God will be blessed.

Other Worship Experiences

Window on the Word

Whatever you do, in word or deed, do everything in the name of the Lord Jesus, giving thanks to God the Father (Col. 3:17, RSV).

Though Protestants do not regard marriage as a sacrament, the wedding ceremony is a genuine worship experience. "Sacrament" means a sacred binding in a covenant relationship in the presence of God. That's precisely what God wants to do in a marriage ceremony. The couple recites vows to each other and to God, and the wedding ring symbolizes that covenant relationship. The people come to the wedding not merely to see a pretty bride and a handsome groom; not just to see a cute ring bearer and a sweet, small flower girl; not primarily to greet the wedding party and kiss the bride. Cake and coffee, nuts and mints, laughter and catching the bride's bouquet—all this God loves. Jesus entered into the celebration of the wedding at Cana where He did a miracle and blessed marriage for all time. Prayers, homily, music, and celebration point to the marriage service as worship.

Funerals, too, call for worship. We commemorate the life of a faithful servant who has died, select appropriate music, preach the gospel of heaven, then bury the Christian departed with ritual readings and prayers. We recognize God himself as the Author of the life lived in Christ.

In weddings and funerals, as in all other types of worship experiences, we focus on God alone, Author and Finisher of our faith. Yes, God alone. Self-referencing easily intrudes itself into public worship—posturing, performance, personal reference—all tempt us to shift our focus away from God himself.

Do you sometimes feel like an unwrapped parcel? A gift from God barely opened? If John of the Cross was right, you may not know what lies in the depths of your heart of hearts. Are you ready to let God, working with the worshiping community, reveal, bless, and use those gifts hidden in potentiality?

— 15 —

Nurtured in Community

First Window on the Word

Dear friends, build yourselves up in your most holy faith and pray in the Holy Spirit. Keep yourselves in God's love as you wait for the mercy of our Lord Jesus Christ to bring you to eternal life (Jude 20-21).

"We are, each of us, angels with only one wing," Luciano de Crescenzo said, "and we can only fly embracing each other."[1]

Luciano was right, I think, don't you? The church must be a lot more than a crowd of saved individuals. God wants to make of us a people committed to God and to each other. God's Spirit is shaping us into a loving community that radiates God's love to all who will see.

The Holy Spirit is sometimes defined as the love and unity that exist between the Father and the Son. While most of us would insist on a more distinctly personal dimension to the blessed Holy Spirit, we can embrace the truth that "by causing us to become brothers and sisters of Christ, the Spirit brings us to share in the love the Son enjoys with the Father."[2] As we follow the Spirit, we participate in the eternal communion between the Members of the Holy Trinity. That lofty purpose is why the Spirit calls us to be committed to each other. We owe each other a fierce loyalty.

How we need each other. John Wesley said, "It is a blessed thing to have fellow travellers to the New Jerusalem. If you do not find any you must make them, for none can travel this road alone."[3] In John Milton's epic poem *Paradise Lost*, we see at the end Adam and Eve expelled from the Garden of Eden. The frightened couple face the sin-cursed world they have been told will be marked by pain and toil: "They hand in hand, with wand'ring steps and slow, / . . . took their solitary way." Sent out into our world of sin and sorrow, our first parents were holding hands. In a world waist deep in rejection and dejection our only hope is to hold hands too.[4] Or, as Crescenzo put it, we one-winged angels must embrace each other if we hope to fly.

ACTS OF BELONGING

Window on the Word

Brothers, if someone is caught in a sin, you who are spiritual should restore him gently. . . . Carry each other's burdens, and in this way you will fulfill the law of Christ (Gal. 6:1-2).

As we saw earlier, few things bring us together like worship and the sacraments of baptism and Holy Communion. But in this chapter we will examine some acts of belonging that both build community and reflect the love of God to the world.

1. *Hospitality.* "Offer hospitality to one another without grumbling. Each one should use whatever gift he has received to serve others" (1 Pet. 4:9-10). The Early Church could not have existed without hospitality. Traveling evangelists, missionaries, and teachers could not have paid the steep prices at the inns—which were usually incredibly filthy and notoriously immoral. Then and now is there any greater gift than the welcome of a Christian home to the traveler in a strange place?[5] In the days of the early Wesleyan movement there was always a room for the traveling preachers. And before we got so prosperous, remember the fellowship at assemblies, conferences, and revivals among those believers and delegates who crowded our houses to sleep on pallets? Hospitality has always been a mark of community among Christians, a sign of belonging.

Author Margie Haack tells a story of true hospitality. She and her husband invited newfound friends to their "ancient" apartment after the Sunday service. They sat on "creaky chairs at a wobbly table in the kitchen" and ate hamburgers, potato salad, and beans from a can. The next Sunday these new friends returned the invitation. Margie and her husband were ushered into an adobe wall-enclosed estate filled with tasteful and expensive furnishings. They sat on leather cushions around a glass table in the living room. "A double litany streamed in my head," Margie wrote. "One flow said: 'You idiot. What ever made you think these people would want to visit the dump you live in? And serving them Coke and burgers? That was like giving dog biscuits to Queen Elizabeth.' The other flow kept saying, 'No. No. Hospitality isn't about status or the stuff we own. Meals shared in love, conversations of the heart in the shelter of homes—this is how it should be.'"

The couples' friendship deepened. One evening the wealthy husband commented to Marge while sitting in her tippy rocker, "Why do I feel so comfortable here, so at home in your living room?"[6]

When Scripture instructs us to be hospitable, it's not talking about entertaining others so that we can show off our silverware, furniture, or good cooking. We don't entertain others so that our social status will increase. Jesus forbade that kind of hospitality when He told us not to invite people just so they would invite us back (Luke 14:12-14). We invite our brothers and sisters into our homes because of Christian love. We listen to their burdens, pray for their concerns, and help them with their needs. The resulting friendships may be sources of encouragement for years to come.

2. *Accountability*. "My brothers, if one of you should wander from the truth and someone should bring him back, remember this: Whoever turns a sinner from the error of his way will save him from death and cover over a multitude of sins" (James 5:19-20). Such restoration should be done gently and in love (Gal. 6:1), but we need to be accountable to each other.

Each of us needs at least one Christian friend who checks up on us, someone who can ask us the hard questions.

At one time, I was in a group of four who met together every week for encouragement and accountability. One member of the group had been delivered from an addiction to pornography. He was now on-line with an Internet service. "Please ask me every week," he said. "Ask me if I've looked at anything on the Internet I shouldn't have."

So we did ask him. One week his answer was evasive: "No, I haven't . . . well, I haven't opened any document and looked at anything."

"Have you gone anywhere on the Net you shouldn't have?" we repeated.

With tears in his eyes he confessed that he had gone to a page listing pornography sites, although he had not opened any of them. The other guys in this group lovingly but firmly told him that he should get off the Net. He did. Now he's on an Internet service with a filter. Without that loving accountability, this brother may have fallen back into sin. Today he's a vibrant Christian in full-time ministry!

3. *Brotherly Kindness*. In Peter's ladder of virtues the second highest rung is *philadelphia*, "brotherly affection" (2 Pet. 1:3-7, RSV). This is the kind of love that does not look at the demands of Christian relationships as an interruption of one's day, duty, or devotions. It is the kind of love that puts the welfare of the person ahead of having a chance to be the first to pass along juicy gossip.

John Wesley writes about a fictitious person called Susurrus—the Latin word for "Whisperer" or "Murmurer." This Susurrus is a pious, temperate man, remarkable for his fine traits. He never misses a worship service, and he nearly starves himself to have money to help feed the poor.

But Susurrus has a tragic flaw: he keeps his ear to the ground for the failings of others. He collects bits and pieces of evil information and can't wait to pass them on. Susurrus appears to have sorrow for the failings of his neighbors, and he readily lets you know about the tenderness of his own heart. After all, he would never have another's reputation damaged. He speaks only hesitantly and would not talk at all if he did not sense inward conviction—a kind of inner compulsion. How he wishes he could hide the bad news!

Mr. Wesley summarizes Susurrus as outwardly compassionate but inwardly jealous and prejudicial. Susurrus makes himself appear as a person of Christian love at the very moment he's whispering evil.

Wesley writes that Susurrus confides in a friend a great secret, something so bad he can't tell it publicly. He declares himself happy that few have heard the awful news and says he hopes it's false, though he feels rather certain of its validity.

But Susurrus's listener answers like this: "Susurrus, you say you're glad few know about this and hope it's not true. Therefore, go home to a private place and pray for this man with the complete earnestness you would pray for yourself in such a situation. Plead with God to favor the man, to save him from false accusers, and to bring shame on all those who tell bad things about him. After all, these uncharitable whisperers, telling secret stories, wound him as if stabbed in the dark."

This admonition impacts Susurrus; he understands the rebuke. Now with a troubled conscience, he almost feels that the book of judgment has opened to him and that God has let him see his self-condemnation.

From that time till now, Wesley says, Susurrus prays fervently and regularly for those he might have talked evil about. He goes through a complete metamorphosis and now can't whisper against another human being any more than he could ask God to hurt one of His children. *Susurrus* has been changed into *Philadelphia*.

Here's what *Philadelphia* looks like today.

"I'm leaving you. I don't love you anymore." That's what Karen told Jason W. the night before he graduated from seminary. "I'm in love with Phil. We've been having an affair. When you get back from the ceremony tomorrow, I'll be gone."

What a blow! After four years of college and three years of seminary your wife walks out. Seven years of hard work (Karen called it seven years of neglect) and before the first day of your first pastorate—she leaves!

What a tragedy. But things changed. The few people who knew about their problems decided to *pray* instead of *gossip*. They decided to play the *Philadelphia* role rather than the *Susurrus* role. Further, they put feet and arms to their prayers.

A miracle happened. Karen repented, Jason forgave and repented of his inattentiveness. They mended their marriage and raised their children. Now, 20 years later, they look back on two decades of outstanding ministerial service. The reason: a half dozen people chose to pray and minister and not to gossip. Philadelphia Christians they were; Susurrus they weren't!

4. *Shared Adversity*. Few things bind people together like shared adversity. Ask any group who have been stranded in a blizzard, or burdened with the survival of a church that is on the critical list. We one-winged angels learn to fly together as we share the hardships and burdens, whether they are emotional, financial, physical, or spiritual. The Bible says, "As we have opportunity, let us do good to all people, especially to those who belong to the family of believers" (Gal. 6:10).

Consider the young family with several children whose car is finally broken down beyond reasonable repair. Can other believers help them get another car? Remember that elderly couple whose children live out of town. Why not visit them or take them out to dinner? Take note of the family who's struggling financially because Mom is staying home to take care of the young children. Could you give them a night out, baby-sitting for them without charge and paying for their meal?

Leo Buscaglia tells about a little fellow who saw an old man crying. The man had recently lost his wife to death. The young boy went into the elderly gentleman's yard, climbed up into his lap, and just sat there snuggled in his arms. Presently the lad jumped down from the man's lap and returned to his mother's side. She asked, "Honey, what did you say to the man?"

"Nothing," the boy replied. "I just helped him cry."

"Rejoice with those who rejoice; mourn with those who mourn." These words, from Rom. 12:15, summarize our mutual encouragement and support in the family of God. How simple and straightforward!

Community on Purpose: Face-to-Face Groups

Window on the Word

May the Lord make your love increase and overflow for each other . . . just as ours does for you. . . . Therefore encourage one another and build each other up, just as in fact you are doing (1 Thess. 3:12; 5:11).

As utterly essential as corporate worship is, the growing believer needs more. Gathering in groups of 100 to 5,000, we can fall into the habit of meeting together, looking at the back of the heads in front of us, shaking hands with the preacher and a few friends, and rushing out to lunch. That's a "Teflon" church. People don't "stick," they slide right through like French toast in a Teflon skillet. They must get involved in face-to-face groups if Christian nurture is going to be done right. Members in Teflon churches can go months without getting within a heartbeat of each other. They are no more likely to get to know each other than spectators at a football game. How could they ever help each other "grow strong in the broken places"?

Face-to-face groups, fostering acceptance, belonging, instruction, sharing, and accountability, are not peripheral spiritual serendipities. They are at the very heart of the church's mission. "One group of ten persons, learning truly to love one another, experiencing an ever-deepening love for Christ . . . will exert more redemptive influence in a community than a church of one thousand uncommitted members."[7]

John Wesley knew this and organized his people in productive small groups. He would not evangelize where he could not follow up with societies, classes, and bands. Wesley was not the great preacher that George Whitefield was. But at the end of his career Whitefield looked back mournfully and said, "Brother Wesley acted wisely. The souls that were awakened under his ministry, he joined in class, and thus preserved the fruits of his labor. This I neglected, and my people are a rope of sand."[8]

Successful nurturing churches today use structures similar to those of John Wesley. To date no one has improved on Wesley's design for spiritual formation, community, and pastoral care. Let's look at his basic structures, not so we can woodenly repeat what he did, but to see how they might inform our mission today.

1. *The Society.* The basic structure for Wesley was the *society.* This was like a local church or a large Sunday School class organized for ministry. Societies ranged in size from two dozen to more than two thousand persons. Wesley's people were, at the start, still members of the Church of England, where they attended on Sunday mornings, and where they received Holy Communion. The society meetings were held on Wednesday mornings and Sunday afternoons. Wesley described the society as a group of persons "united in order to pray together, to receive the word of exhortation [preaching], and to watch over one another in love, that they may help each other to work out their salvation."[9]

2. *The Class Meeting.* Every society member was required to join a class of 12 persons. The class met weekly, and careful records were kept. One had to attend at least 10 of the 13 weeks in a quarter to keep his or her membership card renewed at the examination time by the traveling preacher or the "helper," the lay preacher. The purpose of the class was both spiritual and instructional. One purpose was "to inspect their walking, to inquire of their inward state; to learn what are their trials; and how they fall or conquer by them."[10] The educational aspect of the classes included "to instruct the ignorant in the principles of religion [only 1 person in 25 attended school then]; if need be to repeat, to explain, or enforce what had been said in the public preaching."

A typical class meeting would begin with the singing of a hymn. The class leader would then share the conditions in his or her spiritual journey. Answers to prayer, difficulties, temptations, and spiritual progress, or the lack thereof, was reported in extemporaneous testimonies. Following the leader's example, they would share needs and blessings and then ask questions about Methodist beliefs and polity. Since some of the sharing was quite personal, visitors were permitted only at alternate meetings. The duties of the class leader were to visit "each person in his class . . . to inquire how their souls prosper; to advise, reprove, comfort, or exhort, as occasion may require; to receive what they are willing to give toward the relief of the poor."[11]

D. L. Moody declared that Wesley's class meeting was the best method of discipling converts that the world has ever seen.

D. L. Moody declared that Wesley's class meeting was the best method of discipling converts that the world has ever seen. Henry Ward Beecher said that it was Wesley's greatest gift to the world. Contemporary educator John Drakeford wrote that the openness of the class meeting, where pretense was stripped away, provided the class members with "an experience they would never get in a church today."[12]

Today, some large Sunday School classes organize several subgroups to do discipling and shepherding work that the class meeting once did.

3. *The Bands.* Wesley thought that the Methodists were closest to New Tes-

tament religion in their work in the bands. A band was a "covenant group" of four to six persons (of the same gender) who met weekly to share their spiritual journeys "without reserve and without disguise." They operated on the principle that "God has given us to each other to strengthen each other's hand."[13]

They functioned in harmony with James 5:16, "Confess your sins to each other and pray for each other so that you may be healed." Wesley said that he started the bands because his people in the societies and classes desired "closer union" and a place where they could "pour out their hearts without reserve, particularly with regard to the sin which did still easily beset them, and the temptations which were most apt to prevail over them."[14] Each band meeting began with five questions that each member was expected to answer. Restated in contemporary style, they are:

(1) What spiritual failures have you experienced since our last meeting? What known sins, if any, have you committed?

(2) What temptations have you battled with this week? Where do you feel the most vulnerable right now?

(3) What temptations have you been delivered from this week? Please share with us how you won the victory.

(4) Has the Lord revealed anything to you about your heart and life that makes you want us to join you in taking a second look at what might be sinful attitudes, lifestyle, or motivations?

(5) Is there any spiritual problem that you have never been able to talk about—to us or even to God?

Even today God works miracles through covenant groups. Let me just share one of many.

"I probably will never see you again," Sheila said.

It was Homecoming Sunday, and I had gone back to participate as a former pastor. Taken aback by Sheila's remark, I tried to be cheerful. "Never see me again—what are you doing, moving to Hawaii or something?"

"No," she said. "They tell me I will never get well—six months at the most."

My heart sank. I knew that during the previous year Sheila's only brother and her father had died.

Reading my face, she said, "Don't feel sorry for me. I'm OK. I am stronger than I've ever been. And do you know why? You put me in that Tuesday covenant group—and there I found myself as a person and as a Christian. I could never have made it without that group. But now I am ready for whatever the future holds. I'm going to beat you to heaven, Pastor." Her smile was full of faith and joy.[15]

4. *Twin Souls and Spiritual Friends.* The early Wesleyans were big on two kinds of one-to-one teams: twin souls and mentoring pairs. We will deal with mentoring pairs later. Hundreds of times Wesley put together two Christians whom he thought would help each other on the way. He called them twin souls. Today they are called "spiritual friends" or "soul friends." This is not "spiritual direction," where a mature saint tells a young one what to do. Wesley

thought there was danger in "direction." Twin souls were equals engaging in mutual spiritual guidance.

The Celtic saint Brigit (ninth century) told her foster son, "Go forth and eat nothing until you get a soul-friend, for anyone without a soul-friend is like a body without a head."[16] Though the Celtic tradition was too much in the "direction" mode for Wesley, he would have agreed with the necessity of having a twin soul with whom one could share without reserve and without disguise, with whom one could travel wing to wing and oar to oar. To his banker Wesley wrote, "I am fully persuaded that if you had always one or two faithful friends near you who would speak the very truth from their heart and watch over you in love, you would swiftly advance."[17]

Would a twin soul watching over you in love help you advance?

5. Family Religion. Those who write about Wesley's face-to-face groups almost always forget one of the most important—the family. Family worship and study was recommended twice daily, morning and evening. It was one of the engines that fueled the Methodist revival. The emphasis on this was great, not slight. Besides the twice daily family worship, Thursday night was to be given to one-on-one parent to child instruction. On Saturday night the family was to review all that they had learned during the week. To help with the family worship and religious education, Wesley provided *A Collection of Prayers for Families*, *Prayers and Devotions for Every Day of the Week*, *Prayers for Children*, *Lessons for Children* (200 Bible studies), and *Instructions for Children* (58 lessons on Christian living).

An insightful method of family worship was also provided:

Step 1. A short, extemporaneous prayer.

Step 2. Psalm singing.

Step 3. Bible study. A parent was to read the scripture for the day and *explain* it. Then the children were to explain the Bible passage *back to the parents*.

Step 4. Family Prayer, using both written and spontaneous prayers.

Step 5. Singing of the Doxology.

Step 6. The Benediction given by a parent.

Step 7. The blessing. The parent lays his or her hand on the head of each child and blesses the child in Jesus' name. The blessing in Jesus' name, Wesley charged, was never to be omitted no matter how bad the child had behaved that day. Being blessed in Jesus' name by a parent every day—even on days when your conduct was rotten! Think what a daily parental blessing in Jesus' name would do for a child's self-esteem, for their spiritual health![18]

Christians should feel and act toward each other just as Paul did toward the Thessalonians: "So deeply do we care for you that we are determined to share with you not only the gospel of God but also our own selves, because you have become very dear to us" (1 Thess. 2:8, NRSV). Without the hospitality, accountability, brotherly kindness, mutual burden bearing, and face-to-face encouragement that we need (as one-winged angels), we will crash. But with support groups, twin souls, and the kind of loving community that shares not only the gospel but our very own selves, we can fly, even soar upward, upward in the light.

— 16 —

Nurtured by the Light in the Rhythms of Life

First Window on the Word

Praise be to the . . . Father of our Lord Jesus Christ, the Father of compassion and the God of all comfort (2 Cor. 1:3).

"Everybody gotta be someplace."

Sammy Cohen, in the old vaudeville routine, made this line famous. In the skit a wife was entertaining her old boyfriend. The husband comes home early. The wife quickly stashes her old flame in a closet. The husband, however, opens the closet to hang up his coat, and there stands the sheepish boyfriend. The husband bellows, "What are you doing here?"

Cohen, in the closet, shrugs and blurts out, "Everybody gotta be someplace."

It's true, you know, "Everybody gotta be someplace."

In our journey there are only four places to be in the cycle of life and faith: endings, in-between times, new beginnings, and settled places.

You May Be at an Ending

Window on the Word

We are hard pressed on every side, but not crushed; perplexed, but not in despair; . . . struck down, but not destroyed (2 Cor. 4:8-9).

Meg Woodson, a pastor's wife, gave birth to two children.

They are both dead now.

Both died from cystic fibrosis—CF they call it. Joey died at age 12. Peggy lived to become a college student. She braced herself for her last trip to the hospital by taking a 3" x 5" card with a quote from William Barclay on it: "Endurance is not just the ability to bear a hard thing, but to turn it into glory." How she hoped to turn this hard thing—CF—into glory.

But she spent most of her last few days clutching her quote card and screaming prayers to God to stop the pain. Her mother said that God "decided . . . to let her death top the horror charts.

"I will never forget," Meg Woodson said, "those shrill, piercing, primal screams."

Afterward she wrote to her friend Philip Yancey, "I tell you, Philip, it does not help to talk of . . . God almost always letting the physical process of a disease run its course. Because if He ever intervenes, then at every point of human suffering He makes a decision to intervene or not, and in Peggy's case His choice was 'Let CF rip.' . . . How could God be in a situation like that and sit on His hands?"[1]

Talk about endings. Mrs. Woodson's ideas about God, her world, and herself were permanently changed. She came through it all with a stronger faith. But she will never think the same way about prayer, religion, and God.

Perhaps something in your life has ended; something is over. It is time to take leave of a major role in life. A career has ended, a marriage has failed, a spouse has died, your business has gone broke, or the children have grown up and gone away. An ending is usually unpleasant. It feels like walking over a cliff, or falling down the stairs in the dark. At Job's "ending" he cried out, "What I feared has come upon me; what I dreaded has happened to me" (Job 3:25). When Leo Tolstoy came to an ending in his troubled life, he wrote, "Something had broken within me on which my life had always rested and I had nothing to hold onto. . . . My life had stopped."[2]

Endings create *permanent* changes in our basic assumptions about God, our world, and ourselves. I often employ a "used to think" exercise in which I ask students to finish this sentence: Something that I used to think about God, but no longer believe, is . . . Like my students you would have plenty to write on that subject if you have encountered a few major endings. Endings make permanent changes, hopefully realistic changes, in our way of relating to God.

Endings also make permanent changes in the way you view your world. Your marriage fails—whether a divorce happens or not. Childhood is replaced with the realities of adulthood, or a romance crashes. A leader you trusted turns out to be corrupt, a mentor shows his clay feet. One woman said, "The person who led me to Christ later tried to seduce me. I don't think I can trust again."

Your job is lost to corporate downsizing. Recently a company laid off 5,000 workers. The company spokesman didn't say they were fired; he said the employees were "involuntarily leisured." After such endings our world looks different.

One woman said after an unwanted divorce, "My self-esteem as a woman and as a person, was all tied up in his reactions to me. I didn't just lose a husband. I lost a way of evaluating myself. He was my mirror. Now I don't know how I look anymore."[3]

The most painful endings are those when you, yourself, turn out to be something that you always said, and really believed, you would never be.

You hold this image of yourself as a competent, flawless parent—until your kids turn out worse than you could ever imagine.

You see yourself as an utterly trustworthy friend—but then one day, in order to save yourself, you betray a comrade who always trusted in you.

You see yourself as a faithful spouse—until maximum vulnerability, maximum temptation, and maximum opportunity merge, and then you have to say, "I am the kind of person who commits adultery."

Has an old image of yourself, of the world, or of God changed for you?

We turn now to Scripture to get the climate of endings. Let me set the scene:

Jeremiah sits meditating at eventide. He gazes in contemplation as God paints another sunset. The reddish sun, streaked with narrow strips of cloud, throws javelins of light that pierce the grape-colored haze on the hilltops and sends soft shadows of purple and gold dancing in the valley. Evening quietly claims the land, as welcome sleep overcomes a weary farmhand who lies down at day's end.

Witnessing such ambience, one almost expects to hear a symphony rise from the shadows and come floating into consciousness with hardly a ripple hovering over the innermost being, compelling the heart to stillness and awe.

Most persons absorbing this pleasing tapestry would be tempted to think with Browning's Pippa that "God's in his heaven— / All's right with the world." But our meditating prophet is not so easily taken in. The ironic beauty of the sunset spreads a grimace across his leathery face. He knows that all the red about him is not prismatic sun. Some of it is the blood of men, women, and children slaughtered this day in war.

Even as he feels the cool of the evening march down the now quiet streets, he knows that at any moment a gaggle of grisly soldiers, ravenous with bloodlust, may emerge from the shadows. He is too weary to run or hide if they come. What difference does it make? Besides killing most of the people, the armies of Babylon have destroyed the Temple of God. And Yahweh just sat on His hands while they turned His house into rubble. Nothing is sacred to the soldiers, no violence too sickening, no atrocity stark enough to seize them by the beard and draw them up short. Jeremiah weeps over his homeland, his dead friends, and his fading hope in God. The end has come. The end of the city, the end of the nation, the end of the Temple, the end of David's throne, the end of hope for a Messiah. And he writes:

> How deserted lies the city, once so full of people!
> How like a widow is she, who once was great among the nations!
> She who was queen among the provinces has now become a slave.
> Bitterly she weeps at night, tears are upon her cheeks. . . . There is none to comfort her. . . .
> Those who once ate delicacies are destitute in the streets.
> Those nurtured in purple now lie on ash heaps.
> We have become orphans and fatherless, our mothers [are, NEB] like widows *(Lam. 1:1-2; 4:5; 5:3)*.
> In the LORD's very house they raised shouts of victory. . . .
> [God] withdrew his helping hand when the enemy came on.
> Our days are all but finished, our end has come *(2:7, 3; 4:18, NEB)*.

GROWING DURING THE IN-BETWEEN TIMES

Window on the Word

We were under great pressure, far beyond our ability to endure, so that we despaired even of life. . . . In our hearts we felt the sentence of death. But this happened that we might not rely on ourselves but on God. . . . We were harassed at every turn—conflicts on the outside, fears within (2 Cor. 1:8-9; 7:5).

The only thing worse than an ending is what comes next—the trapeze stage or the in-between time. An ending has changed you. You feel like the trapeze performer who has released the bar he was holding on to, only to look up in horror to find that the bar he expected to grab in this flying leap is nowhere in sight!

After a major ending we feel lost, abandoned, confused. We don't know who we are anymore, nor where we are going. It is a stage of lighting matches and whistling in the dark. We have to learn to walk all over again.

You are in real danger here of becoming bitter, not better. You could be lost, confused, angry, or self-pitying the rest of your life. A list of negative *D* words present themselves in this wilderness between an ending and a new beginning complete with ominous Sturm und Drang rhythms.

Disorientation: You have no idea of what to do next, who to turn to, or which direction to march. God doesn't seem to be answering prayer—after all, He could have prevented the ending that put you in the dirt face first. You are thirsty in this desert, but the streams of cool, living water evade you. Hymns taste like ashes, your prayers seem to mock you, and trying to read the Bible provokes you to frustration—the promises sound so empty, so hollow right now. "The Bible is only answering questions I am not asking," one father who had lost a custody battle said. "Who cares about the names of Benjamin's sons or whether the wine at Cana was alcoholic or not!"

Disengagement: This has both positive and negative dimensions. You need to disengage and spend some time alone to think, to slow down, to listen, to examine your own part in the ending that has happened. Like the crawfish that has cast its shell, you sense your vulnerability, and you need to hide in the rocks. The in-between time is a stage of fertile emptiness that must come before a new beginning can happen. But disengagement is dangerous too. At just the time you need the fellowship and support of the church, you go into hiding. If the ending that plunked you down in the in-between time was something the church frowns on, such as sexual sin or divorce, you are very likely to stay away when you most need support.

Disenchantment: "What did I ever see in this church?" you say when they try to recruit you to make nut cups for Jesus again this year. "The Mother's Day banquet? Look, my house is burning down, and you want me to make party favors?"

You go to church, and the preacher booms, "Rejoice always! Don't you know joy is the mark of a Christian? Where is your joy?" he bellows. You hold your head and feel like standing up and shouting, "Help, I'm bleeding to death inside. My world just crashed, and you want me to clap and giggle?"

And in your quiet moments you think that something is terribly wrong spiritually. Maybe I never was sanctified, after all. Maybe I am backslidden in heart—maybe I'm the only one who gets nothing out of church—maybe it just doesn't matter.

Every false image we have of God He must, in mercy, shatter.

Every false image we have of God He must, in mercy, shatter. How quickly we can lose our footing and see this disenchantment harden into the spiritual sullenness that Thomas Aquinas called the "sour sorrow of the world."

Despair: Spiritual despair is nearly synonymous with depression and is the worst of the *D* words. The religious word for it is *accidie*. Sometimes it is translated "sloth" in the Bible. But "sloth" sounds like soaking too long in the bath or putting off mowing the lawn to take a nap. But *accidie* is one of the seven deadly sins. It means to give in to despair and fling one final comment at the world: "I don't care."

It may help you to know that Christians in every generation have had to wait and wade and work their way through the in-between times. John of Damascus declared that he was "imprisoned in his own confused bewilderment," and his soul was "absorbed by its own indolent dejection." Chaucer said that this spiritual depression "leads to *wanhope* . . . despair of the mercy of God." Archbishop Trent noted that in the throes of spiritual despair "one's own life is a most unwelcome gift."[4]

The trapeze stage is so scary that we want to leap right over it and plunge into a new beginning. But that will not work. We know that a developmental task of one stage left untouched shows up as excess baggage in the next. We need the in-between times. Some wisdom we can gain no place else. That is why God, who is too good to be unkind and too wise to make a mistake, permits, even requires, the in-between times for us.

So don't rush through the in-between time. There is grief work to be done. Serious self-examination awaits. We need to savor the darkness, admit our fear, face our failures, and imagine new possibilities. We must admit that the old is gone and that fashioning a new identity takes time and perseverance. Embrace the "cloud of unknowing" rather than constantly struggling to escape it.

One pastor was voted out of two churches in six years. It was, of course, the dirty work of carnal board members and sinful sneaks who were out to get him. For two years he insisted on this. But finally he had to admit to himself and to others that his insecurity and dogmatism created the problems. He also discovered that it was his father who had called him to preach, not the Lord. He is now a prosperous businessman and a happy tithe-paying member of a local church.

For all the *D* word dangers that come with the in-between time, it can be a fertile time of growth. In many classic stories the hero experiences an extended time of withdrawal for soul-searching before he or she returns to fulfill the calling.

Take the story that you struggled through in high school English class, *The Odyssey*. Odysseus sets out on what should have been a three-week journey home after winning a big battle at Troy, but the journey, a story of transformation, takes 10 years. After winning a battle and then losing most of his 12 ships, he encounters Scylla and Charybdis, the monster and the whirlpool. He girds himself in his armor to fight like a foot soldier when the time for that sort of heroism has long passed. Nearly killed in the whirlpool, the humbler Odysseus clings to the remains of his last ship. Soon he is trapped in a cave by a giant called Polyphemus (Fame). Odysseus tells the giant that his name is Oudeis (Nobody), surrendering his very identity. Finally, after taking a "nobody" name, Odysseus escapes and makes it home to Penelope, a sadder but wiser and more useful man.

Many great leaders had in-between time experiences of withdrawal, renewal, and return. Look at Moses. He fled to the desert, where he stayed and started a family. He herded sheep for decades as he wandered the desert, searched his heart, and communed with God. He returned to deliver Israel from Egyptian bondage.

Consider Paul, the firebrand of a missionary who ran out to win the world before lunch. But before he launched his career, he spent three years praying, seeking, searching in the desert of Arabia.

And what of Jesus himself? Before starting His public ministry, there was a long battle with the devil in the desert and a long time of spiritual preparation —40 days and 40 nights. He returned from the desert experience a Savior!

Similar things happened to Gregory the Great, St. Benedict, and to Abraham Lincoln. Many accounts of Lincoln base his success on his poverty-stricken, frontier childhood. But that upbringing did not produce much of a man. He drifted from job to job, had a troubled marriage, did a poor job in Congress, and was often depressed. It was not an idealized boyhood but a profound in-between times transition in his 30s that brought forth the man who became perhaps the greatest of U.S. presidents.[5]

Wisdom is the honey that the bees of the in-between times make; you can't find it anywhere else.

That is not to say that the trapeze stage works only for the great and powerful. It can become a vale of soul making for any of us. But we must know that the in-between time has meaning. Your life is not a "tale / Told by an idiot, full of sound and fury, / Signifying nothing" (Shakespeare).

Before we can move on to a new beginning, we must let go of the old. Endings are, after all, about death and dying. We struggle in the in-between times to find a new identity, a new direction, and new wisdom. You see, wisdom is the honey that the bees of the in-between times make; you can't find it anywhere else.

We turn again to Jeremiah to taste the flavor of an in-between time:

[God] has driven me away and made me walk in darkness rather than light. . . .
He has turned his hand against me again and again, all day long.
He has . . . broken my bones. . . .
He has made me dwell in darkness like those long dead. . . .
He has weighed me down with chains. . . .
He shuts out my prayer. . . .
He has filled me with bitter herbs and sated me with gall *(Lam. 3:2-4, 6-8, 15).*
He has broken my teeth on gravel. . . .
Peace has gone out of my life, and I have forgotten what prosperity means *(vv. 16-17, NEB).*
You have covered yourself with a cloud so that no prayer can get through *(v. 44).*
My strength has gone and so has my hope in the LORD *(v. 18, NEB).*

Expect a New Beginning

Window on the Word

God . . . has delivered us from such a deadly peril, and he will deliver us. On him we have set our hope that he will continue to deliver us (2 Cor. 1:9-10).

If you can survive the in-between time, a new beginning is what comes next if you wait for God's timing. Ending, in-between time, new beginning, followed by a settled place; that's the cycle of life.

But poor old Jeremiah—how do you find a new beginning in the midst of destruction? I don't know, but it happens. One day you are devastated, and the next day you have new hope, new courage, new dreams. Isn't God's grace wonderful?

Well, I don't know exactly how it happened to Jeremiah, but I know it did.

After he had sat and prayed and mourned over the end of just about everything that mattered until he was numb in body, mind, and spirit, he made a trip to what was left of the business section. There he looked up the Century 21 office. The sign was torn down, and the window was out, but Jeremiah knew where it was. "Azariah, Azariah, is that you in there?"

After a while, an old man comes to what's left of the door. "Oh, it's you, Jerry; thought it might be the soldiers again. What in the world do you want?"

"I wanna buy a piece of land."

"You what?"

"I want to buy a piece of land—big piece."

"Miriam, Miriam, come out here; Pastor Jerry has lost his mind."

"When this city gets rebuilt, there's going to be a real estate boom, and I want to cash in on it." Jeremiah is beaming. "Who knows, maybe I'll donate the land when we rebuild the Temple. How much do you want for Mount Moriah?"

In the wake of utter destruction, Jeremiah, as an act of faith in the future, actually went out and bought a new plot of land. Look at him. There's the old fellow, out at the crack of dawn looking over his land. He has the deed and the surveyor's chart in his hand. He has hauled the real estate man out with him. "Azariah, right over there near the west boundary is where I'll dig the well. The orchard will be on the north side. A row of poplars along the front."

I look back on a time in my life when I had all but given up on ministry. I was discouraged, confused, lost in an in-between time. I didn't want to get closer to God, I didn't want to change, I wanted out—but then in God's sovereign way, in His own time, He reached down and lifted me out of the valley. And overnight I woke up with new hope, new courage, new goals—a new beginning!

How, I don't know—if I did, I'd bottle it and sell it—better yet, I'd give it away. But I have studied the map of the territory between the in-between times and new beginnings. And I have some hints to pass along.

1. You can expect a new beginning any day after you have surrendered everything but Jesus. I spent two recent semesters teaching in the broken heart of Manila. In that city of 15 million people, some 4 million have no permanent dwelling. They will go to sleep tonight in a squatter's hut of sheet metal, plywood, or cardboard. Some will simply pull up a sheet of plastic over them in a parking lot or on the median strip in a highway. It is a city of great wealth for a few, but also a city of 5-year-old beggars and 12-year-old prostitutes. In the middle of this city stands Asia-Pacific Nazarene Theological Seminary, where students study how to take the gospel to the masses of Asia. Through two semesters there my students have taught me one thing. You see, in the U.S. the gospel and the good life get inextricably intertwined. People get saved, stop spending their money on liquor and lottery tickets, and "redemption and lift" occurs. But in Asia you cannot mix the gospel and the good life. You may find Christ, but you will still be poor; you will still be sick. You will still never own a car, or a house, or even an air-conditioner. And you will still die too young.

Your unlived life offers a strong hint about the nature of your new beginning.

And this is what my students taught me. You never really know that Jesus is all you need until Jesus is all you have. Then you know; He is enough. If you have reached that knowledge, expect a new beginning.

2. If you have reached the place where you are willing to give up on being *special* and are willing to settle for merely being *useful*, expect a new beginning. They say that at the heart of most emotional and mental illnesses is the desire to be special.

3. There has to be within you a readiness to change. The first change is to

stop acting like Adam, who blamed both the devil and his wife for his problems. No more pointing fingers at incompetent bosses, bad teachers, selfish spouses, skimpy opportunity—take responsibility for your own failures, sins, needs, and mistakes.

4. To catch the scent of what your new beginning will be like, answer this question: *If your life ended today, what would be unlived?* Your unlived life offers a strong hint about the nature of your new beginning. Suppose you pose as a family friend who got the job of writing your obituary. Suppose the person wrote it accurately. What would he or she say about you? The usual birth date, survivors, hobbies, vocation, honors, achievements, memberships, and so on. Then there is that last sentence: At the time of death he [she] was . . .

What dreams, talents, qualities, convictions of yours are unlived? Look that direction; the sound you hear approaching may be your new beginning.[6]

5. The place to which God calls you to make a new beginning may be the very spot "where your deep gladness and the world's deep hunger meet."[7] After teaching in public schools for 29 years, my friend Bettye Tracy retired. She soon found a new beginning in a series of teaching assignments in South America, Europe, and Asia. A severe spinal disorder threatened her plans to open Y2K with a three-month teaching assignment in the Philippines. But she rejected surgery and refused to let constant pain, steep campus hills, and endless stairs prevent her from carrying out her agreement. Her deep gladness (teaching) intersecting with the world's deep hunger (knowledge) seemed worth the personal sacrifice.

6. New beginnings can come at any age. Gandhi was 50 before he found his mission in life. Miguel de Cervantes was even older when he wrote *Don Quixote*. Edith Hamilton started her study of Greek mythology at 60. At 90 she was still making annual trips to Greece to do further study. Colonel Sanders was 72 when he invented Kentucky Fried Chicken. Grandma Moses was an antique before she started painting them. You never know when a new beginning will take you by surprise.

7. God often sends a person to kindle in you the desire and the energy to imagine a new beginning. It may be a spiritual friend or a family member who challenges you to get off dead center and follow your heart. Perhaps the insight will come from a sermon, a song, or a hallway conversation. God may use a child, a friend, a neighbor, a stranger. Be alert; when you are ready, God will send the witness.

8. The way to make it through the changes of your life is to keep your eye on the Changeless One. Though in the dark night of an ending you cannot seem to see the Light, be sure that He is there. He is steady, He is nurturing you so that the whole experience will make you better, not bitter.

> *Change and decay in all around I see;*
> *O Thou who changest not, abide with me.*
>
> —Henry F. Lyte

9. You need a great principle to hang on to during tough times. When Napoleon collapsed in exile, one observer said, "No great principle stood by him."

Here is the great principle that carried Jeremiah from the lostness of the in-between time to hope for a new beginning:

Restore us to yourself, O LORD, that we may return; renew our days as of old. . . .
Let us examine our ways and test them, and let us return to the LORD.
Arise and cry aloud (NEB) in the night. . . . Pour out your heart like water in the presence of the Lord.
I called on your name, O LORD, from the depths of the pit. . . .
You came near. . . . You redeemed my life *(Lam. 5:21; 3:40; 2:19; 3:55, 57-58)*.
The LORD, I say, is all that I have; therefore I will wait for him patiently.
The LORD is good . . . to all who seek him. . . . Therefore I will wait patiently:
the LORD's true love is surely not spent, nor has his compassion failed;
they are new every morning, so great is his faithfulness (NIV) *(3:24-25, 21-23, NEB)*.

A friend of mine had radical cancer surgery recently. Last week she put her money in a five-year certificate of deposit as an act of faith in the future. Would you this week, this day, affirm your belief in a new beginning with an act of faith for the future?

THE SETTLED PLACE 

Window on the Word

The peace of God, which transcends all understanding, will guard your hearts and your minds in Christ Jesus (Phil. 4:7).

"Everybody gotta be someplace," and the cherished fourth place on the cycle of life is—the settled place. There life is good, the children are good, the income is good, the relationships are good, your health is good, and the spiritual fulfillment is good and growing. Enjoy it if you are there. You know how without any instructions from me.

I do have a word to the wise. God has put us in a world where stagnation is a deadly sin. So look for the cycle to start all over again—anytime!

— 17 —

Nurtured by Disciplined Living

First Window on the Word

And whatever you do, whether in word or deed, do it all in the name of the Lord Jesus, giving thanks to God the Father (Col. 3:17).

When you become a Christian, things get easy. You just turn things over to Christ and set the dial on "Autopilot" and loll back with a book of poetry and a bowl of grapes—right? Not quite; the Christian life requires about all the self-discipline that you can muster through grace.

We would prefer the "Autopilot" mode, but the life of the believer does not work that way. Mark Laaser, author of *Faithful and True: Sexual Integrity in a Fallen World*, spoke of his own battle with sexual addiction. "Some of the spiritual stuff that I was doing was an attempt . . . to manipulate God. . . . I desperately wanted God . . . to remove all my lust . . . so that I'd never have to struggle with it again."[1] But Laaser, along with the rest of us, discovered that holy living requires vigorous discipline.

Augustine is quoted a lot as saying, "Love God and do what you please." "Yeah, that's for me," you say. "Hand me a book on discipline, and I'll drop it like a hot fondue fork." But Augustine was making the point that the heart of a truly sanctified Christian could be trusted to be like Christ. The most dedicated Christian, however, can be tempted to awful sins. More dangerous yet, he or she can be put to sleep regarding deadly dangers—like the famous frog in the kettle. Augustine's own personal life showed a dramatic submission to Christian discipline.

There are those believers who reduce Christian living to a strict code of conduct. But in spite of those who fail to keep perspective, we must open our minds to God's standards for conduct. All areas of life need the Christian discipline. We can treat only a few in this chapter.

The Discipline of Fasting

Window on the Word

When you fast, do not look somber as the hypocrites do. . . . Put oil on your head and wash your face, so that it will not be obvious . . . that you are fasting (Matt. 6:16-18).

Jesus did not say, "*If* you fast . . ." He did not say, "You *must* fast . . ." He did say, "*When* you fast . . ." (emphases added); and He said it twice in the Sermon on the Mount. No debate, no argument, no direct order—just the *expectation* that we would, of course, fast. So fasting in Christ's teaching is squarely between a *choice* and a *command*.

Fasting is not to be done to manipulate God, trigger a miracle, or solve a problem. Fasting is saying no to food for the body so we can concentrate on food for the soul.[2] Prayer needs fasting. "Prayer is the one hand with which we grasp the invisible; fasting, the other, with which we let loose and cast away the visible."[3]

Fasting is two-sided. You forgo one thing in favor of another. Forgoing food in favor of prayer is just one way to fast. Dee Freeborn calls fasting "blessed subtraction." You subtract something in order to make way for something better.

1. *Fast noise and company and add solitude*. You and I live in a noisy world. Stop reading for a moment and count the noises that compete for your attention. Boom boxes, television, radio, traffic sounds, background music impose on our solitude. And there is always a group of people who prize your company. It's hard to find solitude—especially the way we work so hard to avoid it! We will do almost anything to escape being alone. Susan Muto says we shun the silence because "it evokes nameless misgivings, guilt feelings, strange, disquieting anxiety."[4] Until "you can sing and rejoice and delight in God as misers do in gold and kings in sceptres,"[5] you will not "hasten unto Him who calls you in the silences of your heart."[6]

2. *Subtract busyness and add silence*. Christ's mission was a lot more urgent than your job at General Motors, General Tire, General Electric, or the local pickle factory. He had redemption to accomplish. Yet He often withdrew from a hectic schedule to spend time alone in rest and prayer. Matthew, Mark, Luke, and John record at least 10 such occasions. What's necessary for Jesus is mandatory for us. Fast busyness in favor of silence before the Lord. "Busyness rapes relationships. It substitutes shallow frenzy for deep friendships. It feeds the ego, but starves the inner man. It fills the calendar, but fractures the family."[7] Henri Nouwen said, "Silence is the discipline by which the inner fire of God is tended and kept alive."[8]

Henri Nouwen said, "Silence is the discipline by which the inner fire of God is tended and kept alive."

3. *Fast entertainments and add acts of service*. Who doesn't waste too much time half-watching television? David Kendrick decided that knowing how much time you had left might make you invest it more wisely. He invented the Life Expectancy Timepiece. Knowing your birth date and gender, you know your life expectancy. You set the Kendrick "reverse watch," and any time you look at it, it tells you how many days you have left. Would that get some of us off the couch and into worthwhile service?

One pastor fasted television for the month of March. "It was the greatest month of the year," he said. "I'm going to make it an annual event—even [if] my family chooses [again] not to join me."[9]

4. *Subtract acquisitiveness and add sharing.* The ad people bombard us with new products that we just *have* to have—a magic diet pill, a miracle camera, a computer upgrade, a DVD player—but most of that stuff you don't need. So give up shopping for a while in favor of Christian simplicity and good stewardship. One family discovered that they were spending $200 per month of discretionary funds on things that no one really needed. They vowed to cut down and for the remaining seven months of the year give $100 a month of what they saved to their denomination's Hunger and Disaster Fund. Paul said, "I have learned the secret of being content in any and every situation, whether well fed or hungry. . . . I can do everything through him who gives me strength" (Phil. 4:12-13).

Disciplined Entertainment Choices

Window on the Word

For you were once darkness, but now you are light in the Lord. Live as children of light . . . and find out what pleases the Lord. Have nothing to do with the fruitless deeds of darkness. . . . For it is shameful even to mention what the disobedient do in secret. . . . Be very careful, then, how you live—not as unwise but as wise (Eph. 5:8, 10-12, 15).

How difficult even to talk about the objectionable entertainment that floods our world. You can hardly write specifically about the sleazy stuff that shows up on TV, cable, videos, CDs, and the Internet. Describe them, and you are nearly as lurid and prurient as they. As our Window on the Word says, it is shameful even to mention what degenerate and disobedient persons do in secret. But the practice of sensual sin is not kept for the "in secret" venue these days. It is shoved into every home with a TV, VCR, or Internet computer. You can hardly check your E-mail without having to delete unsolicited invitations to click on a pornographic web site.

Therefore, I will not rehearse the vulgar, sexual, and violent sins of the media. But I appeal to you as a thoughtful, honest Christian to discipline your entertainment choices. What you let into your mind and heart shapes you. Here are some questions you might use to examine your entertainment choices:

1. Does this program, film, video, CD, book, song, or movie make sex outside of marriage appear to be the normal and recommended thing by having the "heroes" living together unmarried or ending up in the beach house boudoir?

2. Are sexual encounters portrayed that in no real way advance the plot? Is the message "instant capitulation to the libido"?

3. Do the characters (male or female) dress decently or provocatively? Or do they dress at all?

4. Are gamblers, racketeers, prostitutes, homosexuals, and so on made to look appealing, sympathetic, and admirable?

5. Does society take the blame for wrongdoing, or are individuals responsible for their own behavior?

6. Is the language so vulgar and sub-Christian that you would not let your kids talk like that in your home?

7. How does the family fare on this program? Is this another case of how good and wise and independent the kids are, and how dumb the parents are?

8. Was justice portrayed as violence? (This may be the most important question on this list.) When the bad guy got his, was it violent? Does justice equal bashing? Is violence the only road to justice? The Christian way to justice?

9. Who was laughed at? (Often it is parents, teachers, and clergy.) Who was glorified?

Goianaia, Brazil. Two unemployed men enter a partially demolished cancer radiation clinic. They look for metal that they can sell to junk dealers. They dismantle a cancer therapy machine, put the pieces in an old truck, and head for the dealers.

One junk dealer gives them 25 reals for a stainless steel cylinder about the size of a gallon bucket. Inside the cylinder is a crumbly powder that gives off a mysterious blue light. The junk dealer takes the magic powder home.

His six-year-old niece rubs the glowing powder over her body. She begins to do the bossa nova, "Just like the TV dancers in Rio," she says. Everyone claps as the cute little girl, a dark body covered with glowing blue powder, shifts to dance the *macarena*, "just like the dancers on TV." What an entertaining sight on a laid-back tropical night.

Trashy entertainment can smother the Light within.

The magical glowing blue powder was cesium 137, a highly radioactive substance used to kill cancer cells. It also kills cute little dark-skinned girls gyrating powder blue and incandescent like the Mardi Gras dancers on TV, the junk dealer and his family discovered. The little girl died. Several others who were exposed also died, and more than 200 others got very sick.[10]

A beautiful incandescent dust from an instrument of healing became an instrument of death.

Most of us need less of television, the Internet, and popular music. Can these be as dangerous as the deadly blue powder of Goianaia? Remember the hawksbill turtle that swallowed so much plastic trash that it killed him? Well, trash sometimes looks good enough to eat, or to dance with, all powder blue and happy. But trashy entertainment can smother the Light within.

Disciplined Relationships with the Opposite Sex

Window on the Word

I made a covenant with my eyes not to look lustfully at a girl. . . . Is it not ruin . . . disaster for those who do wrong? (Job 31:1, 3).

I have known several persons who crashed and burned because of adultery. Not one of them woke up one morning and said, "I think I will go out and commit adultery today so I can ruin my life." No, every one of them gradually drifted into an undisciplined relationship with someone he or she admired, worked closely with, counseled with, or "rescued." It is not unusual for adults to spend more waking hours with coworkers and team members than with their spouse. The shared adversities, challenges, corporate victories or failures can draw such persons closer and closer, threatening the marriage relationship. When a relationship begins to move in the wrong direction, the disciplined Christian must deal with it early and ruthlessly. The Holy Spirit faithfully—every time—checks the attentive believer when a relationship starts crossing the line of Christian propriety. To dally along, savoring the flattery and the warmth, will lead to sin. And "sexual sins are the ones we most want to hide, least want to give up, and most permissively excuse in policing our own hearts."[11]

Disciplining relationships is not a prudish frill invented by the Holiness Movement. The Bible says, "But among you there must not be even a hint of sexual immorality. . . . For of this you can be sure: No immoral . . . person . . . has any inheritance in the kingdom of Christ" (Eph. 5:3, 5).

Pamela Condit Kennedy, author of *Where Have All the Lovers Gone?* tells of her own close call in a *Herald of Holiness* article. She met a man when she dropped her daughter off at school. She tells her own story:

> Jeffy was escorted to class each day by his Saks-Fifth-Avenue-looking father. You know the type: square jaw, designer suits, and a perfect smile that would cut through any heart in a flash. Jeffy's father and I found ourselves walking to our cars together day after day. From the very start I was aware of his cordial attitude toward my daughter, Amy, as well as his attentiveness to me. We chatted very briefly at first. It wasn't long until the small talk grew into full-grown conversations. Was he likable? Yes. Handsome? For sure. Wooing? Most definitely!
>
> I admit I began to feel uneasy. But as is common, I convinced myself we were not doing anything wrong. Each time we spoke, my feelings of guilt weakened.
>
> I enjoyed his friendship, this new attention, the secret feelings. I told myself again and again, "This is only a friendship; nothing is going on."
>
> I found myself deliberately getting up earlier so I could spend more time with my hair and makeup. I wanted to look my best for . . . just a friend? Even I couldn't buy that. A light came on inside. I realized where I was headed, and it was not to Bible study.

I changed the time I was bringing Amy to school just to be sure I would miss him. I told my husband about the entire situation. I asked the Lord for forgiveness and thanked Him for opening my eyes in time.[12]

Been there? Done that? Your *Reflecting God Workbook* has more guidelines for cross-gender relationships. Check them out.

RECOVER SABBATH JOY

Window on the Word

If you keep your feet from . . . doing as you please on my holy day, if you call the Sabbath a delight and the LORD's holy day honorable, . . . then you will find your joy in the LORD (Isa. 58:13-14).

American Evangelicals got Sunday observance all mixed up from the start. For example, about a hundred years ago, the faithful Methodists in Baltimore would reserve the public park each summer Sunday. Then the men of the church, armed with bats, would stand guard over the baseball diamond to make sure that no one broke the Lord's day by playing baseball. We have regarded the Lord's day as a hard-to-swallow medicine that we had better take if we know what is good for us. The *joy* of Sabbath as a gift of grace, a time of rest, eating and drinking at the family table, and a day eagerly hallowed for worship got lost in our zeal for codes.

God's Sabbath sets the rhythm of life that speaks to our human hunger for intimacy and transcendence. This "hunger cannot be fully satisfied apart from spacious times of restful presence."[13] The rhythm of our culture, on the other hand, is a "rhythm between driven achievement and narrow escape, a deadly rhythm that threatens to bury ever more deeply the fullness and sanity of our human calling in God."[14] We need the "spacious times of restful presence" that God's agenda offers.

A Tale of Two Sabbaths

Sabbath 1—The Richard Jordan Family

Mr. and Mrs. Jordan are Christians now, but they were raised in Jewish homes. They celebrate the Christian Sabbath, Sunday, bringing some Jewish traditions to it. Step 1 happens on Saturday night and is a simple family ceremony of welcoming the Sabbath. The ceremony includes lighting of candles, usually by Mrs. Jordan. Sometimes they light three, one for each member of the Holy Trinity; sometimes they light five candles, one for each member of their family. Then comes parental blessings of the children: a recitation of Num. 6:24-26.

Next comes a Scripture reading, usually from Pss. 29, 92, or 93. These psalms were used of old to welcome the Sabbath Queen. In the Hebrew tradition the Sabbath is feminine and is welcomed as a royal queen. After the scripture the family sings a song of welcome to the Sabbath. One welcome song they use, singing it to the tune of "Michael Rowed the Boat Ashore," starts:

Welcome, welcome queen of rest, Alleluia!
Guest of joy the Lord has blessed, Alleluia![15]

That's a lot better than *Saturday Night Live*, wouldn't you say?

On Sunday morning the family arises early and observes an hour of silence, each person in his or her own room. After the quiet hour one of the children will read to the family one of the passages of the day from the *Revised Common Lectionary*. Then the family is off to worship at their church.

Sunday afternoon usually finds the family at home for a big dinner. Two Sundays a month a senior citizen who has no spouse is invited to the Jordans' for dinner. The Sabbath helps the family slow down and take time for others.

On Sunday night a "farewell to the Sabbath" ceremony occurs. Candles are lit, a blessing is said. Dessert is served as a sign of the yearned-for marriage supper of the Lamb. Next a little box of sweet-smelling spices is passed around the table. Each family member inhales deeply, remembering the sweet savor of the Sabbath to take with them into the coming week. In the Hebrew tradition, the first three days of the week belong to the Sabbath just passed. The last three belong to the coming Sabbath and are spent looking forward to that spacious time of restful presence. Next comes a prayer that the days ahead will bring "Sabbath sweetness to our lives." Finally the candles are extinguished with a prayer of thanksgiving.[16]

Sabbath 2—The Dale Ferguson Family

Dale describes a Lord's day.

> Last Sunday we got up late and rushed off to church without breakfast. I was late to the class I had to teach, and Beverly was late for choir prep. During the service we kept watching the clock. If the sermon goes past noon, we will be late. Not late to brunch, but late to McDonald's—Lisa, our daughter, works the 1—8 P.M. shift.
>
> We barely got her there on time. By the time that Beverly and I got back home from the Grand Buffet, I had missed the whole first quarter of the Cowboys' game. I covered up with the Sunday paper and watched what was left of the ball game. Then I fixed the switch on the garage door opener and replaced the floodlight on the patio. Jake, our 12-year-old, did his homework.
>
> At 3:30 Bev had to go back to church for a committee meeting, pick up something at the mall, and go straight to cantata practice. She just stayed at church for the evening service. That meant I had to miss half of *60 Minutes* driving Jake to church. He had a party afterward. Thank goodness he caught a ride home. Bev got home about 8:30. Lisa came in about 11, about the time that Jake was dropped off. But by that time I had sent two E-mails to my boss about the sales meeting and, being zonked, I had gone to bed. Monday morning gets here in a hurry, you know.

Which Sabbath appeals to you the most?

Which Sabbath sounds more familiar?

Both the *Reflecting God Workbook* and the *Reflecting God Leader's Guide* provide more information and activities on the Christian Sabbath.

Those who drop discipline like a hot fondue fork should listen to the Word: "No discipline seems pleasant at the time, but painful. Later on, however, it produces a harvest of righteousness and peace" (Heb. 12:11).

PART 4

SHARING THE LIGHT

Christ's love compels us, because we are convinced . . . that those who live [in Christ] should no longer live for themselves (2 Cor. 5:14-15).

If they had Oscars and Emmys for Christian witness and service, my vote would go to Angelina.

I don't know the real name of this Puerto Rican lady, so let me name her according to her angel-like character.

Angelina lives in Hell's Kitchen—that section of Brooklyn where flying bullets and cruising thugs put the life expectancy graph into a sharp nosedive.

But Angelina got saved at Pastor Bill Wilson's church. And you know how it is—you get saved, and you want to give and serve.

With the help of an interpreter she asked her pastor for a job in the church. Not being able to speak a word of English, what in the world could she do? Pastor Wilson told her to ride the Sunday School buses and "love the kids." She did.

Soon she came back and said she wanted to ride just one bus. You see, on that one route was a special little boy who came to the Saturday kids' ministry and to Sunday School every week. He was a sad little guy with hungry eyes who never uttered a sound, not one word, ever.

So every week Angelina held the child on her lap on the bus and loved him the best she could. She even learned one sentence in English to pass on to the boy: "I love you, and Jesus loves you." She told him this over and over, week after week.

One day to her astonishment the little guy looked up into her face and stammered, "I . . . I love you too." Finally! Finally he had responded to love!

That was 2:30 on a Saturday afternoon. At 6:30 that evening, when most Christians were settling down to watch *Wheel of Fortune* or ESPN, someone found the boy's body in a garbage bag under the fire escape.

Someone said that the little fellow had knocked over the last bottle of beer in the house. His mother beat him to death and threw him in the garbage.

Angelina had so little to give. But when God needed someone to be the "light of the world" to a little neglected and rejected boy who had never known love, Angelina was ready. Did she know she was ministering to Jesus himself?[1]

> We must all appear before the judgment seat of Christ, that each one may receive what is due him. . . . Since . . . we know what it is to fear the Lord, we try to persuade men *(2 Cor. 5:10-11).*

— 18 —

Sharing the Light with a Hurting World

First Window on the Word

What good is it, my brothers, if a man claims to have faith but has no deeds? Can such faith save him? Suppose a brother or sister is without clothes and daily food. If one of you says to him, "Go, I wish you well; keep warm and well fed," but does nothing about his physical needs, what good is it? (James 2:14-16).

What a bizarre headline: "Six Egyptians Drown Following Chicken in Well!"

It all started with Ando, a pet rooster. He welcomed the daybreak crowing so energetically that he lost his balance and fell into the well. An 18-year-old farmer, Ando's owner, rushed to rescue the rooster. He climbed down the stone walls of the 60-foot well. There was "ledge room" enough for a surefooted climber, but the young man slipped and fell. He drowned.

Two brothers and a sister, who couldn't swim, tried to help. They, too, drowned—all three of them.

Two elderly farmers saw the commotion and rushed over to the rooster rescue operation. They also fell in and drowned.

The rooster rescue took six lives!

Ando, the rooster, survived.

How many lives is a chicken worth? Who would want to be remembered as a person who did nothing more than try to rescue a rooster? Yet there are many chicken chasers around today. They go through life doing nothing that really matters. They seem to chase whatever chicken crosses their path.

Take Harry I. Jacoby, for instance. He took his own life in his Newark apartment. He left a note that said he was penniless and too proud to beg. So he shot himself. When they cleaned his flat, they found a laundry basket full of losing lottery tickets—$72,000 worth. The chicken he chased wasn't Ando; it was called Lotto.

Then there was the man in Texas, Honorato by name. He spent years trying to build a house out of beer cans. He drank a lot of beer and cluttered up the house with the cans. His wife scolded him, "You've got enough beer cans around here to build a house!" Honorato had just finished a 12-pack, and to him that was a wonderful idea. He started collecting beer cans from everywhere. Using cans, mortar, and welding gear, he started his house. Years later he had most of the walls up. Working late one night, he fell off a ladder and broke his neck. His one contribution: half a beer-can house. His chicken wasn't Ando, it was Coors, Bud, and Miller Lite.

"Life is real! Life is earnest!" wrote Longfellow, and we shouldn't spend it chasing chickens. For what shall it profit a man if he gains a chicken and loses his own soul?

To the early Wesleyans service was as much a spiritual discipline as prayer.

Christians, however, spend their time doing worthwhile things. They are nothing if not predictable. It's been the same for a long time—at least ever since Hadrian, Roman emperor A.D. 117—38, asked Aristides for a report on the Christians. "They love one another," wrote the reporter. "They never fail to help widows; they save orphans from those who would hurt them. If they have something, they give freely to the man who has nothing; if they see a stranger, they take him home, and are happy, as though he were a real brother. They don't consider themselves brothers in the usual sense, but brothers instead through the Spirit, in God."[1]

That's the very kind of religion that fueled the Methodist and Evangelical revolution in 18th-century England. John Wesley declared that they did not "acknowledge him to have one grain of faith who is not continually doing good, who is not willing to 'spend and be spent' in doing all good, as he has opportunity, to all men."[2] To those early Wesleyans service was as much a spiritual discipline as prayer. To them the spiritual life would wither like a leaf without active, sacrificial service.

Were they serious? What do you think? Besides all the teaching, preaching, and meeting in societies, classes, and bands, they engaged in all sorts of service to the church and the world. Wesley and Company established the first free medical clinic in England, they started schools of all kinds, they organized the city of London and appointed sick visitors for every district, they established regular religious services to the poor in the workhouses, established the Stranger's Friend Society (a charity from which no Methodist could accept aid), and distributed food and clothing every day of the year in London and Bristol. Further, they established a hospital for unwed and destitute mothers-to-be, where they gave prenatal and postnatal care, religious instruction, and vocational training. They operated a widows' home, an orphanage, and a poorhouse. They even provided an unemployment plan for out-of-work Methodists, and a loan fund for Methodists who wanted to start their own businesses.[3]

If you think today's Christians don't serve in the same way, you have been asleep. In the past five years I have had the opportunity of ministering in 10 countries on 5 continents, and everywhere I go I see Evangelical Christians pouring out their lives in missionary and volunteer service.

Today's believer focuses on sharing the Light at home, in the church, in the community, and in the world.

Sharing the Light at Home

Window on the Word

If anyone does not provide for his relatives, and especially for his immediate family, he has denied the faith and is worse than an unbeliever (1 Tim. 5:8).

In *Call Me Anna,* Patty Duke wrote about one of her first and favorite film roles. She played Emily Ann, a little girl whom people mostly ignored. The end of the school term came, and Emily Ann, with fear and trembling, looked at her report card. She got promoted to the next grade!

Excited and happy, Emily Ann runs to the dime store where her mother works. But Mom is busy and tells her to get out of there and go home, "Now."

Emily Ann then runs to her girlfriend's house, report card in hand. She knocks and she calls for Sylvia, but no one comes to the door.

So "latchkey" Emily Ann goes home. She makes herself a snack. About that time an old stray cat walks in through the window. The girl gets up and with ceremony pours a bowl of milk for the shabby feline.

Before the cat finishes its milk, Emily Ann swoops it up, gives it a big hug, and says, "Hey cat, guess who got promoted today!"[4]

Four-point quiz: Anyone that lonely in your family? Extended family? Whose fault is that? What do you think God wants you to do about it?

Sharing the Light in the Church

Window on the Word

Christ loved the church and gave himself up for her to make her holy, cleansing her by the washing with water through the word, and to present her to himself as a radiant church . . . holy and blameless (Eph. 5:25-27).

The church will not wax radiant until we learn how to *receive* love. I know, you expected a diatribe on *giving* love. Well, hold on, that may be coming, but first I want you to ponder how hard it is to receive love.

There is a certain superiority when we give love to others, and a certain helplessness when others offer love to us. When we give love, we are in control. We pick the person or persons we will honor with our love, how much we will dole out at a time, and if and when we will give it. When we are on the receiving end of love and assistance, we are no longer in control. The other person decides how, when, and how much. We are almost helpless as receivers, but we must learn to receive love from each other or settle for being a proudly grim bunch of believers.[5]

Chuck Swindoll says that every church can "choose to be a bag of marbles, single units that don't affect each other except in collision." Or a congregation can choose to be "a bag of grapes. The juices begin to mingle, and there is no way to extricate yourselves if you tried. Each is a part of all. . . . And sometimes we 'grapes' really bleed and hurt."[6] In a faith family where people know how to both give and receive love, no one has to bleed alone.

We have seen too many marble-headed church members. Recently in Dadeville, Alabama, two men got into a Bible-quoting contest. Gabel Taylor, 38, the brother of a preacher, got into a shouting match with his neighbor over a particular passage. Taylor pulled out a Bible and showed the other man "chapter and verse." He won the argument—I guess. The loser popped into his apartment, popped back out with a gun, and shot Taylor in the face, killing him.[7] Grapes, not marbles, please.

The French are great cyclists, and the Tour de France is the greatest bicycle race of all. If you watch the French team, you will see the *domestique* (the word means "servant"). He will not win the race. He is not intended to win. Yet mile after weary mile he pedals on. His job is to shield the top cyclist who *will* win the race. The *domestique* shields him from the wind and creates a draft in which the "star" cyclist will ride throughout the race. The *domestique* gets no trophy, no wild cheers from adoring fans. The one he has enabled to win the race is crowned—and that is enough for him. Holy service is all about becoming a *domestique* for Christ and our fellow travelers.[8]

Every local church needs *domestiques*. What church is not in constant need of youth workers, nursery volunteers, Sunday School teachers, greeters, ushers, choir members, office workers, task force leaders, and so on? The church I attend requires 350 volunteers every week just to keep current ministries going. Don't insist on just doing the limelight assignments; settle for being the *domestique*. John Knox, the great Presbyterian preacher, said, "When I think of those who have influenced my life the most, I think not of the great but *the good*."[9]

The "good" describes a woman I know as "Aunt Suzie." I met Suzie in a Louisiana church. She busied herself with baskets for the poor, visiting the sick, arranging better living for the near destitute. I watched her on Sunday morning, before the preaching service, hurry to the nursery to insure that "my little ones have adequate care." She buzzed off to the classes of the older children, wanting to make sure the teachers had arrived and had enough supplies.

The pastor may have noticed my interest in Aunt Suzie. He told me about her. "She's had cancer, you know. But she never spends time talking about it." I stood in reverent silence. "Auntie also lost her husband seven years ago. He was a pastor. She hasn't time to rehearse her grief." Hasn't this woman given herself permission to grieve? I asked myself. Then I saw God thoroughly alive in Aunt Suzie! She worked off her grief and forgot her cancer in good works. I never saw a person more emotionally healthy than Aunt Suzie. In fact, I saw Jesus in her.

Sharing the Light in the Community

Window on the Word

I hate, I despise your religious feasts; I cannot stand your assemblies. . . .
Away with the noise of your songs! I will not listen. . . .
But let justice roll on like a river, righteousness like a
never failing stream (Amos 5:21, 23-24).

What does the community have a right to expect from the church? Plenty—plenty of service beyond vested interests. That is, service that goes beyond recruiting people to pad our rolls and beef up the budget. We must help those in need, whether or not the institutional church ever benefits from the investment. On last night's newscast I saw the story of a teacher who donated a kidney to her eighth grade student. The teacher is White, the student Black. What a selfless, Christlike act!

Can't give a kidney? Lots of other opportunities await the person who is spiritually alert. Take nine-year-old Mackenzie Snyder, for example. She heard that many of the kids moving from one foster home to another had to use plastic trash bags to move their belongings. That touched the heart of the Maryland youngster, and she started collecting suitcases and duffel bags for foster kids. Out of her efforts came the Children-to-Children program that has, so far, delivered more than 1,000 suitcases—with a note and stuffed animal inside—to foster children in the Washington, D.C., area. The Freddie Mac Foundation heard of Mackenzie and gave $15,000.[10]

Consider Bill and Sharon Murphy. Nearly 20 years ago, they got the idea that one way to help families who had no place to live was to let them move in with them and their kids and eat at the same table. The Lord has blessed their selflessness. They now operate 10 houses where 30 families with 59 children live. They also feed 15 other families, operate a clothing bank, and a children's library. This ministry is energized, according to the *Washington Post,* by Bill and Sharon's "religious commitment and a natural affection for people." Talk about radiant believers![11]

Too many are satisfied with an annual excursion into the community where we sing our carols or donate a turkey and then clear out of that part of town until next Christmas. As Jess Moody irreverently put it, anybody can salve his conscience by "an occasional foray into knitting for the spastic home. Did you ever take a real trip down inside the broken heart of a real friend? To feel the sob of the soul—the raw, red crucible of emotional agony? To have this become almost as much yours as that of your soul-crushed neighbor? Then sit down with him—and silently weep?"[12]

Here's another example. Christopher Michael Langan is one of the smartest men in America. His IQ is 195, and that puts him up there with Leonardo da Vinci, Ludwig Wittgenstein, and René Descartes, three of the brightest minds in history. Think what you could do for God and good with a brain like that!

Think what Chris Langan is doing with his gift. Guess what his vocation is. He's a nightclub bouncer. One of the smartest men in history, and he spends his time bouncing bums out of beer joints![13] Three examples: Mackenzie Snyder, Bill and Sharon Murphy, Chris Langan—who do you want to be like?

SHARING THE LIGHT IN THE WORLD

Window on the Word

I will also make you a light for the Gentiles, that you may bring my salvation to the ends of the earth (Isa. 49:6).

I am quite sure that Evangelical Christians are doing more good around the world than all the governments, the International Monetary Fund, the United Nations, or the World Bank. Evangelicals put their money where their love is, and their love is as wide as the world. Find a nation today where Christians are not building hospitals, clinics, schools, and churches, and I'll show you a country that will soon have teams of missionaries and volunteers all over the place. Christians are like that. I have seen them in every corner of the world sacrificing their lives for Christ and others.

They are like St. Francis Xavier, who was working so hard in missionary work that his superiors told him to stop and rest before he killed himself. "I can't slow down," Francis wrote; "I can't take it easy, because the world is full of closed doors and I have to open as many . . . as I can to let the sunshine in."[14]

Consider Beverly Gruver. She and her husband had good jobs as teachers in Newton, Kansas. They had three nice kids and a nice house in the heart of Mennonite country, a nice place to raise your kids. But Jesus called them to become missionaries. They left the quiet security of Kansas. David got a seminary degree. Then they were off to South America. Missionaries at last. Then David got sick. Four days later, he was dead—dead at age 43. There was Beverly, in a foreign country, with a dead husband and three teenage children asking, "What do we do now, Mama?"

What would you do? It was God who called Beverly to be a missionary—so a widow with three kids just keeps on being a missionary. Her children, all in their 20s now, live in the U.S.A. They are proud of their mom—and they should be.

Beverly teaches English at Asia-Pacific Nazarene Theological Seminary, but she does a lot more than that. For example, when I was a visiting professor there, typhoid struck in the women's dorm just 100 feet away from our apartment. That scared me half to death. I scoured Manila for vaccine. None available; I got really scared.

Beverly Gruver's response was a bit different. She went right into the dorm and sat up with the sickest girl. She administered medicine, cold washcloths, and cool fruit juice all night. She carried more than one to the hospital in her car. I could go on and on. Last Christmas Beverly and her grandson visited at our home. Her contract was up in Manila, the typhoid and tuberculosis capital of Asia. Are you going to go back? I asked. I knew what she would say. Hugging that grandson her heart had longed for all those months, she said, "I prayed, and I know my work is not done there."

If you think Mrs. Gruver is a rare exception, I assure you she is not. There's a whole tribe of Evangelical Christians out there pouring out their lives as unnoticed, unapplauded *domestiques*. They make the most radiant section of the Christian choir. They do what others shrink from doing, having turned their backs on the American dream of scrambling to the top of the career ladder or of amassing a financial fortune.

There's a whole tribe of Evangelical Christians out there pouring out their lives as unnoticed, unapplauded domestiques.

Elizabeth Cole spent years as a nurse in an African leper colony. A group of American visitors watched her as she cleaned the wounds of a leper. Unable to even look at that horribly disfigured face, one of the Americans looked away and said to her friends, "I wouldn't do that for a million dollars."

Miss Cole overheard the remark and replied, "I wouldn't either—not for a million dollars, but I would do it for Christ."[15]

Maybe that explains it—this madness among Evangelical Christians these days to give their lives away. Maybe they see in the faces of the diseased, the disfigured, the hungry, the uneducated, maybe in those faces they see the face of Jesus, the Christ. They would do anything for Him. Maybe that's what makes them so radiant.

My life must be Christ's broken bread,
My love, His outpoured wine;
A cup o'erfilled, a table spread
Beneath His name and sign,
That other souls, refreshed and fed,
May share His life through mine.[16]

—Albert Orsborne

— 19 —

Sharing the Light That Transforms

First Window on the Word

Go and make disciples of all nations . . . teaching them to obey everything I have commanded you. And surely I am with you always, to the very end of the age (Matt. 28:19-20).

"How am I doing, Miss Margaret?" the dancing boy asked, face aglow. He put his hands on his hips, pirouetted around, and hopped on one foot and then the other.

Months before, the child had limped into Margaret Sangster's Goodwill Center playroom on a homemade crutch and a cane. A pitiful sight—one foot was twisted completely around, and he could not walk properly. A truck hit him and kept going. His injuries went untreated in his home stricken by the twins of poverty and ignorance.

But that was before Margaret Sangster came into the picture. She recruited doctors to operate and three bankers to pay for surgery. In time, the day came when the boy danced into the playroom as good as new: "How am I doing, Miss Margaret?"

After he had gone, Sangster said to herself, "That's one thing you can *see*. You are always saying that in this work you produce no *visible* results. Well, there is *one definite thing* that you can put your finger on that you did."

Then as Margaret Sangster told her story, she leaned over the podium and said to a deeply moved audience, "Where do you think he is today—the boy that the surgeons, the bankers, and I straightened out?"

Someone in the audience replied, "He's a preacher."

"No," she said.

"A banker?"

"No."

"Governor of the state?"

"No."

"A teacher, maybe a social worker?"

Miss Sangster held her hand up for silence and said, "You'd never guess. He's in the penitentiary for life for a crime so heinous that except for his youth they would have sent him to the electric chair or the gas chamber.

"I spent so much time trying to transform the boy *physically* that I neglected his need to be transformed spiritually."[1]

As Christians we must provide blankets and beans, classes and clothing, medicine and shelter, but our first task is to share the transforming Light that changes persons from the inside out.

THE MANDATE TO SHARE THE LIGHT

Window on the Word

As the Father has sent me, I am sending you (John 20:21).

God the Father sent Jesus Christ to the world; Jesus Christ, in turn, sends us on the same mission. We are to be His witnesses (Acts 1:8). *Martus* is the Bible word that means "proof" or "evidence." We are to be the living *proof* that Jesus saves. The tone of *martus* is not that of a casual witness who just happened to be strolling by and noticed an event transpire. This word pictures a person testifying about deep convictions. From *martus* we get our word *martyr*. A martyr is a witness who backs up his or her testimony with blood. Christ sends us to do whatever it takes to take the transforming Light to every country, town, street, and heart in the world. Jesus' mission included sacrifice and suffering and joy; that's our mission too.

Christ is serious about this; we must go. What if Karla Worley is right? "If God goes anywhere this week, it will be our feet that carry Him. If God says anything to anyone, it will be with our mouths. If God touches anyone, it will be with our hands. And if He loves anyone, it will be with our hearts. We are the Body of Christ."[2]

Some religious leaders appear to hope to preserve Christianity in the world by baptizing as Christian whatever they find thriving in the world: gay rights, sexual revolution, environmental issues, Eastern meditation, and so on. But the mandate is clear: "Go and make disciples of all nations" (Matt. 28:19).

THE MESSAGE WE SHARE

Window on the Word

For what I received I passed on to you as of first importance: that Christ died for our sins according to the Scriptures, that he was buried, that he was raised on the third day according to the Scriptures (1 Cor. 15:3-4).

The message to which we give witness is expressly stated in such Bible passages as John 3:16; 1 Cor. 15:1-11; Rom. 1:1-4; Acts 2:22-24; 1 Tim. 3:16; Heb. 10:12; John 16:7-13. These marvelous passages of grace can be summarized into the message of salvation, the gospel itself, the *kerygma*.

(1) Jesus Christ, the Son of God came to earth.

(2) Demonstrating the love of God, He was crucified for our sins, as the Scriptures foretold.

(3) He was buried and arose from the dead.
(4) He ascended to the right hand of the Father.
(5) Those who trust in Him shall be saved.
(6) He sent His Spirit, to convict sinners and guide and teach believers.

Witnessing for Christ today is not always simple, not always welcome. In our post-Christian, postdenominational, postmodern world, evangelism is frowned upon. "Don't you dare try to share the gospel of Christ with a Hindu, a Muslim, a Jew, a Santero," our pluralistic culture scolds; "they already have a faith, and one spirituality is as good as another." Replacing that "narrow-minded" stance in favor of "broad-mindedness" even wants to become official. The U.S. Congress recently had before it legislation for a "religion-free workplace." The new legislation would require all employees to refrain from saying anything religious to subordinates. Billy Graham said recently that there is now more freedom to preach the gospel in Russia than in the United States.

The Motive for Sharing the Light

Window on the Word

For God so loved the world that he gave his one and only Son, that whoever believes in him shall not perish but have eternal life (John 3:16).

The love of Christ compels us, Paul said (2 Cor. 5:14). Nothing less than divine love will keep us on the witnessing track. Not willpower, not duty, not obedience, not even the urge to please God. The energy for staying power required of witnesses comes from the flame of Christ's love burning in our hearts. John Bunyan, author of *Pilgrim's Progress*, said, "Dost thou see a soul with the image of God in him? Love him, love him. Say to thyself, 'This man and I must go to heaven together.'"[3]

Frank Laubach is the father of the modern literacy movement. He made "Each one teach one" famous in literacy and missionary circles. He was a literacy expert and a dedicated missionary. He was a giant of prayer and the spiritual life. His work was challenging. After going through some difficult and disappointing circumstances, Laubach experienced a deep depression and a bout with physical illness. He accepted a call to do evangelistic work on the island of Mindanao in the Philippines. Since the spot was isolated and dangerous, Laubach's wife, Effa, and their only surviving child (three others had died from malaria) stayed in Baguio, 900 miles away. Laubach was alone in Mindanao, with only his dog, Tip, as his companion.

> **Only the motive that moved God to reach out to us will suffice—love.**

Early efforts to reach the people failed. Laubach's only solace was a regular trek up Signal Hill to think, pray, and try to recover enough energy to continue the work. One December evening during a meditation period, he had a transforming experience. While he tried to pray, the dog licked the tears from the missionary's face. Curiously enough, Laubach's lips began to speak words that seemed to come from God: "My child," my lips said, "you have failed because you do not really love the Moros. You feel superior to them because you are white. If you can forget that you are American and think only how I love them, they will respond."[4]

Laubach's realization that his evangelistic effectiveness was diminished because his love was inadequate transformed him for the rest of his life. Only the motive that moved God to reach out to us will suffice—love.

METHODS OF EVANGELIZING

Window on the Word

I have become all things to all men so that by all possible means I might save some (1 Cor. 9:22).

God uses all kinds of methods to reach hungry souls around the world. Preaching, revivals, small groups, films, personal evangelism, broadcasting—you name the method, and God has Christians using it, even the Internet. Last year Joy Paday planned to visit her relatives in Daet, the Philippines. Click, double-click—she was in touch with the missionaries of her denomination in the Philippines. One thing she wanted to do was to take her relatives to a Holiness church. Bad news—her denomination had no church in Daet. Joy clicked away on the Net until she found out where her denomination did have churches.

Joy and her husband, Nicasio, were not ones to give up easily. They brought Nicasio's brother, Romie Paday, all the way to suburban Manila to attend a Wesleyan heritage church. The church members welcomed the visitors, the singing was happy, even if a little fast and loud. The prayers were fervent—as if they really thought God cared for them—and how the pastor preached! Romie did not know what to call it, but the Spirit of the Lord came. The altar call found Romie—a man with serious drinking problems and acquainted with jail—pouring out his confession to Christ.

God wants you to win others to Christ by turning His love loose on them.

The conversion was real. Romie went back home and started a Bible study in his house. Some 80 people attend. Romie wanted to start a church. A former student of mine at Asia-Pacific Nazarene Theological Seminary graduated and became the pastor of the church in Daet. God uses even the Internet as a tool in His redemptive purpose. We have time and space to cite only a few of the ways God calls us to witness.

1. *Personal Evangelism*. Thirty years ago the personal evangelism star was a person who could wring a confession of faith out of a perfect stranger between the salads and the desserts in the cafeteria line. That mode prompted a

lot of Christians to arm themselves with a canned summary of the gospel and to approach unwary unbelievers. "Too many of us blockheads have rushed into the world with our [evangelistic] techniques and formulas, hardly distinguishable from the sales pitches of soft drinks or Bob's Used Cars."[5] Laymen are embarrassed and confused about witnessing because the gimmicks and formulas given to them seem "unnatural or even phony."

Nevertheless, God wants you to win others to Christ by turning His love loose on them. Your greatest opportunities for evangelism are in your network of family, friends, neighbors, clubs, and coworkers—people who care about you and respect you. Some will listen when you share the Light with them.

Jerry and Charles were bikers, Harley-Davidson men. They had lived rough lives—cocaine addiction had been only part of their sinful past. But Christ had redeemed them. Their hair was still long, and their skin was tattooed. They still rode their bikes. But Christ was in their hearts and on their faces. They wanted to know more about Him. A friend who was discipling them had promised to take them to the minister's house on Tuesday night. They had some questions they wanted to ask. On his way to the meeting, Charles drove down a familiar street that passed the house of his buddy, Jack. Charles had spoken to him about Christ, but Jack just didn't seem interested. The Lord seemed to say to Charles, "Go back and knock on Jack's door."

"Is that really You, Lord?" Charles answered. "OK, if the light's red, I'll go back."

The light was red. Back Charles went. When they arrived at the minister's house, they didn't talk about the questions they had come to discuss. Instead, they helped Jack, who had come with them. He was desperate, full of hurt and anger, and wanted to know how to be saved. Before the evening was over, there were *three* bikers who knew Christ. Charles probably could not have won someone at the nursing home to the Lord. But another biker—that was his network. What's yours?

For models of personal evangelism study John 4:1-29, where Jesus led the Samaritan woman to faith, and Acts 8:26-39, where the Spirit guided Philip, who led a strange man to faith and baptism. You can derive many principles or guidelines for soul winning from these passages including:

(1) Be alert to the leadership of the Spirit (Acts 8:26).
(2) We must go where the sinners are.
(3) Speak to interests held in common.
(4) Be prepared to explain the Scriptures (as both Philip and Jesus did).
(5) We must help the not-yet-saved, not condemn them.

2. *Lifestyle Evangelism*. Just living like a Christian will attract some seeking souls. They see the radiance of God in your life, and they wonder, "Why not me?"

Five elegant and lovely lamps shine in a full-page ad. The all-caps header reads: NOW YOU KNOW WHAT A MOTH FEELS LIKE. You know, "drawn like a moth to a flame." The moth, fluttering in the deep darkness of the night, sees a lamp and—straight for the light. Persons lost in sin and in "darkness that can be felt" are attracted to the Christian who reflects the glory of God like an unveiled lamp in the night.

Do you know someone who wants to be like you? The Lord may be counting on you to share the Light.

3. *Faith Mentoring: The Evangelism of the 21st Century*. In a post-Christian and postmodern culture, mentoring emerges as the most promising method of passing the Light to the next generation. We can no longer assume that Christian faith or values form the common ideals of this culture. We start from scratch, much as the first Christian generation did. That means spending more time with fewer people as we teach the faith by example, counsel, coaching, and modeling.

In times much like our own, Paul urged Timothy, his son in the faith, "The things you have heard me say . . . entrust to reliable men who will also be qualified to teach others" (2 Tim. 2:2). Christians established in prayer and the Scriptures, who are guided by the Spirit, known for holiness of life, patience, understanding, discernment, vulnerability, and the ability to listen, will be our best evangelists as they engage in one-on-one mentoring relationships that last a few days or many years.

Besides the familiar roles of model and guide, faith mentors find themselves serving in these unique ways too:

(1) *Coach*. The mentor-coach instructs on how to play the game. He or she then makes us watch the spiritual game films—in painful slow motion—and shows us how to do better next time.

(2) *Advocate*. As a spiritual friend the mentor offers support and affirmation for the mentee's honest search for identity and meaning even when friends, family, or the pastor may not understand. The Thessalonians found such affirmation in Paul: "We dealt with each of you as a father deals with his own children, encouraging, comforting and urging you to live lives worthy of God" (1 Thess. 2:11-12).

(3) *Sponsor*. Some churches appoint sponsors for youth. The sponsor-mentor is to be guide, friend, colearner, and the one who leads the juvenile into full participation in the church. Paul was a sponsor-mentor to the new believers in Thessalonica: "We were gentle among you, like a mother caring for her little children. . . . For now we really live, since you are standing firm in the Lord" (1 Thess. 2:7; 3:8).

(4) *Guarantor*. Youth and young adults need "guarantors" who incarnate Christian adulthood in ways that encourage young people to grow. Thus they *guarantee* that adulthood is a good place to be.[6]

(5) *Mediator*. One of the basic Protestant principles is the "priesthood of all believers." That doesn't just mean that you can pray to God without going through a priest. It also means that ordinary Christians can become priests to one another.

A faith mentor can *mediate* love, grace, self-knowledge, and discernment of the will of God, as well as acceptance, assurance, and a sense of direction in life. A faith mentor can also mediate between a painful past and a promise-filled future.[7]

Missionary Wilma

The trouble began when Wilma read the announcement in a hurry. Missionary Rally! Great, Wilma loved missions and missionaries. She didn't even notice that it was a youth service. *Wilma was 80 years old.*

She arrived early, not noticing that the crowd was mostly teens. Everywhere Wilma went, the crowd was younger than she. The missionary from Africa delivered his soul in a powerful service. The Spirit came in refulgent waves of glory.

The speaker challenged the young people to answer God's call to missionary service. "If you are willing for God to use you as a missionary, if you are willing to serve wherever He sends you," the speaker cried out, "please stand and come forward." At first 5 students stood, then 10, then more.

Was Wilma willing to let God use her as a missionary? Yes! So Wilma went forward and joined the kids standing before the altar. *Wilma was 80 years old.*

The missionary and the pastors from the sponsoring churches stepped up to pray for and lay hands on the youth consecrating their lives. But there stood Wilma. How embarrassing. Not even God could make a missionary out of an octogenarian. *Wilma was 80 years old.*

Her pastor saw her. Would he tell her to go sit down, that this was just for kids with a lifetime to give? No, he took her by the hand and said a brief prayer. Why embarrass her? She had missed the point. After all, *Wilma was 80 years old.*

What kind of missionary service could she offer at 80? Surely Wilma had been thinking the same thing, but the Spirit and the need of Africans pulled at her heartstrings, so she went forward. She would at least give God a chance.

A few weeks passed. Then one morning her phone rang. It was the pastor. "Wilma, there's a young Black man going on trial in a few days for a serious crime. His mother is a Christian. She is coming for the trial, but she can't afford a hotel. Would you be willing to keep her during the trial?" Wilma said, "Of course."

For four days Wilma delivered the troubled mother to the courthouse and picked her up at night. She cooked breakfast and dinner for her new friend. And each morning and evening they prayed for the wayward son.

The trial was over in four days. The boy was convicted. His mother had to go home to a city two provinces away. On her last day she wept with Wilma and pleaded for her to take her place with her boy. "I can't be a mother to him so far away. Please promise me that you will visit him in my place." Wilma promised.

But she had never been to a prison. The idea scared her, and so she kept putting off that first visit. Then one day in her quiet time as she looked out her window at a Canadian winter snow, the Lord seemed to speak to her, reminding her of the missionary service where she had pledged so much. Wilma decided that though she could not go to Africa, she could call on this imprisoned young man of African descent.

But what could she do for him? After all, *Wilma was 80 years old.* What did she have to give? What was she good at? Grandmothering, yes, that was her talent. So she packed homemade shortbread cookies, a Bible, and a Christian magazine.

She met the young convict, and they soon came to love and appreciate each other. Her visit was the highlight of his week. They chatted, told jokes, read the Bible, prayed, and before leaving, she always gave him a hug in his mother's behalf.

One day he said, "Wilma, I'm so glad that I have you, but I almost feel selfish soaking up your love and company every week. You see, there are a whole lot of men in this jail who don't have anyone. No one cares, no one writes, no one visits, no one reads the Bible to them. Would it be all right if I let some of them join us?"

At first there were 5 and then 10 and then two dozen prisoners who came to sit at the feet of missionary Wilma as she shared cookies, lemonade, grandmotherly wisdom, and the Savior who calls people to service, even in the 80th year of their age.

Now, how old did you say you are . . . ?

— 20 —

Going Forward: Leaning into the Future

First Window on the Word

Our citizenship is in heaven. And we eagerly await a Savior from there, the Lord Jesus Christ, who . . . will transform our lowly bodies so that they will be like his glorious body (Phil. 3:20-21).

Going forward—that's a term from the financial reporters. They say things like, "Going forward, the earnings prospect of XYZ Company look excellent." Or, "Going forward, the economy will continue to heat up." Or, "Going forward, the market share of Widgets Incorporated looks vulnerable due to the launching of Better Widgets dot.com."

So what are your prospects, going forward?

Maybe forward is the only way we can go. But we can enter the future shoulder blades first, or we can lean into the future with open arms and with Easter in our eyes.

The Resurrection Crowns the Cross

Window on the Word

That which . . . we have seen with our eyes, which we have looked at and our hands have touched—this we proclaim concerning the Word of Life. The life appeared; we have seen it and testify to it, and we proclaim to you . . . eternal life. . . . We proclaim . . . what we have seen and heard (1 John 1:1-3).

Judas the traitor is dead. A new apostle must be elected in his place. Did they hire Gallup to do a voters' poll to see which candidate could draw the minority vote? Or to see who had "credibility" with upper-class folks with the deep pockets? How about a screen test to see which candidate had the highest "charisma quotient" on camera? I don't think so.

The nominees had to meet two requirements. They had to have known Christ before the Crucifixion and after the Resurrection. Only a person who had *personally* known Jesus before and after His death could offer authoritative, first-hand evidence of the central teaching of Christianity—the bodily resurrection of Jesus. John the apostle cried out, "We have seen his glory, the glory of the One and Only, who came from the Father, full of grace and truth" (John 1:14).

No Resurrection—no Christianity! The crucifixion and bodily resurrection of Jesus stand alone as the foundation stones of the Church. What about all those commandments, parables, and miracles of Jesus? Without the resurrection of Jesus you would never have heard of any of those—not one! His life and death would have been anonymously buried by the sands of time. Not a footprint would have been left by the Nazarene without the Resurrection.

What Jesus did had never been done before in the whole history of the universe. C. S. Lewis says, "He has forced open a door that has been locked since the death of the first man. He has met, fought, and beaten the King of Death."[1]

Do not think that the resurrection of Jesus proves merely the immortality of the soul. The Resurrection is not about the survival of the human spirit. If that is all that happened, then Jesus simply did what all men do—the body dies, the soul escapes to a body-free, ghostly existence in some never-never land. If that were the case, then the only thing new about Jesus' experience would be that we got to see it happen.[2]

But the resurrection of Jesus included the resurrection of the body. We, too, then, look forward to being "raised imperishable. . . . For the perishable must clothe itself with the imperishable, and the mortal with immortality. . . . 'Death has been swallowed up in victory'" (1 Cor. 15:52-54). We do not know nearly all we would like to about that body, but we do know that we shall be like the risen Christ (1 John 3:2). For those first Christians teaching and preaching about Jesus was primarily proclaiming His death and resurrection. Paul wrote, "I passed on to you as of first importance: that Christ died for our sins . . . [and] he was raised on the third day" (1 Cor. 15:3-4).

Many have written long books trying to prove or disprove the Resurrection. Those dreary and exhausting arguments will not be rehearsed here. Do take time, however, to ponder this excerpt from Peter Marshall's "Grave in the Garden.".

> Is it True?
>
> Is Christ really risen from the dead?
>
> As that question begins to knock—gently—at your heart's door, you realize that you have gone back through the centuries to when the world was [2,000] years younger, back to the country of the camel, and sandaled footprints in the sands of Palestine . . . back to the time of the Roman eagle fluttering over bronze breastplates shining in the Syrian sun . . . back to the days of the Caesars.
>
> And you feel quite funny—almost ridiculous—for you have your microscope in your hand,
>
> your measuring tape,
>
> your litmus paper,

your biology textbook,
your test tube,
and your college diploma.

In the half-shadow in the womb of time your microscope glitters like a diamond.

Your tape measure gleams like a line of gold.

Your litmus paper is a purple ribbon from a royal standard.

Your test tube a silver bugle to sound a lot of triumph. And the noise and confusion of unbelief has died away.

And in the quiet Easter morning you are standing in front of a grave in the garden, and you see a stone in the doorway, but the stone is moving . . . is moving!

And before you are aware of it, you suddenly realize that Someone is standing beside you, and your eyes are fixed on His hand, and you see a mark in the palm of it, like the print of a nail.

And as a great realization dawns over you, you hear His voice,

"Lo, I am with you alway, even to the end of the world." "Whosoever believeth in me, though he were dead, yet shall he live: and whosoever liveth and believeth in me, shall never die."

"Because I live, ye shall live also."

Because you can't stand it any longer—in the secret places of our hearts—we cry out to God for help—and then it comes, the supreme miracle for which we have been seeking.

It is so tremendous a thing that we can't describe it.

It is so delicate a thing that we cannot even bring it into view for anybody else to look at.

We can never explain it to anybody else.

We only know that it is true.

The Voice has said:

"Because I live, ye shall live also."

Our hearts knew all along it must be so.

It was what we wanted to hear, and now that we have heard it, we feel that we have solved the mystery of life.

"If a man die, shall he live again?"

Yes, because the Resurrection is a fact.

And I, too, shall live, because I know it's true.[3]

Longing for Home

Window on the Word

If the earthly tent we live in is destroyed, we have . . . an eternal house in heaven. . . . Meanwhile we groan, longing to be clothed with our heavenly dwelling . . . and would prefer to be . . . at home with the Lord (2 Cor. 5:1-2, 8).

Since Jesus whipped death, hell, and the grave, you and I have eternal life—a gift that Christ hands to us if we will accept it. More than a hope for eternal life, it is eternal life now. We sense it within. Paul described it as the presence of the Spirit, who lives within as a guarantee of heaven to come (2 Cor. 5:5). Joni Eareckson Tada says that it is like "stealing a tiny sip of stew before dinner, it's meant to be a foretaste of what to expect when we get to the banquet table."[4]

God sends us moments that rise above time, experiences of heartbreaking joy in which we see the glow of the divine.

The longing for our heavenly home is also like a radio beam or a lighthouse beacon, or like a spiritual "tuning fork resonating in the soul" that draws us upward. With that resonant chord in our heart that echoes eternity, "He woos us away from the world with that heavenly haunting."[5] We find the confidence Emily Dickinson wrote of:

I never spoke with God,
Nor visited in heaven;
Yet certain am I of the spot
As if the chart were given.[6]

God sends us moments that rise above time, experiences of heartbreaking joy in which we see the glow of the divine. Those timeless moments usually surprise us. We bump into them during a worship service that seems to move no one else, during a sunset stroll, in a child's trusting eyes, in a song that keeps inventing itself in our head, a verse of Scripture that won't stop blooming until it becomes a full-blown Rose of Sharon, or in a night sky in which the stars become the "party lights of heaven." In such moments of spiritual ecstasy we "forget ourselves and yet find ourselves."[7]

Into our hearts high yearnings
Come welling and surging in—
Come from the mystic ocean,
Whose rim no foot has trod—
Some of us call it Longing,
And others call it God.[8]

WHAT IS HEAVEN LIKE?

Window on the Word

The angel showed me the river of the water of life, as clear as crystal. . . . The throne of God and of the Lamb will be in the city, and his servants . . . will see his face. . . . There will be no more night. They will not need the light of a lamp or the light of the sun, for the Lord God will give them light (Rev. 22:1, 3-5).

I read a stack of books and articles trying to prepare to write about what heaven is like. The noble conjectures ranged from humbling to silly. One man, an outdoor type from Colorado, hoped for a heaven that was one long, perfect ski slope that never required him to climb back up the mountain. Perhaps no one has improved on the insight of John Bunyan. In *Pilgrim's Progress* Christian and Hopeful are standing on the "Delectable Mountains." The shepherds of these mountains take them up to the hill called "Clear" and give them a small telescope so they can look at the Celestial City. But their hands shake, and they can barely make out its gate. Our best intimations of heaven are through a telescope held by a trembling hand.

Some ideas do emerge from Scripture and faith about heaven.

1. *The Beatific Vision*. This will be seeing our Lord face-to-face. Songs such as "I Shall Know Him," by Fanny Crosby, celebrate this heavenly hope.

2. *Heavenly Rest*. This world is a vale of tears, a place of struggle to make ends meet, an existence of toil. "We shall rest, and, faith, we shall need it—lie down for an aeon or two." That was part of Rudyard Kipling's vision of heaven in "L'Envoi."[9]

3. *A Place of Work and Growth*. Our talents are not given just for this world. Adam Clarke says that in heaven we will be given greater duties and greater capacity to achieve them. What does the Bible say about Christians being given governmental duties in the next world? Kipling dreamed that in that land we "shall work for an age at a sitting, and never be tired at all!"[10]

4. *A Place of Holy Worship and Pleasure*. "Fullness of joy and pleasures forevermore . . . endless felicity" are other words that Adam Clarke used to estimate heaven. "They fell down on their faces before the throne and worshiped God, saying: 'Amen! Praise and glory and wisdom and thanks and honor and power and strength be to our God for ever and ever'" (Rev. 7:11-12).

5. *A Place of Magnified Creativity*. In this world much of our work is mere drudgery. In heaven we may have creative tasks and multiplied creativity unhindered by human limitations. Kipling yearned for this:

But each for the joy of the working,
And each, in his separate star,
Shall draw the Thing as he sees It
For the God of Things as They Are![11]

6. *A True Heavenly Community*. In this world, at times even in the Church, it is hard to get along with each other. To form the "community" that is the Church's ideal has been beyond us all this time. In heaven the Persons of the Holy Trinity model a true community. There we will finally see true community. Part of that community will be our friends and loved ones—we will probably get along with them better than we did here.

7. *The Redemption of All of Creation*. Not only our bodies and souls will be renewed, but the whole of creation will be redeemed. If you thought that a maple tree in autumn or a May sunset was beautiful, just you wait (see Rom. 8:19-21).

DO I HAVE TO GO TO HEAVEN?

Window on the Word

He who stands firm to the end will be saved (Matt. 24:13).

Heaven lies at the end of the Christ-redeemed, Spirit-led life. It will not be found at the end of *anyone's* self-centered, sinful life.

Wesleyan-Arminian teaching offers a corrective to a warm and cozy myth of popular American Evangelicalism. That is the whimsy that once you went forward or raised your hand or nodded when the preacher asked, "Do you accept Christ?" on the last night of youth camp, heaven is a lead-pipe cinch for you. You have to go to heaven whether you like it or not once you "accepted Christ." We reject that sort of false security out of hand as contrary to the Bible and common sense. Wesleyans (and the Bible, they believe) teach that it is not enough to choose Christ once. You have to keep on choosing Christ throughout life if you are going to make it to heaven.

You can turn from God, choose evil again, and, as Faust did, make *evil* your *good*—and miss heaven. You can turn from God and become a money worshiper, a hate-filled racist, a thrill-seeking hedonist, or, less dramatically, a self-centered sinner.

You see, there is nothing about Christian conversion that takes away your freedom to choose. The Bible and Wesleyan doctrine take free will and individual responsibility very seriously. God created Adam and Eve "able to stand, but free to fall." You are in that same category as a born-again believer. The very essence of Wesleyan teaching is that God gifts us with prevenient grace, the ability to choose God and good—that is, we are not predestined to choose God or evil. We are free to choose and responsible for the choice. Our choices bear eternal consequences.

Not only must we choose Christ, we must keep on choosing Christ if we are to make it to heaven.

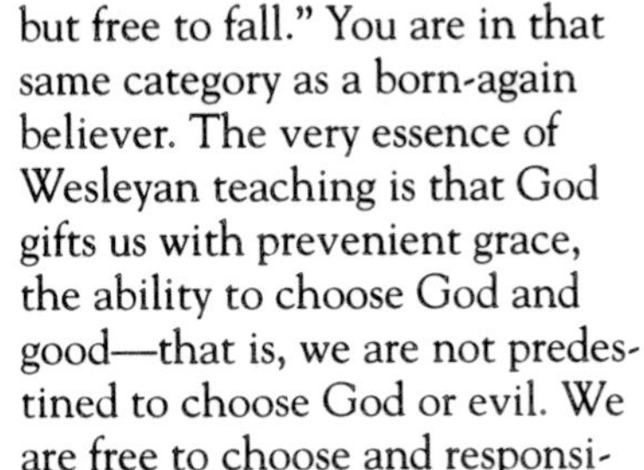

So underline this: Not only must we choose Christ, we must keep on choosing Christ if we are to make it to heaven. The Bible says over and over, "He who stands firm to the end will be saved" (Matt. 10:22; 24:13; Mark 13:13; see Rev. 2:10).

Taking human freedom seriously, as the Bible does, means that "the door to hell is locked from the *inside*," as C. S. Lewis declared. "The damned are, in one sense, successful rebels to the end. . . . They enjoy forever the horrible freedom they have demanded, and are therefore self-enslaved."[12] They may wish to escape, but they do not "will even the first preliminary stages of that self-abandonment through which alone the soul can reach any good."[13]

We don't know much about the details of hell. I am quite sure that the atrocious scenes of torture that a mostly fallen clergy used to terrorize the simple in the Dark Ages don't come close. But Jesus believed in hell, and I, for one, am not going to second-guess Him. Jesus spoke of hell using three metaphors or symbols: (1) everlasting punishment (Matt. 25:46), (2) destruction of the soul and body (10:28), and (3) banishment to the privation of outer darkness in such parables as the man without the wedding garment and the foolish virgins.[14]

Being an optimist, I can still see one good thing about hell—not one single person reading this book has to go there!

Rules for the Road

Window on the Word

Let us hold unswervingly to the hope we profess. . . . Do not throw away your confidence; it will be richly rewarded. . . . Persevere so that . . . you will receive what he has promised (Heb. 10:23, 35-36).

We long for the redemption of all creation, for the new mind, and perfected resurrection bodies the Bible promises. And though we can sometimes hear the heavenly orchestra warming up for the marriage supper of the Lamb, we still have a journey before us, long or short, before we make it home. This whole book, as well as the *Workbook* and the *Leader's Guide*, has been about that journey. We pause now to consider some rules for the open road ahead.

1. *Take the Long-Range View.* My dad used to say when I was about to do something on the spur of the moment, "Son, in the long run, you'd be better off to . . ." It took me years to learn what my father already knew—that it's the long run we are in!

Bill Havens—you've never heard of him, I'm sure. You would have heard of him except for a choice he made when he was young. In 1923 his dream came true: he qualified for the U.S. Olympic team in two water sports events. But when the 1924 games came, Bill did not compete. Bill's wife was expecting a baby right in the middle of the 1924 Paris games. In those days you did not hop over the "Big Pond" in a Concorde or 757. You went by steamer. Bill would be gone for a month and a half. He couldn't leave his wife to face the experience alone. Besides, he didn't want to miss the birth of his firstborn child. So he said no to Olympic kudos and stayed home.

A lot of people thought he was nuts. But he chose family over fame because he felt that it was the right thing to do in the long run. Maybe he was right. Twenty-eight years later, Bill got a telegram from Helsinki, Finland, the site of the 1952 summer Olympics. It read:

"Dear Dad: Thanks for waiting around for me to get born in 1924. I'm coming home with the gold medal that you should have won. . . . Your loving son, Frank."[15]

When Frank Havens won the 10,000-meter canoeing event, his first thought was not of gym-shoe endorsements, athletic gear commercials, or finding an agent. His first thought was of his father. In the long run Bill Havens was right. Keep the long-range view in front of you as you lean into the future.

2. *Run Toward the Roar.* The gazelles never learn. The lion's strategy always works. Downwind several lionesses hide. They send the mighty male lion upwind. He doesn't try to sneak up on the gazelles. He wants to be seen—and heard. When he gets close, he roars with all his might. The frightened gazelles charge off away from the roar—and right into the waiting jaws of the lionesses.

The devil sets traps for you all the time. Wise up; don't keep making it easy for him. Run toward the roar, and break the ambush trap. "Resist the devil," the Bible says, "and he will flee from you" (James 4:7). Now there's a promise for you.

3. *Walk in the Transforming Light.* The Spirit is trying to sculpt you in the very image of Christ. Let Him mold you. Gaze with unveiled face on the glory of Christ in the Word. You will find yourself "being transformed into his likeness with ever-increasing glory," reflecting His radiance like a mirror (2 Cor. 3:18). This is the principle behind Nathaniel Hawthorne's classic story *The Great Stone Face.*

From the time he was a small boy, Ernest had loved to gaze at the Great Stone Face. In the valley where he lived was a great cliff. From the proper angle one could see a great human face on it. "There was a broad arch of the forehead, a hundred feet in height; the nose with its long bridge; and vast lips, which, if they could have spoken, would have rolled their thunder accents from one end of the valley to the other. All the features were noble, and the expression was at once grand and sweet, as if it were the glow of a vast warm heart."

Ernest also loved the legend that someday a person born in that valley would become "the noblest personage of his time" and who would "bear an exact resemblance to the Great Stone Face." Daily after the work was done, Ernest would gaze at the Great Stone Face and hope that he would live to see the prophecy fulfilled.

Several people born in that valley made a name for themselves. Ernest watched and hoped as each of them returned. The first was Mr. Gathergold, a merchant and a banker. The second was Old Blood and Thunder, a famous general. He was followed by Old Stony Phiz, a statesman (or maybe just a politician). The people tried hard to see the Great Stone Face in each of them. But it soon became evident that none of them qualified as the benevolent Great Stone Face. They each displayed a likeness to that which they loved best—gold, power, fame.

Another son of the valley became a great poet. Ernest thought sure he would be the one. But the poet confessed that though his thoughts were noble, his life had not been. One night the poet went with Ernest to a gathering. Ernest was greatly respected for his wisdom and goodness and was often invited to address various groups. That night as Ernest spoke, the poet cried out, "The Great Stone Face! Look—it's Ernest. He is the exact resemblance of the Great Stone Face." Suddenly all could see it. Ernest had so lived in intimacy with the benevolent image that he had come to radiate its very qualities. All believed the poet was right, except one. Ernest could not believe that he had become like the Great Stone Face. But he had.

As you journey on this road, keep your eyes on Jesus. Don't be surprised if some say that they see His Light in your face.

4. *Reach Out to Your Companions on the Way.* Learn to live this song as you go:

I see Jesus in your eyes and it makes me love Him,
I feel Jesus in your touch and I know He cares,
*I hear Jesus in your voice and it makes me listen.**

5. *Do All the Good You Can.* Jesus said it like this: "Come, you who are blessed by my Father; take your inheritance. . . . I was hungry and you gave me something to eat, I was thirsty and you gave me something to drink, I was a stranger and you invited me in . . . I was in prison and you came to visit me. . . . Whatever you did for one of the least of these brothers of mine, you did for me" (Matt. 25:34-36, 40).

These rules of the road will help you make it home.

And just think of stepping on shore and finding it Heaven,
Of touching a hand and finding it God's,
Of breathing new air and finding it celestial,
Of waking up in glory and finding it Home!

—Don Wyrtzen

One for the Road

This course of study, hopefully, will lead you to more adventures of the spirit, more unguessed blessings, and victories of grace. Going forward, take this prayer from Columba, a sixth-century Irish missionary to Scotland. Put it in your spiritual backpack; you'll need the calories it provides soon enough.

O Lord,
Be thou a bright flame before me,
Be thou a guiding star above me,
Be thou a smooth path below me,
Be thou a kindly shepherd behind me.
Today—tonight—and forever.
Amen.

*Sharalee Lucas, "I See Jesus in You." © Rambo-McGuire Music, Nashville, 1986. Used by permission.

Notes

Introduction

1. Annie Dillard, *Teaching a Stone to Talk* (New York: Harper and Row, 1982), 46. Quoted without reference, except a general reference to the historical work of L. P. Kirwan.

2. Brent Curtis and John Eldredge, *The Sacred Romance* (Nashville: Thomas Nelson, 1997), 2.

3. C. S. Lewis, *The Joyful Christian* (New York: Macmillan Publishing Co., 1977), 80.

4. Max Lucado, *Just like Jesus* (Nashville: Word Publishing, Thomas Nelson, 1998), 81.

Part 1 Searching for the Light

1. Howard Thurman, *The Inward Journey* (New York: Harper and Brothers, Publishers, 1961), 118. These lines are adapted from this source and edited to replace generic male references such as "man," "he," "him" with more gender sensitive terms. Used by permission.

Chapter 1

1. Barbara Wickens, ed., "You Scream, I Scream . . . ," *Maclean's* 110, No. 9 (March 3, 1997): 14. Cited by Stanley J. Grenz, *What Christians Really Believe—and Why* (Louisville, Ky.: Westminster John Knox Press, 1998), 18-19.

2. Jean-François Lyotard, *The Postmodern Condition*, trans. G. Bennington and B. Massumi (Minneapolis: University of Minnesota Press, 1984), 81.

3. Saul Bellow, *Herzog* (New York: Viking, 1964), 289-90.

4. J. Richard Middleton and Brian J. Walsh, *Truth Is Stranger than It Used to Be* (Downers Grove, Ill.: InterVarsity Press, 1995), 37.

5. Wesley D. Tracy, *What's a Nice God like You Doing in a Place like This?* (Kansas City: Beacon Hill Press of Kansas City, 1990), 82.

6. Stanley Kauffmann, *The New Republic* 4, No. 420 (August 30, 1999): 24.

7. Barbara Kantrowitz et al., "In Search of the Sacred," *Newsweek* 124, No. 22 (November 28, 1994): 53.

8. Sharon Doyle Driedger, "On a Higher Plane," *Maclean's* 108, No. 52 (December 25, 1995—January 1, 1996): 23. Cited by Grenz, *What Christians Really Believe*, 11.

9. Sharon Doyle Driedger, "Promise of Prosperity: Fad or Fact, Feng Shui Is All the Rage," *Maclean's* 110, No. 17 (April 28, 1997): 56-57. Cited by Grenz, *What Christians Really Believe*, 2.

10. Cited by Grenz, *What Christians Really Believe*, 73.

11. Walter Truett Anderson, *Reality Isn't What It Used to Be* (San Francisco: Harper and Row, 1990), 188.

12. See Middleton and Walsh, *Truth Is Stranger*, 59.

13. Stephen Crane, "A Learned Man," in *Modern American Poetry* (New York: Harcourt and Brace, 1958), 148.

14. Thomas R. Kelly, A *Testament of Devotion* (New York: Harper and Row, 1941), 54.

Chapter 2

1. This true story is based on eight newspaper accounts that appeared in the *Casper (Wyoming) Star-Tribune* and on Max Lucado's shorter version of the case in *He Still Moves Stones* (Dallas: Word Publishing, 1993), 23-24.

2. Rollo May, *The Cry for Myth* (New York: Norton, 1991), 16.

3. Grenz, *What Christians Really Believe*, 25.

4. Shirley MacLaine, *Out on a Limb* (New York: Bantam, 1983), 333. Cited by Grenz, *What Christians Really Believe*, 28.

5. Grenz, *What Christians Really Believe*, 146.

6. Ibid., 27.

7. Carol Riddell, *The Findhorn Community* (Findhorn, Scotland: Findhorn Press, 1990), 30-31.

8. Levi, *The Aquarian Gospel of Jesus the Christ*, 56 (chap. 28: 4). Cited by Grenz, *What Christians Really Believe*, 102.

9. Middleton and Walsh, *Truth Is Stranger*, 123.

10. See J. Kenneth Grider, A *Wesleyan-Holiness Theology* (Kansas City: Beacon Hill Press of Kansas City, 1994), 236-38.

11. Max Lucado, A *Gentle Thunder* (Dallas: Word Publishing, 1995), 122.

12. Middleton and Walsh, *Truth Is Stranger*, 149.

13. Grider, *Wesleyan-Holiness Theology*, 240-41.

14. Ibid., 238.

15. John Wesley, "The Signs of the Times," in *The Works of John Wesley*, ed. Thomas Jackson, 3rd ed., 14 vols. (London: Methodist Book Room, 1872; reprint, Kansas City: Beacon Hill Press of Kansas City, 1978), 6:311 (hereafter cited as *Works*).

Chapter 3

1. May, *Cry for Myth*, 21.

2. *Homiletics*, ed. Leonard Sweet, November/December 1995, 63.

3. Grenz, *What Christians Really Believe*, 122.

4. Douglas Coupland, *Life After God* (New York: Pocket Books, 1994), 359.

5. J. I. Packer et al., *Exploring the Christian Faith* (London, Nashville: Thomas Nelson Publishers, 1996), 151.

6. Maria Harris, *Fashion Me a People* (Louisville, Ky.: John Knox Press, 1989), 55.

7. Packer et al., *Exploring the Christian Faith*, 267.

8. Grenz, *What Christians Really Believe*, 33.

Chapter 4

1. Grenz, *What Christians Really Believe*, 37.

2. H. Ray Dunning, *Grace, Faith, and Holiness: A Wesleyan Systematic Theology* (Kansas City: Beacon Hill Press of Kansas City, 1988), 293.

3. Grenz, *What Christians Really Believe*, 43.

4. Dunning, *Grace, Faith, and Holiness*, 293.

5. Wesley, "The Fall of Man," in *Works*, 6:223.

6. Dietrich Bonhoeffer, *Creation and Fall* (New York: Macmillan, 1967), 38.

7. John Wesley, *Sermons on Several Occasions* (London: Wesleyan Methodist Book Room, n.d.), 629.

8. Morris A. Weigelt, in Wesley D. Tracy et al., *The Upward Call: Spiritual Formation and the Holy Life* (Kansas City: Beacon Hill Press of Kansas City, 1994), 30.

9. Wesley, "The Spirit of Bondage and Adoption," in *Sermons on Several Occasions*, 115.

10. Jesus was talking to rigidly sinful Pharisees; the kingdom of God was hardly within *them*. Jesus was saying that He himself was bringing the Kingdom. "Here it is, here I am, among you right now."

11. Grenz, *What Christians Really Believe*, 39.
12. See Weigelt, in Tracy et al., *Upward Call*, 25-26, 31-32.

Chapter 5

1. As recalled from a story told at a children's ministry meeting by an unknown nurse.
2. William M. Greathouse, *Love Made Perfect* (Kansas City: Beacon Hill Press of Kansas City, 1997), 28.
3. See William M. Greathouse, *Wholeness in Christ* (Kansas City: Beacon Hill Press of Kansas City, 1998). In chapter 1 he cites Rudolf Otto, Norman Snaith, and John G. Gammie on this subject.
4. Dunning, *Grace, Faith, and Holiness*, 187.
5. Roderick T. Leupp, "A Seamless Robe" (a not-yet-published MS written on assignment from *Holiness Today*), 2.
6. Ibid.
7. Dale Moody, *The Word of Truth* (Grand Rapids: Wm. B. Eerdmans Publishing Co., 1981), 104. Cited by Dunning, *Grace, Faith, and Holiness*, 190.
8. "Come, O Thou Traveler Unknown," in *Wesley Hymns*, comp. Ken Bible (Kansas City: Lillenas Publishing Co., 1982), No. 18.
9. Dunning, *Grace, Faith, and Holiness*, 197.
10. Grenz, *What Christians Really Believe*, 79.
11. Ibid.
12. John Greenleaf Whittier, "The Eternal Goodness," in *One Hundred and One Famous Poems* (Chicago: Cable Publishing, 1929), 106.
13. Grenz, *What Christians Really Believe*, 71.
14. Ibid., 72.
15. Dunning, *Grace, Faith, and Holiness*, 223.
16. Ibid., 231-32.
17. Esther De Waal, *The Celtic Way of Prayer* (New York: Doubleday, 1997), 39-40.
18. James E. Lovelock, *The Ages of Gaia: A Biography of Our Living Earth* (Oxford: Oxford University Press, 1988), 218. Cited by Grenz, *What Christians Really Believe*, 81.
19. Grenz, *What Christians Really Believe*, 82.
20. As recalled from a Chicago sermon delivered by Dr. King.

Chapter 6

1. As recalled in an informal testimony at a small-group meeting. All names are changed. Used by permission of the man who told the story.
2. As quoted in *Holiness Today*, "The Quote Rack," August 1999, 19.
3. Cited in Frank Mead, ed. and comp., *12,000 Religious Quotations* (Grand Rapids: Baker Book House, 1989), 90.
4. Words attributed to Jesus in this section are the author's own paraphrase.
5. Marlin Hotle in *The Hunger of Your Heart*, ed. Wesley Tracy (Kansas City: Partnership Press, 1997), 134.
6. Greathouse, *Wholeness in Christ*, 186.
7. This statement of Jesus is not recorded in the Sermon on the Mount but is included here because it shows His interpretation of the fifth commandment, which is treated earlier in this chapter.

Chapter 7

1. Grenz, *What Christians Really Believe*, 86.

2. Ibid., 90-91.

3. John Shea, *Gospel Light* (New York: Crossroads Publishing Co., 1998), 113.

4. C. S. Lewis, *Mere Christianity* (New York: Macmillan Co., 1970), 40-41.

5. Dunning, *Grace, Faith, and Holiness*, 324.

6. T. A. Noble, "Why Did Jesus Die?" in *Illustrated Bible Life*, March—May 1996, 14.

7. Ibid., 12.

8. Grenz, *What Christians Really Believe*, 108.

9. Wesley Tracy, ed., *The Redeemed Will Walk There* (Kansas City: Beacon Hill Press of Kansas City, 1982), 44.

10. Dunning, *Grace, Faith, and Holiness*, 388.

11. Grenz, *What Christians Really Believe*, 98.

12. De Waal, *Celtic Way of Prayer*, 121.

13. See Dunning, *Grace, Faith, and Holiness*, 382.

14. Donald M. Baillie, *God Was in Christ* (London: Faber and Faber, 1961), 177-79. Quoted in Dunning, *Grace, Faith, and Holiness*, 382.

15. Dunning, *Grace, Faith, and Holiness*, 382-83.

16. Ibid., 383.

17. Quoted in J. Glenn Gould, *The Precious Blood of Christ* (Kansas City: Beacon Hill Press, 1959), 103.

Chapter 8

1. Grider, *Wesleyan-Holiness Theology*, 352-53.

2. David L. McKenna, *What a Time to Be Wesleyan!* (Kansas City: Beacon Hill Press of Kansas City, 1999), 29.

3. Wesley D. Tracy, "The Cleansing Blood of Jesus," in *Biblical Resources for Holiness Preaching*, ed. H. Ray Dunning (Kansas City: Beacon Hill Press of Kansas City, 1993), 2:264.

4. Grenz, *What Christians Really Believe*, 119.

5. Wesley, *Works*, 1:103.

6. Ibid., 5:117.

7. Max Lucado, *No Wonder They Call Him Savior* (Portland, Oreg.: Multnomah Press, 1986), 72-73. This story is adapted from that source. Used by permission of Multnomah Publishers, Inc.

Chapter 9

1. Phineas F. Bresee, "The Transferred Image," in *The Nazarene Pulpit* (Kansas City: Nazarene Publishing House, 1925), 148-49.

2. A. W. Tozer, *The Pursuit of God* (Harrisburg, Pa.: Christian Publications, 1948), 45.

3. "Open, Lord, My Inward Ear," in *Wesley Hymns*, No. 37.

4. See Wesley's sermon "Satan's Devices," in *Works*, 6:32-43.

5. John Powell, *He Touched Me: My Pilgrimage of Prayer*, quoted by Joseph A. Galdon, *The Mustard Seed* (Manila: Bookmark, 1991), 128.

6. J. Gilchrist Lawson, *Deeper Experiences of Famous Christians* (Anderson, Ind.: Warner Press, 1970), 320.

7. Cited by McKenna, *What a Time to Be Wesleyan!* 88.

8. Quoted by Greathouse, *Love Made Perfect*, 45.

Chapter 10

1. Maxie Dunnam, *Alive in Christ* (Nashville: Abingdon Press, 1982), 30.

2. Lucado, *Just like Jesus*, x.

3. Ibid., 65.

4. Melvin E. Dieter and Hallie A. Dieter, eds., *God Is Enough* (Grand Rapids: Zondervan, Francis Asbury Press, 1986), 253.

5. John Wesley, "The Scripture Way of Salvation," in *Wesley's Standard Sermons*, ed. Edward H. Sugden (London: Epworth Press, 1921), 448, 457.

6. David McCasland, *Oswald Chambers: Abandoned to God: The Life Story of the Author of My Utmost for His Highest* (Grand Rapids: Discovery House Publishers, 1993), 85.

7. Wesley, "The Way to the Kingdom," in *Works*, 5:79.

8. Wesley, *Works*, 11:430.

9. Galdon, *Mustard Seed*, 5.

10. C. Roy Angell, *Iron Shoes* (Nashville: Broadman Press, 1953), 99.

11. Hannah Whitall Smith, in M. E. Dieter and H. A. Dieter, *God Is Enough*, 249.

12. Dunnam, *Alive in Christ*, 128.

13. Ibid., 60.

14. Greathouse, *Love Made Perfect*, 64-73.

15. Mary A. Reuter, "Formation Through Encounters of Ordinary Life" (Ph.D. diss., Duquesne University, 1982).

16. Wewak (Papua New Guinea: Christian Books Melanesia, 1979). The literal pidgin words are:

Yu bosim mi, God, Yu bosim mi.
Yu Papa na mi pikinini.
Sapos mi gat sin Yu stretim mi.
Mi krai long Yu, Yu kam bosim mi.

17. Stephen J. Harper, "The Devotional Life of John Wesley" (Ph.D. diss., Duke University, 1981), 2:355.

Chapter 11

1. William Barclay, *Flesh and Spirit* (Naperville, Ill.: SCM Book Club, 1962), 22.

2. Ibid., 24.

3. Ibid., 27-28.

4. Leupp, "Seamless Robe," 3.

5. Ralph Earle, "Crucified with Christ," in Tracy, *Redeemed Will Walk There*, 109.

6. Wesley Tracy, "Lili in the Lion's Den," *Herald of Holiness*, May 1996, 2.

7. William Barclay, *Letters to the Galatians and Ephesians*, in *The Daily Study Bible Series* (Philadelphia: Westminster Press, 1959), 50.

8. Barclay, *Flesh and Spirit*, 76.

9. Leo Buscaglia, *Bus Nine to Paradise*. Quoted by Galdon, *Mustard Seed*, 165.

10. Earle, "Crucified with Christ," 111.

11. Ibid., 110.

12. Galdon, *Mustard Seed*, 99.

13. Barclay, *Flesh and Spirit*, 92.

14. Barclay, *Galatians and Ephesians*, 51.

15. Earle, "Crucified with Christ," 111.

16. Barclay, *Flesh and Spirit*, 114.

17. Ibid., 117.

18. William F. Buckley Jr., *Happy Days Were Here Again* (New York: Random House, 1993), 110.

19. Barclay quotes *The Shepherd of Hermas, Visions*, 3:8, 4 in *Flesh and Spirit*, 125.

20. Barclay, *Flesh and Spirit*, 14-15.

21. Paul M. Bassett, "Another Species," in Tracy, *Redeemed Will Walk There*, 53.
22. Thurman, *Inward Journey*, 118-19.

Chapter 12

1. Albert Outler, ed., *The Works of John Wesley* (Nashville: Abingdon Press, 1984), 1:105.
2. Dillard, *Teaching a Stone to Talk*, 24-26.
3. The methodology described in this chapter is traditionally called inductive Bible study. For more guidance in the use of this method, we commend two books: Robert Traina, *Methodical Bible Study* (Grand Rapids: Zondervan Publishing House, 1985) and David Thompson, *Bible Study That Works* (Nappanee, Ind.: Evangelical Press, 1994).

Chapter 13

1. Brother Lawrence (1611-91), *The Practice of the Presence of God*, cited in Mead, *12,000 Religious Quotations*, 342.
2. Frederick Buechner, *A Room Called Remember* (New York: Harper and Row, 1984), 78.
3. Henri Nouwen, *The Genesee Diary*, quoted by Bob and Michael Benson, *Disciplines for the Inner Life* (Waco, Tex.: Word Books, 1985), 74.
4. Richard Foster, *Prayer: Finding the Heart's True Home* (San Francisco: Harper, 1992), 27.

Chapter 14

1. Stephen J. Harper, *Embrace the Spirit* (Wheaton, Ill.: Scripture Press, Victor Books, 1987), 90-91.
2. Evelyn Underhill, *The Mystery of Sacrifice* (Harrisburg, Pa.: Morehouse Publishing, 1991), 71.
3. Ibid., "Introduction."
4. Maria Harris, *Fashion Me a People* (Louisville, Ky.: John Knox Press, 1989), 77.
5. Underhill, "Introduction," *Mystery of Sacrifice*, 1.
6. Nestorian Liturgy, cited by Underhill, *Mystery of Sacrifice*, 46.
7. Liturgy of SS Adai Mari, cited by Underhill, *Mystery of Sacrifice*, 52.
8. Dillard, *Teaching a Stone to Talk*, 40.
9. William H. Willimon, *Worship as Pastoral Care* (Nashville: Abingdon Press, 1979), 22.
10. Albert M. Wells Jr., ed., *Inspiring Quotations* (Nashville: Thomas Nelson Publishers, 1988), 221.
11. Willimon, *Worship as Pastoral Care*, 13.
12. John Telford, ed., *The Letters of the Rev. John Wesley, A.M.* (London: Epworth Press, 1931), 5:116. (Hereafter cited as Wesley, *Letters*.)
13. The *Greek Heiratikon*, cited by Underhill, *Mystery of Sacrifice*, 74.
14. Underhill, "Introduction," in *Mystery of Sacrifice*.
15. Ibid., 29.
16. Ibid., 34.
17. Liturgy of St. Basil, cited by Underhill, *Mystery of Sacrifice*, 73.

Chapter 15

1. Galdon, *Mustard Seed*, 26.
2. Grenz, *What Christians Really Believe*, 127.
3. Wesley, *Letters*, cited by Tracy et al., *Upward Call*, 137.

4. Galdon, *Mustard Seed*, 73.

5. William Barclay, *The Letters of James and Peter*, in *The Daily Study Bible Series* (Philadelphia: Westminster Press, 1976), 254-55.

6. Margie Haack, "Practice Hospitality: Let's Take Our Cues from Badger, not Martha Stewart," *World Magazine* 14, No. 36 (September 18, 1999): 33.

7. Byron C. Deshler, *The Power of the Personal Group* (Nashville: Tidings, n.d.), 15.

8. Holland N. McTyeire, *A History of Methodism* (Nashville: Publishing House of the M.E. Church, South, 1904), 204.

9. Wesley, *Works*, 8:269.

10. From an article in *Zion's Herald* 3:1 (November 21, 1825). It was designated as a reprint from an earlier edition of Wesley's *Arminian Magazine*.

11. Wesley, *Works*, 8:270.

12. John W. Drakeford, *People to People Therapy* (San Francisco: Harper and Row, 1978), 21.

13. Wesley, *Letters*, 2:115.

14. Wesley, *Works*, 8:258.

15. Tracy et al., *Upward Call*, 154-55.

16. De Waal, *Celtic Way of Prayer*, 135-36.

17. Wesley, *Letters*, 3:94-95.

18. For a more complete description and application of Wesleyan family worship see Tracy et al., *Upward Call*, 193-200.

Chapter 16

1. See Philip Yancey, *Disappointment with God* (Grand Rapids: Zondervan, 1988), 156-59 for a more complete account. Also see Meg Woodson, *The Time of Her Life*.

2. William Bridges, *Transitions: Making Sense of Life's Changes* (Reading, Mass.: Addison-Wesley Publishing Co., 1980), 118.

3. Ibid., 95.

4. The quotations in this paragraph are from unpublished lecture notes as presented by Dr. Roy Fairchild, San Francisco Theological Seminary.

5. Bridges, *Transitions*, 140.

6. Ibid., 126.

7. Frederick Buechner, *Wishful Thinking* (New York: Harper and Row, 1973), 75.

Chapter 17

1. Mark Laaser, "Recovery from Sexual Addiction," *STEPS*, summer 1997, 6. Cited in *Holiness Today*, August 1999, 5.

2. E. Dee Freeborn, in Tracy et al., *Upward Call*, 100.

3. Andrew Murray, *The Deeper Christian Life* (Grand Rapids: Francis Asbury Press/Zondervan, 1985), 55.

4. Susan Muto, *Pathways of Spiritual Living* (Petersham, Mass.: St. Bede's Publishing, 1984), 77.

5. Thomas Traherne, *Herald of Holiness*, January 1998, 25.

6. Kelly, *Testament of Devotion*, 102.

7. Anonymous, *Herald of Holiness*, January 1998, 25.

8. Henri Nouwen, *The Way of the Heart* (Minneapolis: Winston/Seabury Press, 1981), 12.

9. Freeborn, in Tracy et al., *Upward Call*, 101.

10. Sweet, *Homiletics*, April—June 1997, 41.

11. Hotle, "Be Sexually Pure and Faithful in Marriage," in Tracy, *Hunger of Your Heart*, 124.

12. Pamela Condit Kennedy, "On Guard," *Herald of Holiness*, February 1994, 17. Adapted from *Where Have All the Lovers Gone?* Thomas Nelson Publishers.

13. Tilden Edwards, *Sabbath Time* (New York: Seabury Press, 1982), ix.

14. Ibid., x.

15. Ibid., 95.

16. The Sabbath observances of a real Christian family, but the name was changed.

Part 4 Sharing the Light

1. As recalled from a 1997 sermon. The speaker referenced *Charisma* magazine. This story also appeared in Tracy, *Hunger of Your Heart*, 163-64.

Chapter 18

1. "Apology 15," in the *Ante-Nicene Fathers*, ed. Allan Menzies (New York: Charles Scribner's Sons, 1926), 327.

2. Wesley, *Letters*, 2:39, July 1745.

3. Wesley D. Tracy, "John Wesley: Friend of the Poor," *Herald of Holiness* 80, No. 2, February 1991, 31.

4. As reported in *Homiletics*, July—September 1996, 39.

5. Galdon, *Mustard Seed*, 15.

6. Charles R. Swindoll, *Dropping Your Guard* (Waco, Tex.: Word Books, 1978), 32.

7. *Homiletics*, April—June 1997, 27.

8. Tracy et al., *Upward Call*, 204.

9. Wil M. Spaite, *Herald of Holiness*, January 16, 1974, 8.

10. *Newsweek*, October 4, 1999, 76.

11. Megan Rosenfeld, "Ordinary People," *Washington Post*, November 28, 1999, F1.

12. Jess Moody, *Quote—Unquote*, ed. Lloyd Cory (Wheaton, Ill.: Victor Books, 1977), 66.

13. Mike Sager, "Ta-Da!" *Esquire*, November 1999, 145. Cited in *Homiletics*, May-June 2000, 65.

14. Galdon, *Mustard Seed*, 215.

15. Cory Abke, *Accent on Mid-America Nazarene College*, 1988, 12.

16. *War Cry*, September 1971, 16.

Chapter 19

1. Wesley D. Tracy, *New Testament Evangelism Today* (Kansas City: Beacon Hill Press of Kansas City, 1972), 10-11. Attributed to C. Roy Angell.

2. Karla Worley, *Glimpses of Christ* (Denver: New Hope Publishers, 1998), 5.

3. Albert M. Wells Jr., *Inspiring Quotations* (Nashville: Thomas Nelson, 1988), 64.

4. Frank C. Laubach, *Letters by a Modern Mystic* (Syracuse, N.Y.: New Readers Press, 1979), 23-24. Also Richard Foster, *Streams of Living Water* (San Francisco: Harper, 1998).

5. Worley, *Glimpses of Christ*, 3.

6. William Myers, *Theological Themes of Youth Ministry* (New York: Pilgrim Press, 1987), 35.

7. For more about faith mentoring see the *Reflecting God Workbook* and Tracy et al., *Upward Call*, chaps. 15 and 16.

Chapter 20

1. Lewis, *Joyful Christian*, 65.
2. Ibid.
3. *The Heart of Peter Marshall's Faith* (Old Tappan, N.J.: Fleming H. Revell, 1964). Used by permission.
4. Joni Eareckson Tada, *Heaven, Your Real Home* (Grand Rapids: Zondervan, Harper Collins, 1995), 14.
5. Ibid., 13, 196.
6. <www.inform.edu/EdRes/Topic WomensStudies/Reading Room/Poetry/Dickinson> The University of Maryland.
7. Tada, *Heaven, Your Real Home*, 117-18.
8. William Herbert Carruth, "Each in His Own Tongue," cited in Tada, *Heaven, Your Real Home*.
9. Rudyard Kipling, "L'Envoi," in *One Hundred and One Famous Poems*, 172.
10. Ibid.
11. Ibid.
12. Lewis, *Joyful Christian*, 226.
13. Ibid.
14. Ibid., 225.
15. Emmett C. Murphy, *The New Murphy's Law* (Worcester, Mass.: Chandler House Press, 1998), 26-27.

Contributing Authors

The principal author of this book is Wesley D. Tracy, D.Min. and S.T.D., former editor of the *Herald of Holiness* (now *Holiness Today*), the magazine of the Church of the Nazarene. He has served the church as pastor, professor, writer, and editor and is a past president of the Wesleyan Theological Society.

Dr. Tracy was supported by a steering committee and board of contributing writers: Gareth L. Cockerill, Ph.D., professor of New Testament and biblical theology of Wesley Biblical Seminary, Jackson, Mississippi; Donald E. Demaray, Ph.D., senior Beeson professor of biblical preaching, Asbury Theological Seminary, Wilmore, Kentucky; and Steven Harper, Ph.D., professor of spiritual formation and vice-president and dean of the Florida campus of Asbury Theological Seminary, Winter Springs, Florida.

CPSIA information can be obtained
at www.ICGtesting.com
Printed in the USA
FFOW05n0316240516

9 780834 118669